Strangers and Pilgrims

Also by Ann Cornelisen

Torregreca: Life, Death, Miracles
Vendetta of Silence
Women of the Shadows

STRANGERS AND PILGRIMS

The Last Italian Migration

Ann Cornelisen   *Holt, Rinehart and Winston, New York*

Published by Holt, Rinehart and Winston, 383 Madison Avenue,
New York, New York 10017.

Published simultaneously in Canada by Holt, Rinehart and
Winston of Canada, Limited.

Library of Congress Cataloging in Publication Data

Cornelisen, Ann, 1926–
Strangers and pilgrims.

Includes bibliographical references.
1. Italy, Southern—Social conditions.
2. Italy—Emigration and immigration.   3. Alien
labor, Italian—Germany, West.   I. Title.
HN475.5.C67   301.32'5'0945   79-16314
ISBN 0-03-044285-0

First Edition

Designer: Jacqueline Schuman
Printed in the United States of America
10   9   8   7   6   5   4   3   2   1

These all died in faith, not having received the promises, but having seen them afar off, and were persuaded of *them*, and embraced *them*, and confessed that they were strangers and pilgrims on the earth.

Hebrews 11:13

Acknowledgments

My debts are many. The most obvious is to the John Simon Guggenheim Memorial Foundation, which, through a fellowship grant, made the travel and research, and so the book itself, possible. Other debts, if less obvious, are just as real and almost always to strangers. *They* are the great discoveries of such a project. Their help, their interest, and their advice, their endless delight in being inconvenienced seem now, in retrospect, even more astonishing than they did in my moments of confusion and uncertainty. I wish I could thank them all. I *do* thank them all, named or unnamed, but especially—Dr. Sergio Angeletti, Dr. Franco Galante, Dr. Ludivico Ortona of the Italian Ministry of Foreign Affairs, and in Bonn, Dr. Francesco Pulcini; John Shirley, Bruno Scarfi, and Bruna Sevini, all old friends, of the American Embassy in Rome; Alec Klieforth of the American Embassy in Bonn, and Paul Tyson, one of those strangers now become, I hope, a friend; Dr. Miklos Frank of *Deutscher Caritas Verband*; Dr. W. Kurt Haerzschel, Assistant Secretary of State for Labor, Health, and Social Welfare of Baden-Württemberg; Dr. Lutz Heidemann and his wife, Bettina, and Ernst and Christa Schwandt, again friends and vital links in their own ways between Italy and Germany; and last, two people, strangers, who were kind, patient sources of information that I would never have found on my own, Dr. Stefano Musolino of Heidelberg and Father Gianfausto Rosoli of the *Centro Studi Emigrazione* in Rome. Grateful as I am to all of them, they are not responsible for any errors of fact or interpretation: those, unfortunately, remain my own.

The Emigrants

Names are much more than convenient labels to distinguish us one from the other. They are, somehow, intrinsic to our personalities, unique symbols of our being, and so, very private. I have invented names for the emigrants that could be their own, but are not. They will be happier with these new, impersonal labels. They will know that their kindness, patience, and trust have not been betrayed. Even disguised and now safe in their privacy, they remain themselves, very real people.

SOUTHERN GERMANY

Michele and Edda

Michele—Chichella's brother, an unskilled laborer
Edda—his wife
Nicola—their eldest child
Berio—their younger son, a painter's helper
Assunta—their fifteen-year-old daughter, just arrived in Germany
Cristina—their youngest child, an elfin five-year-old
Vincenzo—Chrchella's son, who lives, at least temporarily, with Michele and Edda

Therr Friends—"The Regulars"

Pasquà—a Neapolitan mason who has a German wife and five children
Raffaele—a Sicilian construction steelworker
Maria—his wife

Marco—a laborer from Puglia, employed by Fiat
Gina—his wife, who grew up in Germany, but was originally Sicilian

Gaetano and Bianca

Gaetano—a mason who has lived in Germany since 1965 and still
  speaks little German
Bianca—his wife, who has learned German
Nando—their son, twenty, who works in a leather factory
Lello—their son, eighteen, an apprentice mason
Chiara—their daughter, almost seventeen, who went all the way
  through school in Germany
Lisa—their daughter, seven, born in Germany
Martino—their son, five, also born in Germany

OFFENBACH

Paolo and Lucetta

Paolo—once a peasant, now an unskilled laborer
Lucetta—his wife, also a peasant, now an inventory clerk
Bruno—their son, a mechanic, who is married
Domenico—their son, an apprentice mechanic
Rosa—their daughter, who would be engaged

Franco and Anna

Franco—Lucetta's brother, a mason
Anna—his wife, a clerk in a department store
Carlo—their son, who is studying to be a bookkeeper
Antonietta—their daughter in elementary school

DÜSSELDORF

Pietro and Liliana

Pietro—a construction carpenter, determined to find work in a fac-
  tory *and* in a city
Liliana—his wife
Mario—their thirteen-year-old son

Rita—their daughter, eleven years old, who struggles valiantly with
    school
Pina—their bouncy four-year-old

NORTHERN ITALY

Agnese and Her Family

Agnese—the proprietress of a café, whose son, daughter, and son-in-
    law are all, according to her, objects of *invidia*, and her three
    successful sisters, who are, in turn, her own objects of *invidia*

Giulia

Giulia—who has worked for long years in a factory, has asthma, and
    may soon have her pension

Melina

Melina—a recent emigrant to Turin, enchanted with all she sees,
    who is an entrepreneur with ten children

Strangers and Pilgrims

Introduction

Southern Italians have never been optimists. Fortunately. They do what they must. They accept an order not of their making. Vital decisions are few, the choices odious. They accept that too. Whatever frail hopes linger in the dark, secret corners of their minds do not prosper. Thirty years ago it seemed they might under a scheme called The Reform for the South. No one denied it was a political invention. Still . . .

Each new government, by now some thirty, has dutifully presented its master plan for The Reform, each plan more costly than the last, more Byzantine in its efforts to please the Southern political "Barons" who turn out the votes and divide the spoils, and so, less apt to bring *basic* change. It has been an effective, if expensive, mechanism for maintaining the status quo, which had to be the point of the exercise since the new Ministers always turned out to be the same, rotated from armchair to armchair, last year's fiscal expert translated to this year's agronomist. Southerners may have been disappointed, but they were not surprised. The Unification of Italy had offered their grandfathers hope too, hope that evaporated into an all-purpose slogan, "*La Patria*," and the right to emigrate. Several more sweeps around the closed circuit of Italian political solutions and the pageant was revived with new scenery and a new cast. The plot, of course, remained the same. This time Southerners were offered Democracy—and the right to emigrate. If they wanted to work, to eat, if they wanted to join the modern world—not an imagined world, but one they could now see on television—again they had no choice: they must emigrate.

And they did. Exactly how many went where for how long is a secret lost in the jugglings of statistics. A guess, probably an accurate one, is that three million Southerners left their villages bound for Italian cities, especially the Northern cities, where they were (and are) perennial foreigners, put up with grudgingly; and another four million went beyond, to the coal mines of France and Belgium, to the ditches and garbage trucks of Switzerland, and to the building sites and factories of Germany.

Much has been written about them and their brothers in exile, the Turks, Greeks, Yugoslavs, and Spaniards. At times they are made to sound almost subversive. They are said to have caused tragic financial loss to the "country of origin." They disrupt the "host country." They insist on varying from "the norm," an elusive, arbitrary state invented by the social scientists. ("Samplings" must be changed, new "control groups" corralled for new "in-depth" interviews.) Economists, ever impartial judges, discover in the migrations either confirmation of the theory of supply and demand *or* proof that democracy has failed because it does not guarantee an equal measure of security and comfort to all citizens. Emigrants are, apparently, units, like ergs, to be shunted back and forth across Europe as needed—and worse, as not needed.

They are people too. We forget that they would not have left the "country of origin" had it offered work and that, disruptive as the emigrants may be, the "host country" tolerates them, even seeks them, because it needs them. Survival is the question, for the people and the countries alike, and survival is still the one overwhelming human instinct. Statistics, theories, and formulas, which are only arrangements of facts rendered of their humanity, soothe the conscience. Patterns emerge, blame can be assigned impersonally, and people we never knew vanish slowly, silently into the misty anonymity of erg-dom.

But I knew many Southern Italians who emigrated, and because I had known them, cared for their children, worked with them, argued with them, and been infuriated by them, I could not forget them. They remained Mario and Giovanni and Pasquale to me, not ergs or units. They refused to join the percentages, the patterns. "The norm" endowed them with opinions too rudimentary for the intricacies of their reasoning. Failure was too generously heaped upon them—failure to integrate, to send their children to school, to reinvest their capital, to adapt to new ways, to study for higher qualification, to ooze the milk of human kindness, to thank their betters and help those worse off than they. This blurry mass was at fault. "It" had remained as butt-headed, backward, and unmanageable as always. That might be true, though I suspected that the lowest common denominator had worked another of its gray miracles.

Still, the Marios and Giovannis and Pasquales skipped out of lockstep: memories of them superimposed themselves on the neat generalities of the printed page. I wondered what the people who had emigrated, the ones I had known twenty years ago in Torregreca, would be like now. I tried to imagine. Finally I gave up and wondered, instead, if they would talk to me, assuming I could find them. Or would they feel my sudden appearance an intrusion? I had known them for two years, three years, some ten or twelve, in the intimate, yet impersonal way that is the private cross of social workers. I met them first when, as an ex officio member of the housing committee, I visited their old houses in the bowels of the town, the dank, cramped, one- and two-room huts with stone, even dirt floors, leaking roofs, and no plumbing, that would qualify them for new houses in the "Villaggio." Later they came to the nursery each morning with their children and again in the afternoon to take them home. They always stopped to talk—complain mostly—and so gradually I learned their secrets and anxieties. If I had to scold them about the potato peels they heaved out in the streets, or their children's worms or foul hair, there would be a coolness. It never lasted long. Soon they needed help and forgave me. In time we even tried projects of our own: a communal oven, a playground, volunteer garbage collection. They were not always successful. They were not always failures either. But all that was a long time ago. I had known too much about them, they too little about me, for us to be friends, and yet, in a way I cannot define, friends we were. Friendship imposes its own obligations. It was not enough now to imagine what had happened to them as emigrants. I must find them, talk to them, try to talk to them at least. They might be the slugs that obediently filled the slots of all those tabulations. I doubted it. I remembered them so well in the past. They must have a present. And how would they remember me? If they did. How would they treat me? I wondered.

I need not have. My arrival on their doorsteps in Germany, in Northern Italy tripped a mysterious switch in their imaginations. I was not so much a person as part of that past in Torregreca that they loathed and yet cherish. They knew me. I was familiar. They had trusted me once. They remembered. Hesitant questions at first, and hesitant answers. Chronicles of years lost, and they relaxed. I had not changed that much. I might be trusted again. Best of all I came from that other world, the only world real to them, and they could talk. Lonely, diffident people yearn to talk about the past. There is a kind of safety in the past: looking back it seems almost happy. It also leads, finally, to the present, which slips on into the future. All I had to do was listen—and accept the hospitality they lavished on me. They fed me as though I were a goose destined to produce pâté de foie gras. They drowned me in beer and wine. They quietly changed the sheets on the double bed and insisted I spend the night—they would sleep on chairs and sofas in the living room, or on a stray mattress wedged between the legs of the kitchen table. I refused that sacrifice. I was adamant, though twice I lost. They advised me how to get around in these strange places where they had come to live and work. They explained and explained. They explained it all to me. I listened—and gained ten pounds.

They talked and I listened until some evenings my brain

turned to whey. Then after two days, maybe three, I left, knowing that I would see them soon, in Torregreca when they came for the traditional summer holiday; or again in those far-off northern places that would always be temporary, never home to them. I went on to other towns, to other Torresi who accepted me as a friend. By chance along the way I met people I had never known in Torregreca. One woman, who owned a bar and pizzeria across from a railway station, did not believe I was who I claimed to be. "*She* was much younger." My comment that we all were younger twenty years ago did not convince her. Two men I overheard speaking the Torrese dialect in the Düsseldorf station were skeptical about me too, until I proved myself by giving them the mayor of Torregreca's nickname: *Panzachiena*. They reminded me of the suspicion and reticence I might have encountered.

Now more than ever the Marios, Giovannis, and Pasquales are people to me. They have snarled bits of information, experience, and emotion into opinions so bitter they prefer not to discuss them. When they do, they are angry at their own anger; it is so futile. They feel manipulated. They recognize fault and would divide it. They give the "country of origin" its share and the "host country" as well. Their own is less clear to them. "You see, signora, you have to look at it our way. We can't ..." And from their point of view it would be unreasonable to do other than what they have done. It is a narrow perspective, a very human one, that exposes them to the labels of stubborn, unmanageable, backward. They will persist. They can only judge, and judging, act from what they know. They are less inclined to trust than ever. They are not beguiled by promises, but their children ... Hope is only for their children. They accept that they are strangers to their neighbors and to each other. Fate, they say. So much of their lives has depended on what they call fate. They will continue to wander, searching for an almost holy place, one where there is work. Fate has made them pilgrims, too. They do what they must. They work and save, and save, and save: the down payments on their freedom, a decent old age. They cannot plead for themselves. I would make one plea for them: that they be thought of as people, not ergs.

Twenty-five years ago when I first saw it, even twenty years ago when I went there to live, Torregreca was a town of contradictions: a medieval complex—Norman tower, ducal palace, cathedral and all—with electric light; a frayed feudal society that stretched listlessly toward the eighteenth century and another void of pre-industrial existence. Ten thousand people lived there, all waiting for a revolution, though not necessarily the same one. Ninety-nine percent of them were peasants who farmed snippets of land not their own with equipment described in the Bible. Up and down the hillsides they pushed their plows, they sowed, they carried their bushy fagots and their wood. And up and down the hillsides they hoed and reaped and gleaned. Each season was a miniature from a Book of Hours come to life. Rumors of the mechanical Paradise just off, over there, behind the mountains, had reached them, and the hottest days, on the long walk home, they had visions: their children metamorphosed into government clerks or highly skilled, highly paid workers. But only the first five grades of school were offered.

The stumps onto which the missing structures could be grafted were all there. They remained stumps. The Torresi waited. The government would do something. It did, slowly, and in its own arbitrary fashion. Roads were built, connecting the most unlikely places to others just as unlikely: The South had been "opened up." The Torresi had a vague sense that they should go somewhere, but they had no reason to go and no transport. The infant mortality rate was one of the highest in the country; the consumption of sugar, coffee, and meat, the lowest. There was no dependable water supply, almost no sewers, and no work. Still the Torresi waited and the local Minister, who was ever conscious of their needs and next to the Patron Saint the town's most revered being, rewarded their loyalty with an enormous concrete and steel structure that housed all manner of cranes, boilers, bottlers, and conveyor belts. The latest thing, a *Cantina Sociale*, a town winery! It was inaugurated with great pomp one September and closed shortly thereafter—forever. In Lucania grapes are few and wizened. And so—up and down the hillsides the peasants pushed their plows and sowed and reaped and gleaned. The newspapers glorified the Age of Technology.

What were contradictions to me seemed normal to the Torresi, and I should have realized that the opposite could be true. Soon enough I did. For them a woman alone—the younger, the more lustful (and I was young)—must be loose: a foreign woman, therefore a rich woman, *alone*, was beyond comprehension, but definitely immoral. Before I ever walked into the Piazza, wearing my high-necked, long-sleeved cotton dress, I had been dubbed a whore. Later they would marvel at my virtue, never understanding that it was natural enough or that the relentless public display of it had bored and frightened me: was I already or would I become the ultimate prudish Victorian I appeared to be? They invented parental rage over some misalliance of mine. A married man? A gold digger? I never knew. Then they banished me from my father's house with a large monthly stipend which would be paid as long as I abided by one condition: that I never again see this mythical lover. I was a remittance woman! But that came later.

At first only one person in town would take a chance and rent to me. She was young too and desperate, a widow of four months with four young children, debts that amounted to more than she expected to save in her lifetime, and a small apartment in a block of public housing. She would rent one room. Or, *if* I insisted, *if* the price was right ($20 a month, as it turned out) and *if* I promised to hire her, and no one else, for my cleaning and laundry, she would move out. A month-to-month agreement. Clearly I was suspect and would be kept under constant surveillance.

I was wary too and not exactly taken with her. She treated each stage of the negotiations as the climax of a Greek tragedy. Tears that might have been of glycerin, so deftly were they balanced, glistened on her eyelids. She moaned. She chanted. Once she beat her breasts. Her poor orphaned children! Her debts! A widow so young! *Ahimè! Ahimè!* I understood. Those purges of grief were in the finest Southern tradition, a classic technique to pry another thousand lire from me. I admired the performance, for that is what it was, but at the same time I was uneasy: throughout the melodramatics shrewd black eyes watched me very carefully. At the first hint that she had gone too far, that my patience was souring to sarcasm, her features uncoiled and her voice was snappish, all business. "What day of the month would you pay the rent?" Or, "In cash?" She could suspect my morals. I dreaded the daily trauma of her scenes and her connivings, and I knew I would never trust her. *Pazienza!* Neither of us had a choice: we would have to make do with each other.

Chichella was thinner then, as thin as she would ever be. Wasted away, she said, by grief and worry. And by hunger, I found out later. Even so she was stocky and strong with muscular arms and legs and, under her patched black dress, a body solid as a punching bag. Her face was squarish too, or the sharp contrast of her hairline, dark, glossy hair, made it seem so. It was a very definite face. Dark eyebrows lowered over those restless, suspicious black eyes, and the large mouth, its lips outlined by the merest filament of raised flesh, would tighten, concealing all thought and emotion. She could lock herself away at will. The only thing the least ingenuous about her appearance was a sprinkling of freckles. Otherwise she was a stern presence. I am not sure how we got through the first weeks.

We agreed on nothing. She did not approve of the color I

painted the windows and doors, or the curtains I made and hung, or of my rearrangement of the furniture, what little there was. She did not wash the dishes or clean the bath to my satisfaction. She could not read or write. Messages were a daily drama. She spoke only dialect. Italian pronouns were no more familiar to her than advanced calculus, and proper names of no importance because she knew the nicknames. I, of course, did not. Often I was not even sure of my anonymous caller's sex. She decided to clean in my bedroom slippers and stretched them. I did not trust her accounting—to watch her add and subtract on flying fingers is an experience—and insisted, rather pedantically, on writing down every figure and arriving at a total in a more conventional way. She was insulted. I was aloof. Both of us were dissatisfied. Such mutual antipathy and suspicion, heightened by chronic ill humor, are not the common yeast of friendship, and yet, improbable as it seems, we became friends, still are friends and, I think, always will be. How? Why? When? I could offer a hundred explanations that would explain nothing. I am not sure myself.

At first necessity played its part. I knew so little about Torregreca, she so much, and for purely financial reasons she wanted to please me. My casual questions about where to buy wine, olive oil, about a garage I might rent, a plumber who was reliable, a cabinetmaker were answered by the immediate appearance of four half-gallons of four different wines, two gallons of oil, a garage owner, a plumber who smiled and danced with pleasure at the thought of serving me. The cabinetmaker took longer. No one would accept a lira from me. These were tokens of their goodwill. If, in the future ... And they backed out, all but tugging their forelocks. She had the black heart of a con artist! She had not said so outright, but she had insinuated—and I can see her innocently rolling her eyes—that I was very rich, had projects of monumental proportions, which, sometime, in an indefinite future ... A gesture might be remembered ... I raged. She flounced out and slammed the door. She would not be treated like a thief. A few months in Torregreca and my conscience was more elastic. I actually joined her in a mild bit of larceny and justified it with the feeblest excuse: it was not for our personal gain. We needed, that is, we wanted to plant flowers around the nursery. There were none for sale in town. The convent, Chichella said thoughtfully, and waited. I objected, she smiled, and finally I went to the convent with her and entertained the nuns with my chatter, distracted them, while Chichella stepped lightly through the garden stealing seeds—and, I must admit, a few plants. We were accomplices.

Of necessity too, she taught me the dialect, or rather she unraveled it so that I could understand. There was no need to speak it, but I had to understand and quickly, for word of who and what I was, grossly exaggerated, had made the rounds of the town and everyone wanted to talk to me. They stopped me in the streets, in shops, in the café, even when I was driving my car. And they spoke not one, but three different dialects, complicated, it seemed to my untuned ear, by speech defects and mouths full of mashed potatoes. Each evening I arrived home in a fog of uncertainty. Practice may be the best teacher. It also befuddles. Over my morning coffee, some nights when she came for my shopping list, in the odd half-hours of time we both had, Chichella tutored me. Naturally she talked about the town and our neighbors. She skipped from family to family, their nicknames, their relationship to each other, their feuds, their vices, and the gossip about them. She enjoyed gossip, partly, I think, because she had so often been its victim. Also she saw that I was amused. She constructed whole genealogies for me, which I remember to this day. She is a supreme mimic. I found that from her imitations, I recognized people I met, and then, of course, all that other information slipped into place. To have Chichella in the house was like having an encyclopedia of Torregreca. As she said, "If you can't read, you have to have a good memory. Otherwise what do you think about?"

By day she did any work she could find. Entire weeks in the fall she hauled stove wood up five flights of stairs for 1.4 cents a trip. She did laundry. She shopped, scrubbed floors, and washed the dishes for women better off than she in the hope they would give her the pasta left over from lunch. She shucked corn and remade mattresses. If all else failed, she worked by the day in the fields. She dreaded that. From the time she was a half-grown girl she had done nothing else—fourteen years of it. She was too old now, she said, but when all else failed ... She and her children could not live on the $27.50 a month that was her only dependable income (from me). Food was expensive and so were clothes, especially shoes. She must pay her debts, slowly, a bit at a time. They never had enough to eat. There would be no help from her large family either: they had nothing. They had also disowned her. She had shamed them after her husband's death by going to work, by renting the apartment to me. A widow should stay closed in her house—and presumably allow herself to starve to death.

Each evening by dusk she retired to the gloom of the narrow storeroom where she and her children now slept, and sat at the doorway, winnowing her memories. More and more often she was interrupted by visitors, mine, who wanted advice about how to approach me. Was this the right moment? What was my humor? She was my self-appointed doorkeeper. What she told them, I do not know. If she thought I was tired, she put them off, inventing a queasy liver for me or an attack of nerves. I must have seemed oddly subject to the vapors, but in the Italy of that day nervous breakdowns were fashionable, among the gentry particularly, and ran their course from collapse to recovery in one week. If a lone male visitor knocked on my door, I knew that in a few seconds Chichella would pound up the stairs, through the sitting room, and take up her post by the kitchen door. She felt obliged to chaperone me. She pretended not to listen, but she did. Editing facts or slight distortions made her frown. I could accept the signal or not. I usually did, promising some decision the next day. Then I listened to Chichella's rebuttal. She could be very explicit about my visitor's background and what he was *not* saying. She suggested people I might ask who knew all about the situation—and then was too discreet ever to mention the matter again. In Torregreca the "try-on" is a legitimate tool of the poor. Only fools are too proud. As an adept herself, she did not want me taken in—unless for some reason of my own, what I was asked to do suited me. She had my good name to protect: it was also hers.

My contribution to the friendship was as simple as that: standing, respectability. Hers, we found, was connected directly to mine and suffered the same highs and sudden lurching dips that mine did.

She had a direct line to a minor power, who, in turn, knew the mayor, the doctors, teachers, and tax collectors, the rulers of her world. She never gained anything tangible from it, but she had straight information, which was valuable—how and when to file the dozens of applications on which life depends there, when school-children could have their X rays, what the housing policy was—all things that should have been common property and were not. She was an authority in her own right, and she enjoyed it.

Before the nursery could open, every surface had to be scraped and scrubbed and polished. We seemed to have had extravagantly messy workmen. I hired Chichella and let her choose her own helpers. When they had finished, and only then, I said she would be the cook at the nursery. I expected to be attacked by crowds of screaming women who wanted the job for themselves. No one murmured. My choice was accepted as fair: no one could claim to be poorer than Chichella. She is an excellent cook. A generation of children has loved her. If they are hurt or angry they go to her and sob into her apron. She bandages them and teases them and screams at them in fury. They love it. She also understood that with her new job her status had changed and so had mine. In the nursery she affected the same cloying courtesy the teachers used with me. I was the enemy. I saw the things that were wrong, insisted they be done properly, insisted, insisted, insisted—until they all prayed I would leave. But they smothered me with respect and so did Chichella. Her loyalty must be to them. She was even tactful enough not to tattle. By then she knew that I would catch them out sooner or later. She has admitted that she was surprised to find she trusted me. We had come a long way.

Fifteen years ago nurseries became part of the national school system. Our nursery was turned over to the town council of Tor-regreca, and Chichella became an employee of the *comune*. She has almost achieved the Torrese dream, except that hers has always been to escape the town. She has everything the state can offer: the automatic salary raises, sick leave, vacations, the thirteenth—and yes, the fourteenth—month's pay, and soon will be eligible for a minimum pension. If she works longer, it will be larger. She also has all the appliances that are the outward proof of prosperity: a stove, an icebox, a television set. She has not changed a great deal. She is heavier and her hair would be quite gray, if she did not splurge twice a year and go to a hairdresser. Better still, she has not lost the quirky sense of humor that always finds the ridiculous in the schemes and predicaments of the Torresi, including her own. Several years ago she was showing me the new tiles in her bathroom and kitchen, another symbol, that she had always wanted, when suddenly she started giggling. She could not catch her breath long enough to tell me. Finally she blurted out,

"Don't you see what's funny? I'm ... *sono* quasi *una signora!*" I'm *almost* a lady! She gave in to the giggles again. I knew what she meant and was amused, but sad too: she has always been one.

Every few months, over the years, I have gone back to Torregreca for a week or ten days. The town still fascinates me, probably because I know more about it than is quite decent. I want to see how it changes, if it changes, and what becomes of this new generation of young I first met as children in the nursery. It may be a serial story that never ends. And then too, there is Chichella. If it was not for her, I might go less often. We have shared the crises and illnesses and comedy of so many years, that being together, we are reassured and strangely optimistic, we laugh a lot as though we were young again. So I go back to "our" apartment, a member of the family and an honored guest. One evening is enough: I might never have left and that makes a difference.

When I had to search for the addresses of my emigrants, as a matter of course I stayed at Chichella's. She does not hold with abstract ideas and theories, especially mine. For her they are symptoms of an obscure brain fever that attacks me. She tries to be soothing and changes the subject. This too will pass, she seems to be thinking. My curiosity about the actual lives of emigrants was received with that kind of withdrawn patience. She humored me.

In Southern Italy officials think they have a right to know *everything*. If they are not informed, they are suspicious. If they are—at length—they are bored and completely disarmed. The first of my visits in search of emigrants was to the *comune*. I saw the registry clerk, babbled like an ingenue to other clerks I have known for twenty years, and ended the campaign by calling on the mayor. Statistics, addresses, any assistance I might need were at my disposal. They had no specific addresses, only notations of the cities, and admittedly those were out of date. I waited twenty-four hours. News travels fast in Torregreca, almost as though pneumatic tubes connect every neighborhood with the Piazza. Then I went to see the neighbors of the emigrants I wanted to find, the original residents of the "Villaggio." They sent me on to relatives, cousins, or sisters and brothers-in-law. All denied possession of current addresses. Many pretended that they could not quite remember in which country my emigrant had finally settled.

I persisted, going from house to house like the Avon lady. Nothing. I tried the post office and the bank. The directors were courteous and very curious. We had the ritual cups of coffee. They knew nothing, could suggest nothing.

I was worried and that makes Chichella nervous. Against her instincts she asked me questions and then laughed at me. I should wait. Be patient. Had I forgotten? No one is quite sure. They're afraid. . . . I waited. One morning a noncommissioned officer of the Carabinieri stopped me, explained that I did not know him, though he knew of me, and asked if there was any problem about these emigrants I wanted to trace. Had they done anything wrong? Did they owe me or anyone else money? If so, it was a matter for the police. I was startled to hear myself reel through my monologue like an old vaudevillian. He was relieved and overwhelmed by sorrow: the Carabinieri had no records of such matters. I did the only thing I could: I waited.

On the seventh evening the doorbell rang, I answered it, and a young boy, out of breath, shoved a scrap of paper into my hand. Before I could say anything, he galloped down the stairs and disappeared. On the paper in large, unsure letters was the address of a family in Offenbach. Two more arrived the next day in the same furtive way, and three more the day after that. Only one of the messengers was a grown-up, a thin, red-nosed young woman who was shy and a little frightened of me. She was just doing an errand for a neighbor. She knew nothing about it, she insisted, and fled.

Chichella was triumphant. She had told me so. She also admitted that she had had a great many callers at the nursery in the last few days. I know from the past that she receives them out the kitchen window, and the conferences, hissed and emphatic, are very private. She assured me with a smirk that there would be more addresses. I could not wait. She would keep them for me. On the long drive home her last words, joking, but also serious, ran through my mind so many times they became a round I could not escape: "Be patient. You forget, nobody looks for people like us unless there's trouble."

In twenty years Torregreca, like other Southern towns, has changed in all the spurious ways that were not allowed for in the grandiose plans and yet are the direct result of them. Half the people have disappeared. There are few peasants and fewer donkeys. Many of the Land Reform houses are deserted. Everywhere fields are uncultivated. Schools abound. There is no industry, no work. In the Piazza where only two cars used to park—mine and the dilapidated Fiat that served as a taxi and, because of a frazzled exhaust system, delivered its rare passengers in a state of semi-coma—there is now a twenty-four-hour traffic jam. Men still lounge there in the exhaust, but they are not peasants, not even peasants who have declared themselves construction workers. They are the unemployed bookkeepers, would-be surveyors, waiters, and elementary schoolteachers. The Torresi, who remain, are still waiting.

Everyone agrees that something must be done, but not what. One official reform, proof of the goodwill and progressiveness of local political thought, has been carried out: the town Festa is now celebrated in mid-August instead of early October. As a result the emigrants whose holidays usually fall in August are lured back and see the town at its best. And so for the first time in many years I too was lured back for the Festa and, more important, the emigrants.

Torregreca was, indeed, at its best. Tall, lacy ornaments studded with light bulbs arched over the main street. In the sunlight they were grimy and tattered, but at night they glittered so fiercely that their shabbiness blurred into a kind of tinselly make-believe. At all hours crowds of people sauntered back and forth, talking, watching, stumbling along, scarcely moving aside to let the large, quiet, well-sprung cars with foreign licenses pass, then flowing back into a mass once more to go on talking and watching. Always watching. Shops kept unheard-of hours, and their keepers, usually too truculent to waste a "Good day" on customers, were wreathed in pumpkin smiles. Each night in the Piazza the cafés set out chairs and tables, a true first in the town's history and so successful that by ten o'clock people who chose to promenade had only a doughnut of empty space around the base of the monument to the war dead. Off to one side, backed up to a railing, was a large stage. Two rock bands and "The Lioness" of Somewhere were promised for the last night. Gone forever was the old-fashioned band concert—the pagoda-pavilion draped in cardboard icing, the Marching Band, elevated for a few hours to Concert Orchestra, that could not quite stay together for the semiclassical selections, and the soprano who belted out arias of unknown operas. Gone out of fashion. No one minded. They drank beer and ate ice cream cones and peered around through the banks of smoke from charcoal braziers where skewers of sausages and bits of meat were cooking. Children fell asleep, grandfathers dozed fitfully, but the adults, dressed like city dwellers in suits and silk dresses, sat alert, watching for acquaintances and their chance to explain once more how well off they were in Düsseldorf or Turin.

Most of my emigrants had come home. They too were elegant in dress and speech. Few had cars, but, they hastened to tell me, their sons did. The younger children never seemed to play. They sat, neatly dressed in what a few years ago would have been called their Sunday best, on the front steps of their houses, waiting for someone to speak to them, waiting to be on show. Several of the men and women apologized for their cousins, their sisters who had been reluctant to give me their addresses. "They weren't quite sure. You understand how it is, signora?" I did. They hoped I would come to see them. I could tell that they did not expect me to: this was only a temporary aberration of mine. To my surprise every one of them had left Switzerland. They were all either in Northern Italy or Germany. They were very watchful, not antagonistic, but tense and subdued, and they all said exactly the same things: as long as there was no work at home, they could not think of coming back. They wanted to, they would someday, not now. They were doing well—some boasted of property they had been able to buy or small businesses—it was a hard life. They must give their children the start that they had never had themselves: a few sacrifices now. *"La vita è così per tutti, no, signora?"* Life is like that for everyone, no, signora? I heard it so often that I began to wonder if the lines had been memorized. Could they be so patient, resigned, and prosperous? And so detached?

Was this the truth, their truth? If so, they had nothing else to say. If not, they were determined to claim it as their truth, and there was little chance that I could break down their resistance. My dreams became long, exhausting sequences, always the same: I was in Germany, asking questions of faceless Torresi, waiting in a shrill, sirenlike silence for answers that never came and then asking another question.

The last night of the Festa, Chichella agreed to go to the Piazza. When we arrived, every table and chair was taken. We could neither stand nor sit. We went wherever the crowd shoved us. People offered tables, bunched together themselves, requisitioned chairs for us in the kind of respectful courtesy that is so embarrassing and undeserved and yet so comfortable. It is easy to be spoiled. All evening at our table people came and went, stopping to talk, ordering beer for us until we were giddy, talking about the "old days," teasing Chichella and asking me questions that ranged from how was my mother to how could they get a disability pension. (That particular pension has become the local hobby and a national scandal.) The *notabili* bowed: I bowed. Emigrants, the ones I had seen and many I had not, came to sit and tell each other how well off they were. We talked of sacrifices and savings and giving the children a chance, and what they would do when they came home, which seemed to be gloat.

The rock bands blared, and we talked. The Lioness of Somewhere was breathlessly awaited. The chairman of the Festa committee whispered that there was a problem. Modesty required that the Lioness wear a cloak of some kind, at least a chiffon scarf. There would be a delay. Finally she stumped up onto the stage, a bulgy, tough lady with long black hair and a raucous voice—and a cape that she swirled in ever wider, higher circles, revealing a lot more than anyone wanted to see. Boos and hisses. She shouted on, striding back and forth across the front of the stage, stopping every few measures to exchange insults with the audience, the men in the first rows. A young actor, who was in town making a television short, so people said, jumped up on the stage. He was drunk. He harangued the crowd: they had been duped; the town council had cheated them, made fun of them. Then he slipped off into garbled Communist slogans. The Carabinieri appeared. They seemed to swarm out from under the stage, armed for battle. They carried off the Lioness of Somewhere and the actor turned Castro, both shouting obscenities over their shoulders, and we all went home, satisfied that it had been the best Festa ever.

My dreams turned to nightmares and the still predawn hours were interrupted by the banging of car trunks, whispering voices, and the hoarse starting of engines. The emigrants were leaving, returning to their real lives. Chichella heard them too and surprised me one morning, a few days later, as I was drinking my coffee, by speculating out loud about their lives. What they were really like. They made money. That she did not doubt. But she wondered ... My brain fever was contagious. And then I had one of the better inspirations of my life: why shouldn't she come to Germany with me and see for herself? Without realizing it, she forces people to talk. I had seen it that night in the Piazza. She gave them no peace until they reacted. They must react. Sooner or later they do. She did not quite believe me at first. She? Go to Germany? Her brother, her elder son, they were both in Germany. Could we see them? Could we do a thousand things? Of course we could.

We left four weeks later on what she calls with audible capitals, "My First Trip Abroad."

As we crossed the Swiss border at Basel into Germany, nothing changed. I cannot think now what I expected. Perhaps I have lived in Italy too long. Perhaps the reminiscences of too many Southern Italians about Germany have left me with an image, a naïve stylized image like a child's painting:

A black cloud boils over a landscape of unlikely, utopian neatness in which factories belch out smoke while men and women scamper around, doing their chores to the manic rhythms of a runaway metronome; much larger figures, some in uniforms, all with their arms crossed, are strategically placed to scan even the farthest reaches. They view the scene with puritanic disapproval. Some last wisp of common sense had saved me from large heraldic beer steins and mountains of potatoes, and the fairy-tale Gothic spires that everywhere pierced soft-looking clumps of trees had been my own embellishment. All a mirage, that vanished instantly.

The already gray sky did not turn to gunmetal, nor did officials, uniformed or otherwise, order us with belligerent efficiency to prepare for inspection. The sky that stretched in front of us was light, more curded than cloudy, and the only officials to be seen—carrying clipboards and quietly, rather slowly examining the under-bellies of thirty or forty trucks parked in long lines—ignored us. In a nervous urge to please, or at least establish my good intentions, I held our papers out the window, the "Green Card" for insurance conspicuously on top. No one was interested. Uncertain what to do, I eased the car along between the narrow concrete curbs that isolated my lane. The driver of the car behind us tootled. A Frenchman, not a German. A customs guard straightened up from a truck tire, laughed, and waved me on with emphatic gestures. We were in Germany.

At least technically. We had exchanged the green and white thruway signs of Switzerland for the drabness of another European border village whose buildings, always of indefinite architecture, look as though their backs are turned. Windows are shuttered. There seem to be no front doors; the shops are so deserted they might be no more than street dressing. Few people venture out and those few reluctantly. They wear shapeless clothes, seldom shift their eyes from some invisible object in the middle distance and acknowl-edge no language. Apparently the only defense against life on a border is physical and emotional withdrawal.

By a vacant lot whose weeds, empty bottles, and dross of plastic gave it an international character, I found a parking place and turned to look at the shops, one by one. Of all the signs I understood only two: BÄCKEREI and APOTHEKE. If I could trust the German on thousands of Italian bank windows, WECHSEL was what I wanted. I looked along the other side of the street. The offerings there were just as mysterious. Why on other trips to Austria and Switzerland had English, Italian, and my palsied French solved my problems? Ah, but that was different. There were friends and English-speaking concierges, and I was a tourist on vacation. The first chill ripples of defeat tickled the back of my neck. I glanced at Chichella, prepared to meet the same bewildered, anxious expression I knew must be on my own face. She turned back from the street, smiled, cocking her head in a motion that asked "What's wrong?" and suddenly I real-ized that what was so unnerving for me was, for her, a constant state. She cannot read. She does not expect to understand signs, even in Italy.

"Wait here, I'll be right back," I told her and got out of the car. She settled herself comfortably to wait.

"*Fai! Fai!*" She encouraged me as though I were off to some amusement. She was neither bewildered nor anxious. And this was my second surprise: she felt entirely safe as long as I was managing our affairs. The idea amused me. So far my record had been mixed. My performance in Switzerland—gas stations, a bank, two stores, and a restaurant where we breakfasted—hardly seemed enough to counteract the misadventure of the night before.

At dusk we had been 980 kilometers from Torregreca, our starting point of that morning. Milan was behind us. I did not want to go into the city of Como, so I pulled off the thruway at Saronno and considered myself lucky to find a very nice-looking modern motel in a grove of trees. Something about me disconcerted the clerk, sitting behind a console complicated enough for the largest organ. To his right up a short flight of stairs was a comfortable bar and presumably, beyond, a dining room. Nothing but double beds. I was tired: I assumed he meant two to a room. He accepted our documents.

I went back to the car and waited for the barrier to lift and allow us to pass into the compound. Each parking space had rippled plastic shields screening it from its neighbors. Novel, I thought, but of course I had not seen the room. The switch inside the door produced a baffling pink glow from a long glass-encased light over the bed, the only bed. I fumbled until I found another switch. Pink changed to eerie blue. Finally in the bathroom, which, I found out later, functioned as well as one might expect, there was a bright white light. It revealed a row of wardrobes set in the wall opposite the door and a strange hatch with a knob. I pulled the knob. Nothing happened. Beside it were complicated instructions for ordering any one of four meals, the only meals, served only in this way—at exorbitant prices—which would be put into the space behind the hatch by unseen personnel and could, at the sound of a buzzer, be withdrawn by you without your being seen. Back in the room I found Chichella frowning up at a mirror on the ceiling. I knew then—long before the noisy comings and goings of our neighbors interrupted my nightmares—that, more than a motel-hotel, I had chosen a *casa di appuntamento*, which catered to rich adulterous Milanese.

Walking along the street of that German border village, I laughed at myself. A very good dinner, not served by the minions of the hatch, revived Chichella's sense of humor enough for her to call us "the odd couple," but nothing will shake her old suspicion, now proven, that only women of light virtue take rooms in public accommodations. (Decent women have relatives or friends who offer, insist on offering, hospitality.) I cannot blame her. It was the first night she ever spent in anything that might be called a hotel.

Out of the corner of my eye I caught the last word, or as it turned out, syllable, of a very long gold and white sign that ran the entire length of a shop above its two windows and door: something, something, something . . . bank. As I crossed the street I noticed that the venetian blinds were closed, never a good omen. I tried the door: locked. It was 12:30, and my guidebook said banks closed from 1:00 to 2:30. Lesson number one: guidebooks are fallible. I had intended to celebrate our arrival in Germany with a real lunch, but being a cautious traveler (I was stuck once *in* the Mont Blanc tunnel), I had also bought the makings of a picnic, just in case the unexpected happened. It did: no money, no restaurant; and so, although I did not know it, I lost my only chance to have a an entire "German" meal on this first of my visits to Germany.

The sun had come out to light a flat, misty landscape with soft-looking clumps of trees, pierced by Gothic spires just as I had imagined. Small villages, their steep circumflex roofs jutting up in neat rows, dotted the fields where tractors worked back and forth harrowing. Entire families picked apples in orchards and mounds of potatoes waited by the roadsides for trucks to take them to market. Behind rose low wooded hills to complete the kind of sunny tranquillity usually found only in calendar pictures.

We had our lunch along with a dozen German families in one

of the many parking areas equipped with tables, benches, garbage cans, and even lavatories. Chichella ate automatically and said almost nothing. She concentrated on our neighbors, their clothes, which I think she found odd, their fitted picnic kits, and their Thermos bottles. With our brown paper bag we looked like vagabonds, and the Italian license plate on the car would not improve our status. There were a great many polite, quiet children and a surprising number of dogs; even they, going off into the woods behind the lavatories, seemed polite and quiet. As each family finished, the women brushed off the tables and benches and collected their wrappers, paper napkins, and heels of bread, which they dumped carefully into the garbage cans, and there was one for every three or four tables. With dignity that just escaped mockery Chichella performed the ritual for us. When she came back, she was shaking her head.

"Never work in Italy. One day and it'd be a garbage dump with flies—and rats," she said in an excess of self-criticism, she embodying, for the moment, her entire country. *Autocritica* used to be a ploy, almost an art form, of the Italian Communist party, which allowed the revision, or with care the absolute reversal, of inconvenient dogma. More extreme groups, and that there are such is another Italian anomaly, have taken it up as though it were Scrabble or. backgammon. Radio and television have obligingly overused it, and here we are with a new national panacea, which is like a dose of emotional salts and may replace confession. It has one great advantage: everyone can play. "We don't . . ." but she stopped and a gleeful grin spread over her face. Her eyes twinkled. "Eh, *lo sapete voi, signò*, if they put out trash bins as good as these, they'd disappear the first night."

I sent her to look again: the containers were shackled to their posts—even in Germany.

An hour later, about forty kilometers north of Freiburg, I turned off the autobahn and, as I had been instructed in Torregreca, took the first left after the bridge. To my surprise I ended up exactly where I was supposed to be with the railroad station in front of me and the Gasthaus Krönen in back. The proprietor of the *Gasthaus*, I had been told, would give me further directions.

Once through the door I was in a ginger den—ginger linoleum on the floor, the wainscot and tabletops, ginger Formica, the walls an unfortunate ginger-mustard mix. Only the chrome of the table legs and chairs anchored the room to the ground. Two men at opposite ends of the bar that ran along one wall looked up. They stared at me in silence and wonder, and for several minutes, until the proprietress appeared, all I could do was stare back with desperate composure. From beyond the swinging doors at the end of the bar came muffled sounds of washing up. Lunch, years of lunches and beery evenings, had left a heavy acrid musk about the place, which time had converted into a viscous substance, or so I imagined, and which was even now curling around the fibers of my sweater like smoke from an oil lamp.

Finally a large blond woman, perhaps forty, although her shapeless figure and even more shapeless cotton dress made it hard to tell, appeared in the doorway, wiping her hands on her apron. When she looked up, I was surprised to see the face of a china doll twenty years later, aged and bloated. She did not come toward me or seem the least interested in serving me, so I was forced to say the only thing I could.

"Do you speak English?"

"*Nein*," she answered with indifference and started swiping at the bar with a wet rag. What it really needed was cleansing powder and a lot of patience.

"Do you know where these people live?" I showed her my notebook with the name and address clearly written. She glanced at it.

"*Ja*," and she returned placidly to dragging the rag around a steel service sink. She had answered my question. She felt no need for further comment. If we had to play Animal, Vegetable, or Mineral, I was the automatic loser. The two men still stared at me. The woman squeezed out the rag, dropped it into the sink, and whirled around with her back to me. She gave out with a great rattle of German, which, of course, I did not understand, and wild gestures to her left.

"Unh," she grunted, pointing a long peremptory finger. "*Und unh! Gut?*" For the second turn to the left she pulled her elbow in by her side, from which I gathered I was not to go far along that road, then she pointed down: the address I looked for would be right there. She repeated the performance several times, each time the gestures were broader, her voice, louder. I nodded and smiled reassuringly, delighted that the theory of loudness—the louder a language is spoken, the clearer the sense will be to someone who does not understand—is not just an English fixation. I thanked her and left. The two men still sat, staring at me.

That was my first adventure, but *Gasthäuser* and hotels in the out-of-the-way places I would be staying were to prove my nemesis. Later that same afternoon I went off to a nearby town, no more than a large village, to look for a room. I had found my Italian friends; they had conferred and decided that if I must stay in town, then I should go to the hotel, although, they admitted, they had never been inside it. Too expensive. Such things are relative, but I was discouraged to find the hotel was at the intersection of the town's two main streets and drove on in search of another, twisting around narrow lanes, admiring the steep roofs, the timbered walls, the white curtains, and the window boxes with their cascades of ivy geraniums or pink and blue and white petunias. It was the antithesis of an Italian village. There were very few people about, none ambling down the middle of the street, no noise, no maniacs on scooters. Timbered houses and flowers and the sun shining—it was a travel poster. Suddenly in front of me on a slight rise was the ornate façade of a church, which, planned or otherwise, was the hub of all the lanes, each ending at the bottom of the stairs that surrounded it on three sides. And just there was a *Gasthaus*. I parked the car at the door and went inside.

More Formica and linoleum, this time tending to ochre, surprised me, but not as much as what happened next. Two older men with caps were seated at a table, drinking beer and talking to a young woman with long dark hair. The man with his back to me turned and shouted at me,

"*Nicht Italiene. Nicht! Nein! Nein!*" The sight of me enraged him further. His eyes bulged and the end of his nose became very red. As though beyond speech, he started waving vehemently toward the door.

[*26*]

"Why?" I asked in German, bewildered. My face must have shown my confusion and surprise, because my enemy put his head down on the table and laughed and laughed and laughed. Finally he lifted his head, said something to the others, and then all three laughed. I stood there, waiting without knowing why except that I refused to be driven off that easily. To say I was not Italian seemed cowardly. Probably they would not have believed me. To insist I was American might have stimulated greater rage (or do I mean prejudice?). Besides I did not want to be acceptable to them. I only wanted to know why "No Italians."

"Why?" I asked again. The young woman looked up at me for the first time, her eyes narrowed and spiteful. When I did not move, she pulled back the curtain and pointed down into the street at my car.

"Nicht Italiene! Nein! Nein!" She waggled a long index finger at me. *"Nicht Italiene!"* And, in case I had not understood, she jabbed out a stiff hand toward the door. As I closed it, I heard them burst out laughing again.

The second *Gasthaus*, in a quiet street a block or so closer to the center, did nothing to batter my ego further, but did not produce a room. Once more there was the Formica and linoleum, which I had come to expect, and also eight or nine young boys, students I imagined. A blond young woman, hardly more than a girl herself, puzzled over my double-room-single-room, with-bath-without-bath level of German and finally told me they had no single rooms and would charge the full price for a double even though it was occupied by only one person. She was not sorry to see me go, but she was courteous.

And so I ended up back at the hotel where there was no Formica and the floors were gleaming dark wood. In the hall-bar-dining room at a large round table sat two men and a heavy woman, perhaps sixty, with blond hair going white. (Had I been in France, I would have thought her a tired provincial Simone Signoret.) They were having afternoon coffee, but morning or afternoon, one of the men, presumably her husband, was always there, drinking something and talking to friends who wandered in to join him.

[27]

When the woman came over to a counter in the middle of the room to talk to me, she walked slowly, jerkily. Even in felt slippers her feet hurt and her joints were stiff. Still, she smiled. We both smiled a lot, and I was given a single room with linen as white as detergent makers assure you it will be, a creaky floor, a basin with hot water, a shower down the way, and breakfast of good German coffee and fresh rolls. Outside my window was a box of petunias and by the end of my several stays Frau-owner and I could discuss whether I had slept well—punctuated by many tentative smiles. I learned what I should have known. By 8:00 P.M., even at the main intersection, a German village is as quiet as a museum. I also learned once and for all, contrary to the helpful advice I had been given, that everyone in Germany does *not* speak English. In fact only twice on the entire trip did I find anyone who did: once in a bookstore in Offenbach and once in the ladies' room of a gas station on the autobahn when a woman desperately needed to borrow ten pfennigs for the toilet stall. If there is fault, it is mine, and fortunately it made slight difference. On other trips I would arm myself with interpreters and try to find out what the Germans think of their *Gastarbeiter*, their "guest workers."

On this first trip I wanted to slip back into the lives of Southern Italians, if they would have me. For all their smugness in Torregreca they must still struggle with their hopes and feuds, their discouragement, their misconceptions of both Italy and Germany, and their plans. Their own plans; or, as before, would they be the plans of others into which they must fit? I speculated ... but I am getting ahead of myself.

I was standing in front of the Gasthaus Krönen about to get in the car, make two left turns, and look for number 82 Hauptstrasse. Chichella looked relieved to see me. I followed the directions: two turns brought us to a plowed field on our right and on our left a row of houses. The first number was 84. I eased on; the second was 86. We passed several more and then houses began on the other side of the road. Perhaps, as happens in Italy with each epidemic of renumbering, 82 had been left on the wrong side of the road. I went on, knowing I would have to turn around, but intrigued by the tall, timbered houses, each with its garden and hedges and its gate. At every window were full, white curtains and window boxes, even at the miniature town hall, which was new and had been built in an official utilitarian adaptation of the same timbered style. There was a school, a nursery, a grocery, a baker's shop, a hairdresser, and a bank in a small cottage set back in some trees. On the gate a sign advised that business hours were only three afternoons a week. There were also two cemeteries, more or less in the center of the village, both very green and well cared for, with small chapels of their own.

Two blocks beyond the town hall we were again in the middle of fields, and hardly more than two blocks farther, we came into another village, much like the first except that the timbered houses were arranged in neat spirals around a low hillside. At the top was a "castle," or more properly a manor house, of dark mossy stone.

On our return trip, when we were already in the eighties, a car pulled away directly in front of us, revealing a gate we had not been able to see before and the number 82. This, then, was Michele and Edda's. Behind a tall hedge, the front section newly trimmed, the sides, scraggly in the extreme, only the eaves of the two-story house were visible. Approaching it from the railroad station, as we had the first time, two large trees screened it from sight. It was much like the other houses in the village except that the timbers needed oil, the plaster a coat of paint. My first thought was uncharitable. Southerners are allergic to maintenance: they will let a house fall down around their ears, and when it does, they curse the builder, usually these days the state. Later I learned that the house belongs to a Frau Schmidt, a much older woman of limited means who plans to leave it to two nephews in Hamburg. She cannot afford repairs; the nephews are interested only in selling. In compensation she has given Michele and Edda as much land as they want for a vegetable garden, where, even in September, there were tomatoes, salad of all kinds, basil, squash, and the last of some dwarfish grapes.

Chichella got out of the car and began shouting singsong, "Oy, Ed-DA! Oy, Ed-DA!" just as though she were in Torregreca, standing in the middle of the Via Appia Antica, trying to bring her sister-in-law out on her balcony for a chat. A man on a bicycle stopped ped-aling to stare at us disapprovingly and then wobbled on, shaking his head. Chichella laughed at him and howled all the louder.

"Oy, Ed-DA! Ed-DA! Ed-DA!"

"Oyee, Chichel'!" came the booming, flat voice that is Edda's only tone. To her, volume, not nuance, is important, so sympathy, secrets, and tirades are delivered in identical, most unmusical bellows that make her seem witless and stubborn. "We didn't expect you until next week." She had come to the side door toward the back of the house and, still shouting, looked out. Automatically her next remark was louder, the slight variation in cadence implying some emotion—surprise? pleasure? nervousness?—which would remain un-certain. "And the *sig-nor-a!*"

Edda's appearance always surprises me, partly because I hear her before I see her and, as well as I know her, am again unprepared for her smallness. She is little more than five feet tall with a fine, slightly arched nose, small, intent brown eyes, and blond-streaked brown hair that could be attractive if she did not favor kinky per-sian-lamb permanents and occasional quick washes in the kitchen sink. Twenty years ago, when I first saw her, though she was almost pretty, there was also a sadness in her face which I always attributed more to the structure of her mouth, which is wide and thin-lipped, than to any emotional cause. Time, anxiety, and perhaps disappoint-ment do not improve anyone. Edda has had the added misfortune of losing her upper front teeth, so that her mouth is wider and straighter than ever, not sad now, almost bitter, but she herself is not a bitter person. Noisy, thundering she is, but she is also good-humored in her bluff way, quick to rage, quick to voice it and just as quick to forget it. Her motto, if she had one, would be "Ah hell, what's the difference," a point of view that makes her both amiable and infuriating.

For a moment, as she bounded down the stairs and across the yard, I had an odd feeling we were back in Torregreca. What she wore was identical to the clothes of years past: a striped blouse tucked into a black skirt that was held together by an enormous safety pin; backless slippers that slapped against her heels. The only change was that the safety pin did not just replace a missing button; it functioned as a gusset to accommodate a small, melonlike tummy.

Behind her came a tall, very muscular man/boy wearing blue jeans and a work shirt. He had to be about twenty, which meant he was their younger son, named Tiberio because to his mother the name sounded exotic. Everyone calls him Berio. The five or six years since I last saw him had been crucial. The small brilliant-blue eyes were the same, but the thick brown hair, the bristly moustache, and the muscles were all new. He had grown into an extremely hand-some boy. I must move my car immediately. I was blocking the bicycle path, he shouted at me in a hoarse booming voice, like a seal's, that confirmed he was Edda's son and also that he had been in Germany a long time, at least long enough to lose the Italian's casual disregard for regulations. (Berio was also conscientious about the village council's decision that, to avoid the expense of a street sweeper, each family must be responsible for the verges and paths in front of its own house. He even gave me a solemn lecture on the civic responsibility of neighbor members of a community, which amused me: eighteen years before in Torregreca I had harangued my neighbors in public housing and later the new residents of the "Vil-laggio" with the same theory—to no avail. They thought I was daft.)

After he had opened the gate, and I had obediently moved the car, we unloaded Chichella's suitcase and the boxes crammed with cheese, *salame*, pickles, olives, peppers, and relishes in oil, which had been dragging at the trunk like sea anchors. Everyone took some-thing, and we trooped toward the side door, where a tall, dark-haired girl of fifteen waited listlessly. Assunta had only been in Germany six weeks. Her dislike of it had brought on an almost per-manent silence. The only time she said more than a few words was one evening when, before anyone noticed, she managed to gulp down four glasses of wine.

The door led to a glassed-in corridor that ran the length of the house along the back, the garden side, past a formal "front door," which was never used, to the end where there were three doors: to the left, a storeroom; in the center, the nonflush toilet; and to the right, the kitchen. It was not a large room (9' × 12' maybe) with faded tan linoleum on the floor, white curtains at the window, a four-burner electric stove with an oven, a steel sink, and the arrangement I was to find in every Italian-German kitchen, an L-shaped bench covered in plastic with an extendable table, so that no corner space was lost. Along one short wall were cupboard doors, which opened onto shallow shelves and, in the corner behind a door into the hall, a small wood-burning stove. Edda, who had already decided that I must be bullied into giving up my idea of a hotel and stay with them, insisted on an immediate tour of the house.

The hall, parallel to the glassed-in corridor, was bare except for a chair and a mirror—that evening I would learn their function. To the left was the living room, again not a large room, but a very bright one with sun flooding in through a window and a French door that opened onto a small balcony-porch completely taken up by a derelict sofa. Again, there were sheer white curtains. (Southern Italians like to watch their neighbors and have always been happy without curtains. If, indeed, they have them, they are inclined to loop them together in a high knot to get them out of the way. But not in Germany. Everywhere I went, they had borrowed the local custom of shielding their rooms, and so their lives, from intruders and put up immaculately white curtains. In part these are a substitute for shutters, but only in part, because the women were very proud of their curtains and recommended them to Chichella.)

The furniture was a heterogeneous collection of styles and shapes, which puzzled me. It was beyond me to ask directly where they found it all, but, as so often happens, patience was rewarded. One evening, when I was visiting in a different household, one of the men started laughing about the Turks and their willingness to do *anything* to make money, accept any salary with or without insurance, cut any kind of figure. (Prosperity had dulled his memory of the days when it was the Italian who was willing to accept *any* paid work.) As an example he cited the Turks' Saturday and Sunday sideline: they take carts and go through the villages collecting anything bulky that people want to dispose of and then sell the same things to emigrants. When I mentioned the story to Berio, Edda interrupted to say that all their furniture, even the icebox, had come from the Turks' carts, except, of course, for their double bed. That was new.

Her sofa and two chairs upholstered in knobbly beige were the square lump style that used to be called "moderne," while a rattan table completed the "suite." Just inside the door of the living room was another small wood-burning stove, and beyond it, stretching all the way to the corner, was a bed with a bright red coverlet. Diagonally across from it, an old icebox with rounded corners and a large pull-down handle served double duty as a television table. Next to it was a "buffet" of sorts, an example of seventies' sophistication in black and white plastic and smoked glass. Of course on the floor was the ever present linoleum.

Next to the living room was a bedroom large enough for the usual "matrimonial" bed, the obligatory wardrobe and the lone chair that must sit at the end of the bed. Again at the windows, gleaming white curtains, on the floor, linoleum.

A curved wooden stairway, very solid and waxed to deadly slickness, led to the second floor where over the living room was another bedroom that Berio and Vincenzo, Chichella's elder son, shared. They had painted it and almost plastered it with posters. By each bed was a sagging overstuffed chair and a pile of comic books, but the obvious focal point was the elaborate tape deck and radio enshrined on top of the only dresser. Berio had bought it with his first paycheck.

Another bedroom next to theirs was empty except for small mounds of beans, three or four different kinds, some chick-peas and ditty bags and cardboard suitcases that I recognized from trips on Italian trains with emigrants. A third bedroom was kept by Frau Schmidt for storage of her own possessions.

I admired everything quite sincerely. Edda's answer was always the same: "Yes, but the house is old." When we came back downstairs, I was still insisting. At the foot she turned to shout at me once more, but she hesitated for several long seconds.

"Well, if you look at it." She waved her arm in a broad general sweep, by which I gathered she meant Germany. "Then I guess, as far as the house goes, we're better off. All this room and the garden—and everything. We've got rabbits in a shed out there too. Michele keeps talking about chickens." As she came to the end of this admission, she frowned, perhaps about the chickens, or she may have remembered she had not shown me the bathroom, which had to be between us and the kitchen. I waited. She stopped outside the only door that could lead to it and deafened me with a torrent of curses against what she was about to show me.

It *was* the only bathroom I had ever seen that lived up to that name and only that name. It was a closet just large enough for a huge old-fashioned tub and a wood-burning water heater.

"It has one advantage, Edda. That's a lot bigger tub than the one you had at home," which in fact had been a sitz bath. I waited for the abuse my cheerfulness would bring down upon me. Instead she guffawed.

"Yes, and I've got plenty of well water to fill it too. Not like down there. Come on. Assunta will have coffee ready by now."

Back in the kitchen we sat around the table, Chichella and I drank thimbles of black coffee, which are the bracers offered to travelers, and argued about my going to a hotel. Berio shouted fabulous prices, Edda was raucously offended, Chichella tried to take up my part and occasionally, when the racket subsided, I repeated that it would be easier for everyone if I stayed in a hotel. When we reached a stalemate, I found an excuse to go out to the car and left Chichella to settle the matter. From past experience I know she invents idiosyncrasies for me, tailored to the situation. It is a system that always works and did again. Later she admitted she had not been forced to use her imagination. She simply told them that I like to read in bed at night—until all hours—which is true enough. She considers it one of my most bizarre habits.

Berio, who was employed as an unskilled construction worker and was normally attached to a painting crew, had fallen off a low scaffolding that morning and scraped his arm. Although it was more like an extremely bad rug-burn than an open wound, he had been sent home for the day. Now it had stiffened and hurt. He wanted to buy bandages and some ointment in town. He had also told Chichella about a store there that had everything—with price tags. You did not have to explain to clerks. Chichella cannot resist such carry-everything stores, like Sears or the English Marks and Spencer. This was the first of many forays. We promised to be back before Vincenzo and Michele came home from work.

One cold, rainy fall morning in 1959, when I had lived in Torregreca less than six months, I drove into the upper Piazza and found the parking spaces blocked by a truck loaded with a large mechanical something—all outsized wheels, ratchets, and belts working shafts up and down—that looked like a homemade torture device. Whatever engine propelled it had given up combustion for explosion. I parked the car somewhere and, since my errand was at the post office, returned to the Piazza. The machine was still grinding and snorting along. Each cycle seemed to end with a thud and a metallic sound. Finally, by following the belts and gears, I discovered a long metal spear, like the bit of a pneumatic drill, that was raised by one of the shafts, then released to disappear behind the workings in a propelled free fall. A second later came the metallic clank.

Around on the offside of the apparatus I found a man surrounded by wood that had been cut the thirty-centimeter length required for stoves and then split lengthways into two or more pieces. As the bit rose he grabbed another log, placed it on its end, and held it for the bit to skewer, then split it and hit the metal plate below. The bit lifted, the man threw the pieces aside, reached for another log, placed it, waited for the splintering crash and the lifting of the bit. Farther toward the front of the truck was a large pile of sawdust and above it a saw blade set at right angles to the truck floor and apparently driven by another series of wheels and belts. The man, of course, did not look up from his lethal drill, and I went on about my business.

By that afternoon I was very interested in finding him because I had realized I was almost out of stove wood myself, so I went back to the Piazza. If he was not there, someone would tell me who he was, where he lived. The machine was still there, banging along in its erratic way, and its attendant was still placing logs carefully under the falling bit. I need not have worried. The Bishop intended to stay warm that winter: his order would take three days to split. To get the man's attention without causing an accident, I stood near him, where he could see me, and waited. He was sturdy, not very tall, with wavy brown hair and a broad, almost square face very clearly defined by heavy bones, although his features were even and not at all large. When he flipped the switch on that remarkable engine and looked up, I saw that he had very, very blue eyes.

Seldom has anyone been rude to me in Torregreca, but this man had a courtly, almost protective manner. True, he listened to me with his eyes on the ground, the workman's stance I dread as the prelude to objections, doubts, and often refusal. He heard me out, never lifting his eyes. When finally he did, he gave me the sweetest smile, as though I were a child asking once more for his help. The amount I wanted was easy to supply. He might even be able to find that much dry wood, instead of this wet stuff. He jerked his head back toward his mechanical monster. Two more days would see him through this order. The day after that, maybe sooner, he could bring mine. In any event he would let me know the night before, so that I could have someone there to carry the wood upstairs, something I had not considered in my plans. Above all, I was not to worry. I would have wood before I ran out, and if I had been that little girl, he would have put his arm around my shoulders to reassure me. Instead, he lowered his voice and gave me firm instructions about negotiating with his padrone and about the fair price. I was not to pay one lira more. Did I understand? I said I did and to convince him repeated the price. On his way back to the log splitter he turned and called after me, "Remember, you're not to worry. I promise we'll be there." I was more puzzled than worried.

The next morning when I was having my breakfast, Chichella came in and bustled around rattling pans and clattering dishes, actually doing nothing, which with her is a sure sign of ill humor. Eventually, resigned, I looked up from my book and asked what was the matter.

"Why didn't you tell me you wanted wood?" How had she found out? "That man you talked to yesterday—in the Piazza—he's my brother, Michele. He came by last night. Said he's having them bring it this evening just as he gets off work. That way, we'll load it up ourselves." And she marched off to make my bed, leaving me properly scolded and contrite.

Twenty years and a great many marriages later I can even keep the spouses of the nieces and nephews more or less straight, but at the time it seemed to me that every man I talked to was related to Chichella and too often to be quite possible was a brother or brother-in-law.

Michele was one of the six brothers (and one sister) who grew up with Chichella in that one large, windowless room they knew as home, where the donkey slept in an improvised stall at the back, separated from his owners by a low partition, and where chests and benches served as beds for the children at night. There was no light, no water, and the fireplace was the kitchen stove. (Several blocks down the cobbled street were the public latrines, always foul, cold in winter, fly-infested in summer.) All that happened in the private lives of two adults and eight children—their conception, their birth, their illnesses, and their rages—happened in that one room, while the chickens pecked about in the cracks between the stones that were the floor and the donkey chewed, brayed, pissed, and plopped.

For a while Michele must have lived in the cradle suspended by ropes over his mother and father's bed. If he cried, a pull of the rope tied to the headboard sent him rocking and lulled him back to sleep. Later, when his mother went to cook and clean for the padrone (her services were part of her husband's contract, and unpaid), she took Chichella with her—she was too ambulatory and mischievous to be left at home—but he could stay, immobilized by his swaddling, asleep on her bed.

Michele remembers Chichella teaching him how to warm his feet on cold mornings by sticking them in the ashes of the previous night's fire. It helped. There were not always shoes enough to go around and the rag wrappings that bound their feet did not keep out the damp, much less the chill of a Torregreca winter. He did not take to school. In the end he did not finish the fifth grade, but he worked, even as a little boy, for his father in the padrone's vineyard.

Then the war came. Antonio, the eldest son, was killed, their father died, and Chichella, more by sheer force of will than any right, took over the management of the family.

Chichella worked on a women's crew at a large *masseria* in the valley far below Torregreca, where the fields were fertile—and malarial. There she lived much of each year, sleeping on the floor of a loft, a sack of corn husks for a mattress and a large communal sheet of canvas for warmth. Each girl tried to add whatever chewed-up blankets and sweaters she could to this basic bedding the padrone supplied. The work schedule was simple: from daylight to dark the girls hoed, or picked, or reaped, as the season required. Their meals were simple too: a daily ration of a kilo of bread apiece, peppers, tomatoes, or occasionally a bit of cheese to put on it, and in the evening a dribble of oil for the bread and the right to use a gas burner to make soup of it. Now Chichella would starve rather than eat soup. Fourteen years of it were enough. All this for pennies a day. If it rained, they were given their ration of food, but were not paid. And it was there that Chichella decided to take Michele, when he was thirteen, and Sabatino, another brother, who was twelve.

The padrone would not hire them. They were too young for a real job, but they were not too young to work and learn. He allowed them to sleep in the men's quarters, a kind of one-room "bunkhouse" with tiers of wooden platforms, four or five to a row, for beds, and eat whatever the men cooked up at night—at best pasta, at worst bread soup with maybe a plug of *salame*. By day the boys chored for the animal keepers, or helped the shepherds milk and graze their sheep.

Two years later Chichella became the "boss" of the women's crew and argued and fought and bargained with the padrone until he agreed to take on Michele and Sabatino as shepherds, for a fixed annual amount of grain and salt and oil and a small payment in money, no more than a token. With their supplies in sacks slung over their shoulders, they left, driving their small flocks to the grazing land some fifteen or twenty miles away from the *masseria*. One of Chichella's duties each week was to carry their ration of bread across the bare, rocky hills to them. The trip alone frightened her, but she knew those two boys were more alone and frightened than she. Once a month, sometimes more often, they came back to the *masseria* to get clean clothes, supplies, and maybe a hot meal.

This is not a medieval tale: it happened in the mid-1940s. To avoid self-congratulation on recent progress in what has always been called a "depressed" area and should in today's jargon be labeled a "non-emerging" area, I offer this article from the *Corriere della Sera* (one of the Italian papers of record) of November 17, 1976, page ten. It happened less than fifty miles from Torregreca. Italy does, of course, have child labor laws: the legal minimum age is fifteen. The increases in prices paid for Michele Colonna reflect inflation (and fluctuations of exchange) rather than compensation for his improved skills.

SOLD AT 11 YEARS, SUICIDE AT 14. ONE-YEAR PRISON SENTENCE FOR THE "PADRONE."
One year for Giacinto Lorusso, padrone of the *masseria* "Selva" of Altamura, a town 46 kilometers from Bari; one year for Francesco Colonna, also a landowner; six months for Marco Pignatelli, Lorusso's overseer [factor]; and eight months for Michele Di Benedetto, a leaseholder. Fines and damages to the family. This is the outcome of the trial that saw the four accused of mistreatment of a minor, Michele Colonna, born in 1960, hired as a shepherd for a flock in the country outside Altamura. "Bought" in the piazza by a private agreement, made to work for fifteen hours a day without rest, not even on Sunday, he came home only once a month to change his clothing. He was without either a work book or social insurances. Michele Colonna, after three years of this life, killed himself the 6th of November, 1975, with a shot from a shotgun. He had found the weapon in the house of his last padrone, Giacinto Lorusso, who entrusted the management of the *masseria* to Pignatelli.
Michele Colonna was 14½ when he killed himself. But he had been working from the time he was 11. His is a poor family: his father is a janitor at the Agricultural Cooperative, his mother, a housewife; three children remain (the youngest, 12, works in the fields with his father). Francesco Colonna, the first

padrone, "bought" Michele in Piazza Duomo the 15th of August, 1971 (the designated day for the market—i.e., sale—of workmen) for 40,000 lire [$64.52] a month and a few kilos of cheese annually. Di Benedetto, in 1973 [bought him] for 70,000 lire [$112.90] and an annual 8 kilos of cheese and a lamb; Giacinto Lorusso, in 1974, for 125,000 lire [$156.25], 10 kilos of cheese, 15 quintals of wood, 12 kilos of oil, and 12 of salt. The money, each month, was given to the mother. Before buying him they looked him over and considered him carefully: "One cannot assume the responsibility of taking on a boy for heavy work"—one of the defense lawyers stated—"without being sure that he is able to bear physical and moral suffering."

... Michele's day began between three and four in the morning: 200 sheep to milk and then follow for kilometers while they grazed. At lunch a piece of bread. After 15 hours of work ... in absolute solitude and in whatever weather, he returned to the farm. For dinner a plate of pasta. Michele slept in the stall with the cows and calves: in the same excrement, mud, and stench. He was locked in from the outside. The last stall got its only air through a small hole high in the door. On the moors in the winter the temperature reaches as low as -10°C [roughly 16°F] and the boy had to stay without a fire for fear of choking the animals. Alongside him they even threw dead animals that were to be fed to the dogs.

And still the last padrone, Lorusso, had a nice house above the stall: he came from Bari with his friends for excursions. The defense exalted country life where the young do not take drugs, do not smoke, dress up, where corruption and dishonesty are not the order of the day. The defense also praised the will of a boy who, refusing schooling and progress, must lead a difficult life. The 6th of November was a day like any other. Toward four o'clock Michele was severely reprimanded. "After all you're a man, and you will have to act like one." At six o'clock he disappeared. For three days no one looked for him: Sunday morning they found him dead 15 kilometers from the inhabited area. He had killed himself with Lorusso's shotgun: he had propped it between two stones and then tied a cord, one end to the trigger, the other to a stone. Michele threw the stone and the shotgun fired. He bled to death.

... His mother does not accept the death of her son: "He was happy in his work. He chose it after the fifth elementary grade. He wanted to buy a *masseria*: someone killed him."

... The defense has insisted on the innocence of the four accused, repeatedly citing the commonness and diffusion of the practice and [also citing] social conditions.

Our Michele and Sabatino were more fortunate in many ways, not the least being that Chichella bargained for them. As soon as they were old enough and strong enough, she argued until they were given yearly contracts as *salariati*, salaried general workers, like our "hired" men. They were still paid in a mixture of money and kind, but they lived at the *masseria*, had a hot meal every day, one they could add to from their "in kind" supplies if they wished, and had fixed days off. Chichella watched over them to be sure they did their work as they should—and for several years she collected their money and doled it out to them as she saw fit. She was the family dictator: no one objected; they were all young.

But Michele began to grow up. He was very handsome and, to his and everyone else's surprise, had a good singing voice. He was in great demand for dances—after weddings, during Carnival, and especially at summer harvest. Somewhere, not even he remembers just where, he started playing the drums, which he had to borrow from the regular drummer during intermissions, or as he soon learned, he could invent them from pans, pails, barrels—hollow anythings. And there were girls. He was restless. He did not want to stay stuck out in the country at a *masseria*. He also wanted his own money. Chichella must have been cross. She still complains that the boys spent all their money. "They were young. When you're young, a package of cigarettes, a glass of wine, they're important," she admits. "But I was young too—and saving to buy sheets and things for my dowry. Eh, no! Everything I had went to feeding them at home and buying us clothes. I got pretty sick of them." She may have, but she knew they were lucky to have work and some kind of life.

So did Michele. He drudged on, hating the endless days and waiting for a chance to escape, which came, as it did to almost every young man his age, in the early 1950s with the advent of public building. It was supposed to be a "program" to stimulate development, industry, and so employment (and incidentally supply schools, housing, and roads, as all such schemes do). Instead it has become a here-again-gone-again phantom, a celestial signboard that flashes on every few years, as new funds are allotted, and as suddenly disappears when the main switch is flipped off again in Rome. Michele did not know, nor did anyone else, that its most lasting effect for him would be a love-hate relationship with the employment office, and, eventually, brief periods of unemployment compensation.

He applied and was hired as an unskilled laborer on the first of the housing developments. He was the right age, strong, tireless and, because he wanted to escape the fields, uncomplaining.

On the strength of his new prosperity, he married Edda, who was small and blond and pretty. There were no houses, so they crowded into two rooms with her family. Her father is a precise little man who has farmed other people's land with the same precision that he lavishes on his own small strip of vineyard (and, as I found out, that he would also use when the *comune* hired him on partial pay in one of the unemployment campaigns, to dig and hoe the nursery garden). For him precision is a cast of mind. He carries on long, didactic discussions about whatever interests him at the moment, which must be entirely for his own satisfaction because no one has the patience to listen to him—and he knows it. Edda's mother is a heavy, dark-haired woman with moustaches and the crabbed expression of someone who feels perpetually ill used. (It may be only an illusion created by eyes too close together.) It cannot have been a gay household, and even less so when, two years later, the housing construction was completed and Michele signed up, along with most of his friends, at the government-run employment office. They were in line for the next public construction, but no one knew when, if ever, that might start.

Eventually Michele found seasonal work with a man named Fiore, who had cornered the firewood market. He needed strong men, willing to cut wood, load, saw, and split logs—for seven months of the year. What they did (or ate) for the other five months was of no concern to him.

Michele has never said so, it is only my supposition, but I believe that he and the others were not insured, that they were hired to work a day at a time. Probably they were paid a premium on their day's wage not to insist on insurance. The system was (is) dangerous for the employer, but often made (makes) the difference between a slight profit and absolute loss. Insurance payments would produce the loss: permanent employment of the workmen, automatic bankruptcy. The choices were evil for the men too: accept the day's pay and its premium or refuse and have nothing. At the end of the season the men could denounce Fiore, but their chances of gaining anything (especially since insurance payments are made to the state) were slight and their chances of alienating their employer, and so any hope for a job next season, certain.

Michele understood the system: he was careful to stay on good terms with Fiore. Years when there was construction work, he took it and then worked overtime, Sundays and holidays, cutting wood. Years when there was nothing else, Fiore always had a place for him. It was a kind of insurance for a man who already had two sons—Nicola, who, on my first trip, was away in Italy doing his military service, and the roaring Berio. By then Michele almost never sang or played the drums, except occasionally in the winter. Most nights he fell into bed with the sound of the bit still clanging in his ears.

In the 1960s Italy was in full boom, the "Italian Miracle." The industrial gold rush was on, bringing with it a most un-Italian hysterical optimism. Even Torregreca quickened from torpor to something approximating activity. There was a new epidemic of public building and the relaxation of emigration laws (notably to Switzerland, before the Common Market agreements) brought remittances. The Torresi plastered their houses and bought new kitchen stoves, and Fiore expanded his firewood business into a small sawmill. Michele was one of the first permanent workmen hired and as though some bureaucratic fairy had waved a magic wand, he was given an apartment in new housing for insured workers. I do not mean to suggest cause and effect, but he also had three more children, all girls, the eldest, young Assunta who is now in Germany. With a permanent job, health insurance to take care of most medical expenses, contributions toward an eventual pension, and the subsidy the government paid for each minor child, Michele had only one complaint and he seldom mentioned it: he was slowly going deaf in one ear. The crashing and banging of the infernal splitting machine was taking its toll. Instead of complaining he smiled that same gentle smile and shrugged: it was one of the hazards of the job.

In 1966 the sawmill was prospering in its small way. The equipment was still rudimentary, but Fiore had saved and ordered a new power-saw table. With luck he would be able to pay for it in three years. Old habits, old economies are hard to lose. Fiore hired a young boy on the old system—technically day by day, without insurance—to do manual work: hauling, loading, whatever needed to be done. He was *not* to go near the machinery. One day, of course, he did. No one noticed him until there was a shriek and he was pinned to the floor, a metal bar driven through his stomach and out through his backbone. He died. Fiore was tried, convicted, and ruined. Michele was unemployed again.

There was no work in Torregreca: friends who worked in Germany told him that there, there was only the embarrassment of choice. When they went back in the fall, he went with them, discouraged and sick at heart, and shared their quarters at the same Gasthaus Krönen where I asked for directions. That sounds rather elegant for emigrant workers, but they did not rent rooms that a traveling salesman or a stranded tourist might take. Theirs were low, narrow cubicles up under the eaves of a long wooden shed that stretched out in back of the *Gasthaus* and served as a catchall for chickens, cases of beer, customers' cars, if any, and abandoned farm equipment. Just outside the back door of the bar, by the garbage cans, was a rickety staircase, the one entrance to the upper regions. They had a gas ring and could cook, which saved money, and they had a wood-burning stove that, stoked until the metal glowed red, still could not counteract the drafts that siphoned through the floorboards and walls as easily as water through a fish's gills. Michele worried about that stove. He had never lived in a wooden building. It seemed very temporary and frail, perfect touchwood for an overheated stove. He never slept well in the attic above the shed.

He had other worries too. The embarrassment of choice had evaporated in one of those sudden slumps that the construction business is subject to in any country. No choice, just the desperate scrabble for a day's work here, another there, never quite legal, never paid a full wage, never insured, and never permanently employed. The others were no better off than he except that they understood more German, which he was finding hard to learn. The constant change of jobs—each with a new foreman and new crews and the special terms of the trade that even an unskilled workman has to understand—made the language seem more complex than need be.

As winter settled in and with it the tension of unspoken fear, the men in the attic grew short-tempered. Arguments exploded over ridiculous nothings. Who hadn't washed his plate? Why were socks hanging on the towel rack? No one had any money to spare. They had no way to escape the attic, so, more often than not, they ate dinner and for the sake of peace went to bed. Some nights when they were sound asleep, they would wake up to thumping footsteps on the stairs, followed by fists banged on the door.

"You in there" came the shout of a German voice. "Anybody want to work tomorrow?" They stumbled to the door. Sometimes they knew the man, often they did not, but they all wanted work. "Be out on the road by six-thirty. A truck will pass by and pick you up, but it won't wait." And the man thumped back down the stairs to disappear into the night. No one asked what they were to do. It was pointless: they could not refuse. So for a few days they worked in the tanning factory, or loaded sacks of potatoes or mixed cement, dug foundations or cleaned sewers—anything, and always at cut-rate.

Michele smiles now at the idea. "Today they have to go to the Turks. They'll take anything—like us a few years ago—but you won't find an Italian who'll go along with it now. They ran us like blacks. When we got sick or hurt, they didn't know us. They know us *now*, and we know what the law says. There's one thing in Germany. What the law says is what is done. So they go straight to the Turks. They'll take anything—like hungry dogs."

That first spring, construction picked up as unexpectedly as it had slumped, and Michele found steady work, with his taxes and insurances in order, as a laborer assigned to a stone mason. He made money, sent some of it home, ate better, bought a winter jacket and, like the others in the attic commune, his temper improved. Now on Friday and Saturday nights after dinner they even went down to the *Gasthaus* bar and drank beer with other Italians, some old friends, others new. They shoved two tables together in a corner and laughed and shouted and yarned and of course drank beer until the good Frau decided to close up for the night. They were noisy, but good stories have to be appreciated—and topped. Animation generated more animation and more noise, but their noise was cheerful, never drunken, because like most Italians they drank beer to have an excuse to get together, rather than getting together to have an excuse to drink. Most of the German customers knew them, laughed at the din, and shouted louder themselves.

One night everyone had gone home. Michele and his friends were finishing the last beer before carrying out the bins of empty bottles for their landlord, when the door from the station square opened and four very drunk young Germans came in demanding to be served. The Frau-owner started to refuse, then shrugged and agreed. They could have chosen any table in the room, but they came and sat next to the Italians. The woman brought their beers and, as she turned back toward the bar, made signs with her eyebrows which Michele and the others understood to mean Stay here until they go.

They settled back in their chairs to wait and talked more quietly, speculating in broad dialect about how much trouble their neighbors might create. One of the group, a short, sturdy Neapolitan called Pasquà (for Pasquale) who had already been in Germany for seven years, had married a German girl, and worked as a qualified mason, warned that the Germans were looking for a fight. They were starting with anti-Italian insults. He advised his friends to ignore anything that was said, pretend not to understand even if they did. The others nodded and tried to keep up a normal conversation. If he said ignore them, they would. Pasquà was no coward.

In his bachelor days he had earned a reputation for being able to defend himself. Young Germans did not appreciate his way with their girls, nor did they see his charm, which must have been of the Neapolitan *putto* grown up. Now, in his late thirties and gone a little plump, he still has it. Brown curly hair, enormous, literally liquid brown eyes that offer doelike tenderness one second, and the glitter of malice and fun the next. A small arched nose, perfect even to flaring nostrils, and a red, red mouth, stronger than a cupid's mouth, something only a sculptor could mold. And he loves to dance. He discovered early that fat women often are better dancers, so before he could say "Good evening" in decent German, he dragged staid, plump ladies usually ignored out on the dance floor, then progressed to their daughters and so the trouble began. He danced on, ignoring the scowls, enjoying the lady in his arms, and if another beer turned the scowls to courage and underestimation of his strength, he enjoyed the fight that followed. No, Pasquà was no coward.

Suddenly, unexpectedly, one of the Germans turned with his mouth full of beer and sprayed it all over Pasquà. He wheeled around, his face flushed, and said very slowly,

"If you do that again, I'll hit you." His voice was quiet and though even to me his German has some Neapolitan sounds, he is fluent and understood instantly by everyone. The Germans roared with pleasure. Pasquà pulled out a handkerchief and wiped his face while his friends held a muttered conference about what they should do. Nothing, he told them. Pretend it didn't happen.

"So the little cock speaks German," one of the Germans jeered at him. Pasquà ignored him, as he ignored the flood of obscenities that followed, but his face grew redder and redder. The same man, again with his mouth full of beer, turned and sprayed Pasquà, whose control through the whole affair seems quite Olympian: he ignored him. The third time, however, that the man spewed beer on him, Pasquà stood up and hit him so hard that the man's chair flew over backward, still carrying its load. The man was out cold, but Pasquà did not have a chance to enjoy the scene. One of the Germans crashed a chair down on his head, splinters skittered all over the room, and Pasquà crumbled. Michele had dumped one man hard on his back on the floor. Two of his friends were sitting on the man who had been knocked out, chair and all. Two others were just barely holding their own with one of the Germans. That left one.

[47]

Michele glanced around and saw the fourth coming at him with one of the jagged spindles from the broken chair. He held it like a dagger. The man lunged against him, slamming him into the wall, and then brought the spike down hard—just missing Michele, grazing his jawbone and digging a deep furrow under his left ear. At that moment the front door opened again and the police arrived.

Unknown to anyone, when she saw the German squirt the first mouthful of beer over Pasquà, Frau-owner had called the police. They separated the men, lined them up on opposite sides of the room, and then took inventory. They cleaned off Michele's scratch and decided it did not need further treatment. Pasquà's victim had lost a tooth and leaned against the bar screaming threats. Chairs and tables were broken. The floor shimmered with the glass of shattered beer mugs, and the police wanted to know what happened, how had it started—from Frau-owner, no one else.

I have now heard the story from four of the men involved, separately, and each remembers what happened next in exactly the same way, with the same sudden fear.

Frau-owner looked at the Germans, blood-spotted and mad, wanting revenge, and she looked at the battered Italians, who certainly would have fought on if they had had to, but she said nothing. Michele, Pasquà, and the others all had the same sinking intuition and were cold and afraid. It would be so much easier, they realized, for her to say the Italians had insulted the Germans, had insisted until the Germans were forced to defend themselves. Instinctive loyalty: one's own must be protected. She hesitated one long minute more, eyeing them, and then said,

"That man," and she pointed at the German who had lost his tooth. "That man spit beer on the short Italian—three different times. The third time the Italian hit him."

The Germans paid the damages, a tacit admission of fault. Several days later, sober, they came and apologized to the Italians. It was probably an honest apology (Michele and the others took it as such), but they may also have wanted to stifle any bitterness that could lead to assault charges.

After that Michele and his friends still went to the bar sometimes early in the evening. They were quieter and a little wary. As the crowd grew and with it the first sullen quarrels, they took their friends off upstairs to the attic. Whatever happened below, their stories and the squalls of laughter that followed would not irritate the locals, jarring dull resentment into venom. They still went down and helped Frau-owner carry out the bins of empty bottles and if the customers got out of hand *and* she called them, they even served as bouncers, but they had sensed once and for all, more than they had ever sensed at work, that they were strangers.

Michele worked straight through the summer. When his friends went home for August, he stayed on, working for pay and a half. He had made his calculations. With the extra money and what he had saved, he could afford to go back to Torregreca. If need be, he could support his family for a number of months while he looked for work. This year there would be work at home, surely there would be work. But there was none, and so began a period of years when he was on a seesaw between Torregreca and Germany, always putting off his departure until he had almost run out of money, always returning with enough money to allow him months of looking for work. Once for a year and a half he was employed on the construction of a school in Torregreca. When that was finished, there was nothing more, and he was at the tail of the employment lists. He left again for Germany.

During those years I saw him occasionally, most often on the road near his house. By his walk I knew whether I dared ask about his job or had better be doggedly interested in children and weather. That gentle, thoughtful smile could still light up his face and his optimism bordered on folly. It'll get better. Something's bound to change, signora. You'll see. Next year ... But the slight creases of his frown had settled into furrows and at his temples wiry tufts of gray hair refused to stay slicked back, which, if they added a certain character to features that had been almost too smooth and undisturbed, also added years he did not yet deserve. Edda, with five children now and a husband too often unemployed, was almost invisible, except for her twice-weekly trips to the oven with a long tray loaded with wheels of bread dough on her head and her sprints to the market to buy whatever was cheapest. She had already lost two front teeth and was inclined to frown too in a half-cross, half-worried way that in her case did *not* add to her attractiveness. It was understood that Germany could not be mentioned to her. Anyone who dared was treated to a bitter tirade which could only have been perfected to such readiness by repeated stormy scenes with Michele. No, she would not go to Germany! She would not sacrifice her children! They had to go to school, to an Italian school, and they needed her with them. There was much to be said for both arguments, but no one dared to express an opinion, certainly not I.

I do not know what final dose of vetch brought on Michele's decision. Perhaps nothing specific, just the combination of negatives. He left in 1970 determined he would stay in Germany and he has. He lived again in the attic, then for a while he boarded with a friend and his wife, which is an arrangement that seldom lasts. (If by some miracle the family has been without tensions, the outsider soon generates them, often through no fault of his own.) Michele moved soon enough for them to remain friends and, again paying his part, went to live with a brother and sister-in-law. They left Germany, and he went back to the attic over the *Gasthaus*. There were times it seemed he might live in that attic forever. On his arrival in Torregreca that August for his vacation, he announced that Nicola, their eldest child, who had finished the *terza media*, the equivalent of our eighth grade and the end of obligatory schooling in Italy, would return to Germany with him. If Nicola wanted to be a mechanic, as he had always said he did, he could go to school in Germany, complete the minimum required there, and pass on into a professional school, a system that provides for half the day studying, half working.

It was a stormy visit, but when Michele left, Nicola left with him. In August of 1972, he took Berio back with him. He too would go to professional school. They all lived in the attic, Michele acting as mother, father, cook, and tyrant.

Edda's surrender seemed only a matter of time. Once she did make the long, dreary train trip, just, as she specified beforehand, for a visit. Later she admitted Germany "wasn't bad." She had expected it to be different somehow, grim, dark. She was not sure herself what she had imagined. The attic—now that was another matter; and we understood that she would resist yet a while longer. Cristina was born in 1972. The endless months, which could now only stretch into years of children—cooking and washing for children, squabbling with children, preaching to children, fighting for children with the neighbors, with teachers, even with other children—were eroding her determination. She saw too much of her parents, who now lived on the same staircase and had appointed themselves the defenders of her honor and the critics of her children's deeds, or more often misdeeds. For the town she was a *vedova bianca*, a white widow, and subject to an unwritten code almost as strict as official mourning. This was no life. If Michele could find a house...

In 1973 Michele rented the house Edda now apologizes for as old, and she and Cristina, hardly more than a year old, moved to Germany, leaving the three little girls, seven, eight, and ten, to live with her parents and obey their draconian rules. She sublet their own apartment with all the furniture so carefully chosen, so laboriously paid for over the years, to a midwife. The neighbors below complain that her schedule is erratic and that she wears wooden clogs in the house. Chichella brought that message once more and Edda erupted in a shriek of exasperation

"Always them! Always complaining. Nothing's ever right! My kids dirtied the stairs. If we walked around at night, we kept them awake. If we listened to television, we kept them awake! If I did the laundry, I took all the water! Always, something's wrong! Always!" And she made the abrupt half-circle gesture that, starting at the floor and finishing in the unknown, relegates pests to the inferno. "Tell them to get used to it. It'll be another ten years before we go back, and they can pick on me." She has accepted that, barring some unlikely miracle, they will not leave until Michele has a pension.

In these last eight years Michele has always worked as an unskilled laborer for contractors, usually as a helper for one or more masons. Five years ago he found a small firm he particularly likes and has stayed with them. His only transportation is a bicycle. A

Volkswagen bus meets the men in the middle of the village at 6:30 A.M., takes them to work, and brings them back. The salaries, with taxes and required insurance payments already subtracted, are promptly paid. A reasonable excuse gets time off. The foremen, the "Chefs" who were to haunt hours of our conversations, are all German, decent, friendly, and now passionately fond of spaghetti. They have their grumpy days, like everyone else, several drink on the job, have their hangovers and their problem wives, but I heard no one complain about them.

Michele was not to be spared the recession. Four years ago, at its peak, the building industry faded and the contractor was forced to let four men go—logically, the last hired. Michele had worked longer than the other three and was promised his job back as soon as there was any improvement. When that would be, no one knew. For the first twelve months he would be paid unemployment compensation, which, after his experiences at home, was small comfort. But he was in Germany. At the labor office officials told him that he would be paid 80 percent of his normal salary and had the right to do any odd jobs he found as long as he did not work more than twenty-two hours a week. They also warned that inspectors would keep track of exactly what he did: it speaks well for both that Michele was meticulously careful not to exceed the limit. Why should he? He was rich. Unemployed he had more money than he had ever earned. Everyone needed repairs, windows put in, walls built. Six months later he was almost sorry to have his job back— except that it was now permanent.

Michele *is* unskilled, so after four years he is paid 1,200 DM a month (about $600).* His rent is 120 DM a month ($60), his taxes and deductions, close to 60 DM ($30).

His elder son, Nicola, on his return expected to work for the same garage where he had been sent by the school for his half-days of practical training. By the spring of 1978 one more salary of ap-

* The DM was then the equivalent of 50 cents. Subsequent variations have brought it to 55 cents on January 1, 1979. The lira is more volatile. Between 1977 and 1979 it fluctuated between 800 and 890 to the dollar. During the 1950s and 1960s the lira had a stable value of 620 to the dollar. In all references to those years I have used that exchange.

proximately 900 DM ($450) would be added to the family income.

Berio had already moved from a leather factory to a contractor. He does a bit of everything, but is supposed to be a painter's assistant. His salary is 900 DM.

Edda is picked up every evening along with other women at 6:00 P.M. and driven to a large town nearby to clean one of the everything-under-one-roof, Sears-like stores. Each night when she comes home she has found some irresistible bargain, and on Saturdays the management urges the women to take as many roast chickens as they like at half price, so while I do not know her actual salary, she is fortunate to break even. Assunta either will join her mother on the cleaning detail or spend the mornings taking care of a teacher's child.

Vincenzo, Chichella's son, pays room and board from his monthly salary of 1,200 DM. (He has worked a shorter time than Michele, but is a qualified construction carpenter.)

By the winter of 1978 the combined incomes of Michele's household (not including Vincenzo's) were, after taxes and deductions, roughly $1,400 a month, plus Vincenzo's room and board and Edda's bargains and roast chickens. Everyone works and everyone saves. Their clothes are nice; they buy new ones. There is pasta on the table and meat every night, lots of it, a luxury no Torrese ever imagined would be part of his life. There is more coffee, *Schnaps*, beer, and cigarettes than is good for them, more dances, *Diskotheks*, and cinemas than they have energy for, medical insurance that actually covers them, and a local hospital that actually cures them. In nostalgic moods they wish they were back in Torregreca. Remember the time...? Whatever became of so-and-so?

Michele listens to them and laughs. "Which one of you wants to be the first to give up eating?" he asks them, but with a smile. "Get it into your heads *now*. Torregreca is a place to die, not to live."

By 5:15 that first afternoon we were back at Edda's, sitting in her kitchen while she peeled potatoes, Chichella made sauce, Assunta followed their shouted orders, little Cristina, next to me at the table, played with my keys and later, when my attention wandered, with the contents of my purse, Berio, on my other side, bellowed in my ear, and across from him a dark-haired youngish woman in a striped sweater and black pants, both too small and too tight to conceal a bulging stomach, tried to tell a long story to the cooks. She smoked one cigarette after another, jabbing each in the air to emphasize the details no one heard.

That day I knew nothing about her and at the same time a great deal. Her name was Maria, she had been in Germany twelve years, had five children, worked, had taken an hour off that afternoon to go to the hairdresser, and hoped to God she never saw Southern Italy again. Had I ever been in a Sicilian village? Did I know what it was like? The gossip? The backbiting, the envy? *Figurati* now! She smokes. She drives. She goes to dances with Raffaele. (Raffaele who? Presumably her husband, but I could not be sure.) If it weren't for his mother, she'd never go back, even for a visit, never, and if *her* family wanted to see her, they could come here—but they won't. They didn't care any more about her than she did about them.

Surmounted by a firm pagoda of hair, her face was round and crinkled all over when she laughed, which was often, and her full mouth, even in repose, remained a crescent. I imagined it attached by a secret network of muscles and nerves to her gray eyes that flashed and flicked across our faces in a most ungraylike way. Everything seemed to amuse her—jokes, illnesses, outright disasters—or if they did not, she was determined the next subject would. She allowed nothing to discourage her good humor or its magic store of energy, which in spite of her intention to share it, wore her friends down to an exhausted docility.

So far Chichella, who surrenders to no one, had watched Maria with a slight frown. She winked at me and then, turning back to her sauce pot, relaxed into skeptical silence. She had decided to relinquish the floor for the moment. She would take it back whenever she chose. Without recognizing it, Maria had met her match. All I had to do was sit and enjoy the sparring, but I had calculated without Berio, who took advantage of a slight lull to claim my attention in his imperative way. As I soon learned, his vocal cords needed very little rest.

Twice that afternoon he had been complimented on his German: the first time by the owner of the hotel, when he helped me with my bags; the second time at the store where he had herded us past the cashier. Praise had gone to his head. How did I think I could get around Germany without the language? It was ridiculous. I should have studied it before I came. Reminding myself that he was young and I must be patient, I asked if he had found it difficult to learn. No. Hard to write, but not to speak or understand, except all the dialects. They change from place to place, village to village. You've seen how close together the villages are? Well, that next one, not more than a kilometer away, has a different dialect from this village. Impossible! Not like Italy. Oh, really? My patience was a bit threadbare that day. Would he then claim that Venetian, Abruzzese, and let's say the Torrese dialect of the Rabata were equally clear to all Italians? The Rabata doesn't have a special dialect, he objected. (It is one of the *three* Torrese dialects.)

"The Rabata doesn't have its dialect? Is that so?" Chichella shouted from the stove, and I realized that she was blocking out all the other voices to eavesdrop on us. "Signò, like I keep telling you, a little schooling, a little Italian, ruins them every time. Tiberio," she lingered solemnly over each syllable, then liked the effect so well she repeated it. "Ti-ber-i-o wouldn't understand Rabatana if he heard it, and if you took him as far as Calciano, he'd never get back...." What further scorn she might have heaped on him, I cut off with a scowl. She laughed at his red face, but turned back to her sauce.

I asked if he had liked school. So-so. He'd made a lot of friends. Germans too. Still saw them, did things with them on weekends. What he hadn't liked was the job in the leather factory. Nothing but Turks. Can't talk to them. Have to watch them all the time. If you don't, they'll undercut the wages. You know, offer the boss their cousin for 100 DM a month less than you get. Sure, the German's interested in saving 100 DM. It's logical. Besides the work was foul.

What did they do on weekends? Well, he liked the *Diskos* best, but they were pretty expensive and he didn't have a car, so he couldn't always go. He had a friend, a German boy he knew at school, who had a car and usually came by for him Friday or Saturday night, then they hit them all. One after the other, as many as they could in one night. It was a real gas. He went to the films sometimes, but you might as well watch them on television. Probably the *Fests* were the most fun. *Oktoberfest* is the one everyone knows about, but they have them all the time. For new beer, for new wine, for this and that. They have these long metal sheds, like the ones they put up for factories (an elaborate variety of Quonset hut). There's one in every village. Every time there's a *Fest* they open it. Hundreds of people go—sometimes thousands—and they have beer and wurst and schnitzel and fried potatoes and music. They dance and sing all night and dinner costs almost nothing. You can even have two if you want. They drink beer and everybody gets drunk. So drunk they wander off into the fields and you don't see them for two or three days, until they sleep it off. The *Oktoberfest* is in a couple of weeks. You should stay. You've never seen anything like it! *Everybody* gets drunk.

The idea was not tempting. When Berio talks, he stares at you with those sharp, blue blue eyes until you find yourself staring back, bolted into position and at his mercy. Only the violence of the thump beside me freed me. Cristina had dropped my purse on the floor. We both went under the table to retrieve the oddments that had scattered about, among them my lighter, which she found intriguing: push the button and flare, push the button and flare. As we resurfaced I took it away from her and, putting it on the table, asked her not to play with it. She might hurt herself. She looked at me with defiant little black eyes that could just barely see out from under a black fringe of bangs. She clamped her mouth together and stared at me, estimating, I thought, just how far she dared push me. I almost laughed. She is a very fine-boned little thing with her grandmother's (Chichella's mother) small, pointed features and her same habit of squeezing them tightly together as though that would help her achieve maximum concentration. In Cristina this adult look of wisdom and shrewdness was disconcerting. For a moment she seemed about to—but she decided not to test me. Instead she put her hands in her lap and waited.

Do you go to the nursery I saw down the road? She shook her head. But you're old enough? She nodded, sitting up proudly. Don't you want to go? Oh, yes! She inspected me through her bangs, then hurried breathlessly on to explain. Oh, yes, but Mamma doesn't want me to go because she says it's too far and besides I can go to school next year. That's soon enough. And I can play *here*, but it's not the same. I want to go to the nursery. My friends go. And her face puckered up in real or mock suffering that might have turned to tears if the door had not opened to produce a new interest. Vincenzo was home.

He kissed his mother as though he had seen her that morning and shook hands with me. Except for his wide smile, it might have been any other evening. He just stood there in his baggy work clothes, which had once been blue twill, with his brown hair, eyebrows, and even his bushy moustache floured blond by brick dust and cement, looking at us like an amiable clown. I knew that in a second he would find something to do, something abrupt, that would rescue him from the need to express any pleasure.

Vincenzo, at twenty-six, is much like Vincenzo at seven, not that he is in any way retarded, but rather that his character and looks followed certain distinct lines early. Time has only accentuated them.

He was a slight boy with tawny eyes and a broad, generous mouth, which, if he did smile, seemed to light his face with a gentle, ambiguous glee. He smiled seldom enough that we were never sure if his reaction was to something external or to a more secret source. He was simply, for that moment, happy. He has grown into a muscular, not overly tall man who smiles more easily, and still we are often not sure why.

He was always shy, and if he no longer lowers his eyes and lapses into silence at a question, his answers are succinct. He shunts away from emotion with a skill that betrays him more surely than anything he could say. Stubborn as a boy, he still is: right is right, wrong, wrong. Practical things appealed to him. He hated school. He nailed together every board and crate stay he could find. He made sledges, boats, trains. He started bonfires and led his friends up muddy hillsides, waving a wooden sword, in search of hidden treasure, but he hated school. Chichella beat him, quite literally, through his eighth-grade certificate and now is as surprised as I to find her son is a man, who follows without seeming to the quirks of men's hairstyles and the cut of trousers and even wears glasses, as he should have for years, if the world was to be more than a blur for him. And not just any glasses: his are the drooping, wraparound kind with delicate frames that television announcers affect. He is a quiet, almost morose man, who feels, as he has ever since his father died twenty years ago, that he is the head of the family. He wants his mother to spend the money he earns. She refuses. He intends to take care of her. She intends to take care of herself. He will not consider the idea of marrying until his sisters are settled. He has certain obligations, which, long before we were aware of them, he had accepted.

Yes, he is almost a man and, somewhere along the way in his struggle to grow up, thank goodness he discovered that people are very funny. Maybe it was the surest defense, maybe Chichella's sense of humor is contagious, but however he acquired it, nothing is ever so serious as to be without its ridiculous element, that he can winkle out and play with, turning and twisting it until he is satisfied. If and when he decides to share his prize, he lowers his eyes shyly, as he did at seven, and whether others understand or not, I know he is amused, and I wonder now if this was the explanation for those rare, gleeful smiles he used to give us: we were funny.

"Where do you want this lunch pail?" he asked of the room in general, waving a battered briefcase with the neck of a bottle sticking out at one corner. He had found his escape. Maria took it from him and held it on her lap as though it were precious. Vincenzo disappeared into the hall, and Berio reclaimed my attention. He could teach me German easily enough and over my objections launched into an explanation of declensions. Vincenzo slipped in beside him on the bench with a bottle of beer and two glasses in his hands.

"The water hot?" he asked. Berio shrugged without looking away from me.

"You know I don't take a bath Fridays. It's one of my practice nights."

"You won't go with your arm bandaged like that."

"No, but I'm not taking a bath, so I didn't start the fire." Berio ignored Vincenzo's irritation to explain to me that he is a new member of the local soccer team. It meets twice a week to practice. Afterward he takes a shower in the locker room, but, of course, with his arm he wouldn't go this evening. As a topic I preferred soccer to grammar. Was his team good? Not bad, not bad. It is supported by the local athletic society and has a decent field with a clubhouse about two kilometers away. He is the first non-German player, he added proudly and, before I could stop him, slipped back to declensions. Vincenzo, who had pushed his way out from behind the table, grumbling that some people were pigs, and disappeared, banged back into the kitchen with an armload of firewood and screamed for Assunta. She was standing right in front of him, but I could not blame him: the babble was stupefying. Maria was once again trying to tell her story, which was interrupted every few phrases by Edda explaining to Chichella who the people were, and of course Berio was still roaring declensions in my ear. Cristina had given up trying to talk to anyone and was singing at the top of her voice, or what I hoped was its top.

After Vincenzo had shouted his instructions to Assunta about lighting the fire in the water heater, he slid back into his place beside Berio and opened the bottle of beer. Berio pulled the second glass over in front of himself, ready to have the beer poured.

"Dummy, it's not for you," Vincenzo grunted at him. "It's for the signora." Berio flushed, but held his own.

"Yes. Yeh, sure. I was just going to pass it."

"I bet."

Berio pushed the glass across to me and went on with his lesson. It seemed we had already reached adjectives. He explained at length and with many examples that they must agree with the nouns they modify. I listened, but watched Vincenzo, who was rubbing his left thumb with his right hand as though to warm it. Last June his hand had slipped when he was using a power saw and he lost the first joint of his left thumb. I broke in on Berio to ask Vincenzo if it hurt. He pulled his hand away from the thumb and I saw that it had a leather shield held on by two laces tied around the hand.

"Doesn't hurt exactly, but it gets numb." He twisted around trying to see the back of his hand to untie the laces. When he pulled the shield off, he stuck the finger over for me to see. "They did a good job, and ... well ..." He shrugged. "If I had to have an accident, this was the best it could be. Doesn't keep me from working, gave me a paid vacation—and here's the part I like—in forty years, mind you, forty years, I'll get ten marks a month extra on my pension." He looked down and smiled at the beer in his glass. "By then ten marks won't buy a package of cigarettes."

Berio wanted to return to adjectives. This had to stop. I told him it was useless, there wouldn't be time for me to learn, especially for me, because I am a slow learner. He mustn't worry, I would get along somehow.

"No, come on! It's easy once you get the declensions." I shook my head and held my hands up in front of me as though to fend him off. "You've probably never tried to learn another language, a *foreign* language. That's why you think it's hard. Now, take the numbers—"

"Professor Tiberio," Vincenzo broke in quietly. "Shut up! You're making a donkey of yourself." Berio looked startled, but Vincenzo had already turned away to call, "Hey, Ma, did you hear what Professor Ti-ber-i-o just said to the signora?" And he barked the phrase. " 'You've probably never tried to learn another language, a *foreign* language.' That's what he said, Ma. Would you believe it?" Chichella's eyes started to dance. My laughing was no help to her, but she kept her face straight and leaned toward Berio, waving the wooden spoon from her sauce as though it were a pointer.

"Professor Ti-ber-i-o, you have been talking to the signora ever since we arrived. True?" She spoke slowly, very clearly, in as close an imitation of my quite precise Italian as she can manage. "You have not let anyone else talk to her. True? Then tell me, Professor Ti-ber-i-o, *what* language does she speak to you?" Vincenzo pounded the table triumphantly. Berio looked at him, then at me, then at Chichella, frowning. The wrinkles were just relaxing, he might have a clue, when the door opened and a deep voice called,

"*Ma, in somma*, do you have to yell *all* the time? I could hear you clear out at the gate." Another door opened and bottles rattled. "I don't suppose anyone thought to put beer in the icebox," and Michele finally came in carrying an armload of bottles. "Owee, look who's here! Chichella—and *la signora*! Who'd ever believe you'd get Chichella this far?" We freed him of his load and he threw his arms around his sister with the kind of spontaneous excitement that Vincenzo had not dared show. Was she tired? Had she had coffee? Why was she cooking? She could sit down and rest, at least. Have a beer. She laughed at him: he must have forgotten who she was.

As though a new set in some ruleless game had started, everyone shifted. Maria decided that she was late and must go home, which she did with surprising speed and no wasted words. Berio withdrew to the living room where he played a rock tape so loud that we finally had to close the door. Cristina went with him to watch television, probably without the sound, and fell asleep. When it was discovered that the hot-water heater had gone out, Assunta followed them into exile. As we talked, the room suddenly seemed almost too quiet.

"*Scusate*, I shouldn't sit down this dirty. Maybe..." Michele's apology was not necessary. His work clothes were baggy, like Vincenzo's, but much cleaner, and his hair, now grayer than when I last saw him, had been carefully combed down close to his head. With his face pink from the sun, in looks and manner he might have been a distinguished banker, relaxing after a day of hunting. Again we settled down around the table—this time Michele, Chichella, Vincenzo, and I—while Edda leaned against the stove, listening. Michele's level eyes, still very blue and normally so serious, twinkled as he teased Chichella. Would she have her driver's license soon? Where was she planning to go on her next trip? Paris? Oh, New York. Eventually he asked what brought me to Germany. The question was so tactfully put that I could have avoided it, but I have always told them the truth and in detail if they, the Torresi, were involved. Certainly in this case they were: I had come to see how they fared in Germany.

Anything he could tell me he'd be glad to, and he leaned back as though he expected to be quizzed. I hesitated. Solemn investigation, set questions and bland answers were not what I wanted. If they could forget I was there with my project. . . . So I asked several formal questions to which I already knew the answers and finally worked around to where had he lived when he first came. (One night years ago on Chichella's balcony he had talked to me about the attic, but he would not expect me to remember. It is their absolute conviction, not false humility, that nothing about their lives is so important that you should remember it.)

Help came from an unexpected quarter: Vincenzo. When he was eighteen, he decided he could not wait forever in Torregreca for a job. He had two years before he would be called up for military service. Money was tight, prices high, and his brother and sisters needed things their mother's wages could not possibly provide. He went to Germany in search of work. He too lived in the attic. Michele and another uncle cajoled their contractor of the moment to try him—as a construction carpenter. Not that he was one or had ever actually worked as one, but he had wangled a certificate of qualification from the *comune* of Torregreca. It was a nervous time for the uncles who were not too sure of their own jobs. They watched him. They advised him. For a while they supervised every nail he drove and every beer he drank. Eventually he rebelled and fled to Turin, where less domineering cousins rented him a quarter of a room, but he remembers his sixteen months with his uncles, the work, and the attic, and even the story of the brawl. And he admits now that his uncles and their maddening fussiness taught him his trade. Whether he did it consciously or not, I do not know, but he started saying, "Remember when ... ? Didn't you tell me ... ?" And soon Michele had forgotten me and my project: he was reminiscing.

The kettle on the stove came to a boil and Michele looked surprised. His shaving water. He took the kettle into the hall, and suddenly I knew why the chair was in that most inconvenient place just outside the door, under the mirror. They could put·the basin on it and see themselves to shave.

Vincenzo told me about running off one weekend when he was so exasperated with his uncles that he had to escape. He got up very early one Saturday morning and took the first northbound train that came through the station. He didn't know where it was going, didn't care. He rode until he was hungry and then got off in a large town somewhere near Frankfurt. There, by chance, he found some Torresi not much older than he and spend the weekend and a bit more—until Monday afternoon—drinking beer with them. Michele stuck his head around the corner into the kitchen. He had taken off his shirt and was busy lathering his face.

"And when you came back, what did we do to you?"

Vincenzo grinned at him. "You took all my money and hid it. And then for weeks you never let me have more than enough for a couple of beers. No more trips. Remember the night you caught me trying to fish your billfold out from under your pillow?"

"Sure. I came down so hard I almost broke your arm."

"And my birthday? When you wouldn't let me walk that girl home? Said I'd get her in trouble, so you came with me. Both of you!"

We could hear Michele chuckling in the hall. I have seen pictures of the party: happy drunken faces taken by a shaky-handed photographer. The men had given a dutch-treat party, fifteen or twenty of all ages and four or five girls, some daughters of the men themselves, and at least two German girls, one of whom Vincenzo was determined to walk home.

"You were drunk," Michele commented, half-shaved.

"Eh, so were you."

"Maybe, but I didn't want to take the girl home."

Vincenzo's shaving water was boiling now. Soon the bath water would be ready and Edda was restless. In a few minutes her bus would come and take her to clean the store. She would put the water on for the pasta.

"Leave it, Edda," Chichella said. "The signora doesn't want to eat yet. It's too early."

"*Chichella*, you can't say things like that," I objected, surprised and irritated. She was right. I did not want to eat at 6:00, but as a guest I would eat whatever I was given, whenever it was given to me. "It's not your house. You can't give orders like . . ." Chichella had jumped up quickly and gone to the sink, which put her slightly behind Edda. Her agonizing facial gymnastics told me to keep quiet. Michele came in wiping the lather out of his sideburns.

"No, you're wrong there. Wherever I live, she can give orders. After what she did for me when I was little, just a boy, I'll even *take* her orders." He smiled, but he was more than half-serious.

Later they explained to me that they—Vincenzo and Michele—had both whispered to Chichella, "Thank God we won't have to eat so early tonight." Edda was in the habit of shoving their dinner on the table before she left for work and they hated it. Our visit and Chichella's proven ability in the kitchen would be an excuse for change. (By the time we left, Chichella had taught Assunta the not-very-mysterious secrets of cooking pasta and warming the meat and vegetables her mother had already prepared. Dinner was at 7:00 or even 7:30, and the men were happier, except for Berio. He had to eat cold pasta two nights a week after soccer practice.)

Edda seemed subdued. When the men talked, they had excluded her, and now we had changed her dinner plan. It might be tactful of me . . . I asked how she found the Germans. She hunched up her shoulders.

"Beh, è brava gente." They are good people is noncommittal praise, the least that could be said of any country. I waited. "They're good people—but that's about all I can say. They're ... well ... different, that's all. They eat different things—all that lard!" She wrinkled her nose. "They think different. They're ... they're cold people. That's it. They're cold. A man's wife died here, oh a couple of weeks ago, and the day after the funeral—you know what he did? He went back to work. It's that kind of thing. They're cold." She looked at me, waiting, expecting me to agree with her. I said nothing, which, uncomfortable as it is, I know is one way to force people to justify themselves. Finally pointing at Michele and Vincenzo, she said, "They can tell you. If there's an accident on the job, someone gets hurt, they leave him lying there until the ambulance comes, or the doctor arrives. Not allowed to touch him, to help him. Just leave him there, and everybody goes back to work—like nothing was wrong. *That* couldn't happen in Italy—the men would gather around, try to help him there, make him more comfortable, but not *these*. They don't care. They're cold."

"But Edda," I objected. "That's undoubtedly the law. By moving a man you can make his injury worse—like a concussion, for instance, or broken bones."

"*No, no, ti dico io, signora, quest' è gente dura, gente fredda!*" These are hard people, cold people. Nothing would shake that conviction, nothing would soften her scorn. This was the first of dozens of times I would hear the same judgment, supported by the same kinds of examples. In the case of work accidents, occasionally people admitted that I was right, that there is a law prohibiting nonprofessional aid and requiring workmen to return to their jobs. It is the law and—this said with infinite relief and respect—in Germany no one tampers with the law, but even the law did not excuse the harshness, the coldness of the people.

A horn tooted outside the house. Edda grabbed her jacket and rushed out, shouting last-minute instructions to Chichella, who just smiled. Vincenzo was still in the hall, shaving, but as soon as the door closed, he said, "I sure didn't need a bunch of people standing around moaning when I hurt my finger. What good would that have done? Beh, for me the foreman did the right thing. Gave me a clean handkerchief, shoved me in his car, and drove me to the hospital. *Va bene*, he did dump me in the first-aid section and rush back to work. Maybe an Italian would have stayed with me. No maybe, he *would* have, but signò, you should see the first-aid room! You should just see it. Everything you could ever need—right there—doctors too. Not like Torregreca. In half an hour I was sitting up in bed, having tea and watching television. I didn't *need* the foreman."

While Vincenzo bathed, we stayed at the table, talking about old times and new: about Chichella's two daughters and their projected marriages to boys they had chosen and she would not have; about Michele's unexpected prosperity under unemployment compensation and his work. He was uneasy about something. There was no way to guess what. He insisted we must be tired, which Chichella denied with her usual energy. Well, uh ... Edda would be back before nine, but he ... he had ... Chichella did not hesitate to ask what was wrong. As it turned out, nothing. He had been late coming home that evening because the foreman had asked the men to work half an hour extra to finish a roof, which meant that the customary rooftree party would be tonight, rather than Monday. It suited the German workers, he thought, to have their Friday-drunk free on the owner's beer, when he would have preferred Friday with his friends. (The contractor undoubtedly saw it from a different point of view: the men could have their hangovers on their free time rather than a workday.) Still, Michele had to go, at least for a while, right after dinner. We could go with him maybe, he added tentatively. He could not leave us alone. Now the dilemma was clear: his duty as a host required that he entertain us, his duty as a workman, a foreigner at that, required he attend the party. The chance to see one in Germany delighted me, but I knew that not even the men's wives are included. For him to explain why he had arrived with two women, one neither Italian nor German, could be embarrassing and difficult. When I said my time was so limited that I thought I should call on Gaetano and Bianca, a Torrese couple who lived in the next village, he looked relieved. Chichella volunteered to stay with me, to make sure I "found my way," which invited more teasing from Michele.

She sent him off to bathe, recruited Assunta from the living room, and together they began the final stages of our dinner. No one would allow me to do anything, so I sat watching Vincenzo "blow-dry" his hair in front of the mirror with an electric dryer and a round, professional brush. I had always thought that, at best, his hair was combed. Instead it is coiffed. The forelock is carefully spread not too low, not too high on the forehead and then fluffed and un-fluffed, blown, rolled, brushed, and patted innumerable times until some indefinite something happens that suits him. The collar-length remains are swirled around, curled under, brushed, and deflated—and when he is all through, I still think it looks as though he had combed clean hair carefully, but perhaps that is the idea. Through the process he grumped about German barbers and their lack of patience. At home they *understand* hair: here they hack it.

Berio was roaring in the hall that he needed the dryer, for Vincenzo to get out of his way, nothing could be done to improve the mess *he* had made. Michele and Vincenzo joined me at the table, both now dressed in gabardine slacks, knitted shirts, and sweaters. German clothes fit them a great deal better than anything they ever wore in Southern Italy, but even this preview did not prepare me for Berio's splendor in a gaudy satin shirt of imitation snakeskin, yellow, brown, black, and tan scales overlapping in terrible reptilian *verismo*, tight yellow pants that belled, and orange and yellow pointed shoes that looked like Western boots, but had elastic at the sides and no legs. A cowboy would have said he was "all duded up": I dreaded to think what a German would say. He smiled at us shyly, a little shamefaced, I thought, and said,

"Hans will be along later and I wanted to be ready. You coming with us?" This last directly to Vincenzo who shook his head. "Aw, come on. You had a good time the other—"

"Yes, but I'm going with them." He nodded at me.

"You'll be sorry. Think what you'll miss." Vincenzo shrugged.

That night when we came back just before midnight, he called me in from the kitchen. He wanted me to see what he had missed. Berio in all his finery was asleep in front of the television set. Hans had never come.

Vincenzo had me turn off the main street soon after the town hall. The land was as treeless and level as a bulldozer could make it, and still we were gliding around curves, evenly spaced, uniformly flat, an occasional split, curves left, curves right. Why was it familiar? Ah, yes. Garden estates—anywhere in the world. The curves are the conceit (or the condescension) of modern architects who would convince us that we are unique, that our house is really not like any other. To confound us they avoid straight lines now and the humiliating mirror images that result, and we, wanting to be confounded, agree that it is very pretty—quite like living in the country—and very genteel.

On later daytime visits I decided that whoever had planned the subdivision should be forgiven the telltale curves, even the dreary alternation of a single freestanding house with a double house, obtained with stunning economy of imagination by locking two singles together, because he had been loyal to the local architecture. The units were all half-timbered, white plaster with high pitched roofs. Except for their unrelenting symmetry they could have been part of the natural expansion of the village, houses that local bakers, teachers, or clerks might, at any period in history, have built for themselves. Each had its front walk of concrete and multicolored round stones, not quite set in patterns but fussily casual, flanked by squat hedges, and its side garden which, from the way it was planted, allowed immediate identification of the tenant. The Germans preferred low-growing, colorful flowers that formed a carpet as distinctive in pattern and concept as English borders. Where there were several rows of taller flowers along the front, you could be sure that they were a nod to custom and a blind for the peppers, tomatoes, zucchini, eggplant, lettuce, parsley, and basil planted behind by a homesick Italian. At the back of the houses were yards with very green grass, no weeds, and small brick terraces protected by bushes. Children might play there. On warm evenings families even sat there. But the front, all brown and white order, white curtains with their deep flounces of embroidery rippling at every window, offered a veiled, almost hostile neutrality. Do not bother us. You are nothing to us. We are not interested ... and yet, whenever I went, curtains twitched and eyes scanned their neighbors' doorsteps. The speculation I knew must follow was almost reassuring: after all, it is not people who vary so much from country to country as their machinations for respectability.

Standing on Gaetano's front steps, visible, even conspicuous in the glare of a light above the front door, Chichella, Vincenzo, and I must have piqued the neighbors' curiosity. We were an incongruous trio. They had to be *paesani* of Gaetano's; what about me? I do not fit the Mediterranean stereotype. I turned quickly toward the street. Three distinct triangles in three different windows disappeared with the gentle lapping of curtains allowed to fall back into place. Vincenzo rang the bell again. As I swung around toward the door expectantly, I caught the faintest swaying of white at the window just to my right. They too were peeping at us. A deep voice rasped something in German over the intercom. Vincenzo replied, "*Amici!*" For a brief moment I imagined we were Mafiosi, then the door was thrown open and Gaetano in a turtleneck sweater, gray trousers, and slippers peered out at us.

"I don't believe it," he muttered. "I just don't believe it." Over and over again he would repeat that one phrase as though trying to convince himself that we were not amiable lemures who had come to tease him of a dark evening. He could not fuse the shadows of his memory with the faces before him. Eleven years were not to be denied. We had changed without knowing how or when, as Gaetano himself had changed.

As a young man Gaetano was an exception in Torregreca: he was a mason who usually had work—if the weather was decent. Four months of the year it is not, so even his was a precarious life. Like the others he fleshed out his income with odd jobs, which explains why we first met over the nursery cesspool. I had tried to find someone to empty it, and when all else failed, had gone to the mayor, who said there was only one man with the stomach for such a job. He would see to the matter. Several days later, after a sleet storm, one of our standard winter delights, I came around the corner of the nursery to discover a tall, blond young man standing on a plank across the open cesspool, reeling in a rope. Below him on the hillside, where I had not immediately seen it, was a scooter with a small truck body attached at the back on which four old oil drums had been set, wedged tightly together. The bucket appeared at the end of his rope, he dumped its contents into a drum and let the bucket drop back out of sight. Then, very slowly, he stepped off the plank, pulled out a handkerchief to blow his nose, and saw me. He shook his head and smiled slowly, deliberately, as I was to find he did everything. It was a very crooked smile that, at its fullest, almost closed his heavy-lidded green eyes, but it was a real smile. I do not remember our conversation that day. I must have thanked him. I certainly did not ask how much he would charge: I would pay whatever he wanted. I do remember the soft, deep voice and the clearness of his Italian, which was unusual in a town where everyone speaks dialect.

As so often happens once you meet someone you have never known, the theory of probability collapses: suddenly, wherever I went, there was Gaetano. In the Piazza, on the road, in the post office, the bar, all places where we exchanged the ritual nods, which in a village turn a casual walk or the morning errands into a puppet show. And even finally one snowy morning at the hospital. He had brought his mother to see the doctor and introduced me to a minute woman in black, whose translucent skin was crisscrossed by a tracery of fine lines and whose piercing blue eyes seemed to look beyond me as though already gazing into another world. For several minutes we talked, she in a thin, reedy voice. She hoped this would not be another winter like 1956. Did I remember the blizzards? Ah, but I had not been in Torregreca that year when death seemed inevitable and the only choice had been the means—by freezing or by starvation. Terrible, terrible! But this year we have enough wood. She smiled at her son, then added, "And he will see to the rest. I'm quite sure of that." She offered me her hand, a mere brush of the fingers, and with tiny, light steps she glided off toward the street, a curious, wispy figure of stateliness that was much more imposing than the vague exhausted dignity natural to the old.

In Southern Italy there are no secrets. I found out easily enough that Gaetano's mother had been born in a nearby town, one of several daughters of a prosperous family, not gentry, everyone was quick to note, but prosperous. They owned the flour mill, to which in later years they added an oven. The daughters grew up without schooling, which was normal, and with great leisure, which was less so. A servant girl did the housework and except for acquiring a certain facility with the needle, the girls simply marked time until they were old enough to marry. They did, and all went well for the first years. At the death of their father, however, the brothers-in-law quarreled over the estate and finally divided it. Gaetano's father had schemes for investing their share, schemes which he followed faithfully into bankruptcy. The last years of his life he spent in Torregreca as a clerk, no more than a scrivener, in a government office, and died young in the middle of the war, leaving his widow with five children, Gaetano, at thirteen, being the youngest, and no assets.

In postwar Lucania no one prospered. As soon as there was any chance of emigration, one of Gaetano's brothers went off to Venezuela in search of his fortune. A sister married and took the other sister with her as a companion. A brother, who was never actually employed, married and almost immediately died of cancer. Gaetano was left to support his mother and share two airless dark storerooms with her at the back of one of the town's ramshackle "palaces."

Recently, more than fourteen years after his father's death, he had married a young girl named Bianca. Small and dark with black eyes and buck, almost crossed front teeth, she was known as "*La Profuga*" (The Refugee) because, during the war, her parents had been pushed behind the lines, south to Torregreca, where they stayed to raise thirteen children and live in public housing, complaining all the while that the government should "repatriate" them. They were a family of marathon talkers, as I had every reason to know living just opposite them, and Bianca was no exception. Our neighborhood was kept up to date on all the minor and most of the major events of Gaetano's and her household. There was some justification for her complaints. Their quarters were cramped. The arrival of their first child did not improve matters. Gaetano was always worried and so inclined to be cross. There was never enough money. Her mother-in-law, who might know what should be done, but could not herself do it, waited for someone else to perform the simplest tasks, even the preparation of a cup of coffee. Before Bianca's second child was born, her mother-in-law became too weak to get out of bed. Another burden was added to the day, and Bianca had less time for talk and less desire.

Gaetano and I kept up our nodding acquaintance and *in extremis* I would beg his help for stubborn bits of maintenance at the nursery that defied the attentions of more available and theoretically more skilled workmen. He always came, eventually, and drafted me as an apprentice-assistant. While I handed him hammers and pliers and wire, we talked, or better, he ruminated out loud and I clucked at what I hoped were the right moments. I learned that he had no sense of humor. His ponderous, step-by-step reasoning through every situation excluded it. And besides, humor was frivolous.

I met him once at a crossroads waiting for a lift, or in due course a bus back to town. When I stopped to offer, he considered me very solemnly for what seemed several minutes and then said No, he guessed he'd better not. He'd wait.

[72]

"Oh, come on. Bianca won't mind," I answered unthinkingly. If I meant anything at all, it was the mildest kind of joke.

"I'm afraid she doesn't see things the way you do" was his enigmatic comment. I let out the clutch and sped on, wondering if Bianca was a jealous wife, something I had never thought of and could hardly imagine, or he so obsessed by appearances that he would wait an hour by the roadside rather than accept a lift from that most exotic of all creatures, a foreign woman alone. Nonsense. Even to the Torresi I was respectable. Banter might be unbecoming to a lady, I decided, but it was just as true that there was nothing lighthearted about Gaetano, except his broad, lopsided smile.

Six months after she was confined to her bed, his mother died, and I remember the sad little funeral procession, not more than a dozen people, most of them old, stumbling along the side of the road. Drivers did not bother to stop their cars in the usual sign of respect. Illogically I was sorry for *her*, as though she knew that there were so few who mourned her and suffered for it.

Bianca had a third child, a girl finally, followed by a series of violent hemorrhages. She was rushed to the hospital in Bari. It was only a gesture, everyone said: she could not live. But she did. She was warned that another pregnancy would be fatal. Gaetano spent weeks in a daze, first of grief, then of surprise. He was content with three children. When suddenly he was assigned a small apartment in public housing, something he had almost given up hoping for, he began to see the world as schematic: tragedies are followed by rewards. He prepared to enjoy them and, among other things, came to see me, to discuss his children's chances of coming to the nursery.

It was an extraordinary interview. Normally I asked the questions: the nursery was for children with the greatest need (not always financial), so the child, or his parent for him, had to qualify. Instead Gaetano might have been entering his children in an expensive private school. He wanted a full explanation of the schedule, the food supplied, the methods used, and the eventual responsibilities of the parents. He asked for a formal tour, ignoring the many times he had been there to fix things. I did not resent his questions. They were, after all, very much of a piece with his personality, but I refused to give him any definite answer, telling him, as I told everyone, that when the time came, a place for his eldest would depend on what other children had applied. Most of us prefer fairness when it is practiced on other people. Certainly Gaetano did. He was offended, would almost have argued, but his nerve failed him, and I realized he thought that because he knew me, he had only to ask for a place. He forgot that everyone in town knew me.

In 1962 I moved from Torregreca and for the next few years spent only part of every month there, always busy with the teachers and the technical problems of running a nursery. I lost the daily contact with the children and their parents, which had always been the part of my work I enjoyed most. Gaetano and Bianca's Nando did indeed come to the nursery, admitted in the normal way, and in time so did their Lello.

I remember hearing that Gaetano had had an accident and was in the hospital in Bari. He had, it seemed, lost his balance and stepped back with one foot into a vat of lime, burning his leg and ankle badly. When I met Bianca on the road one day, she railed at the ineptitude of the local doctors, who in a year had been unable to heal the sore that had formed from one of the burns. They had waited to send him to Bari until the bone was exposed and amputation seemed the only solution. Typical! she snarled at me. Butchers, all of them! They botch something. Refuse to admit it. Lose time. Wait until the patient is a corpse, then ship him off for emergency hacking that might save his *life*, when *they* should have saved his *leg*. And why, when you get right down to it, did they send him away? So he won't ruin their statistics here, that's why. Same thing they did to me! Always the same! There was too much truth in what she said, but it would help no one to agree: I tried to be diplomatic and in the end felt hypocritical.

Several months later, during the Festa, I met Gaetano in the Piazza, very red-faced and quite drunk. He was gayer than I ever remember seeing him. He did still have two legs and, like everyone else, he worried about the building slump, but he was not as pessimistic as I would have expected.

In the fall of 1965 he disappeared to Germany. A year later Bianca and the three children—Nando, Lello, and their little sister,

Chiara—followed him. Since then she and Gaetano have returned only twice to Torregreca.

Now Gaetano was heavier, not fat, but burly in the way of middle-aged men who do physical work. His shoulders were padded, boneless; the trunk of his body was too long and broad and solid for his legs to support. The only superfluous weight seemed to be on his cheekbones, making his face round, and in repose, as when he opened the door, a bit flabby and inclined to jowls. Whether it was this extra unsupported weight or some permanent inner heaviness that pulled the corners of his broad mouth down, was hard to tell, but slowly, very slowly, one corner began to lift in the old lopsided smile.

"Michele said something—but I never . . ." And calling over his shoulder, "Bianca! BIANCA!" he grabbed Chichella and me by the arms and dragged us inside. The neighbors probably assumed we had tried to escape.

In the hall we almost collided with Bianca, who was leading a small, blond boy, maybe five, by the hand. His face was the deep thunder-red of a child who intends to have a tantrum. His eyes, which had been screwed shut in anticipation, opened just enough for him to squint at us. Curiosity got the better of him. The flush began to fade and the eyes, now much wider open, were brown and decidedly crossed. We all talked at once, explaining and exclaiming, no one listening to anyone else, until we drifted into a large, very modern kitchen where a little girl who sat on the floor, surrounded by books, was sorting through her possessions and, when satisfied with some quixotic cataloging of her own, methodically putting them away in the lower compartment of a cupboard. After a glance at us she decided we were of no interest and returned to her chore. The next time I noticed her, she had, without a word, climbed into Chichella's lap and started what was to be a long, loving bilingual conversation which both enjoyed and neither understood. Once some instinctive sonar device in Lisa's little head had identified Chichella as a sure source of love and attention, she spent most of the evening astraddle her knees, gibbering at her when she had her attention, or when she did not, cuddling, half-asleep, against the warm capacious bosom so conveniently close to her face. Chichella talked merrily over her head, stopping only to roll her eyes and purse her lips at the child in a warning to be quiet. Then they both would smile in complete satisfaction with the arrangement. Martino, the little boy, flitted petulantly from one adult hip to the next, never quite managing to distract anyone enough to suit him, ever closer to his tantrum.

Bianca was fussed by our sudden arrival. She smoothed her cotton dress. She smoothed her hair, started to make a pot of coffee, forgot she was doing it, and finally sank down on a chair to stare at us. She had changed very little. She had thickened slightly, her short brown hair was waved and set with a rigidity that excluded grace, and of course nothing, not even time and the inevitable slow shedding process that Southern Italians undergo, had altered her prominent, jagged teeth. Her large black eyes still had the wary speculative look I remembered from other years and now, added to it, was a physical stillness that betrayed chronic tension well controlled. Remembering the doctor's warnings after Chiara's birth and the hemorrhages, I was puzzled by Lisa and Martino. Whose children were they? Maybe a neighbor's. Gaetano ignored them. Bianca spoke to them with clipped authority in German.

"We don't owe anyone any money" was the first thing she said directly to us and then, realizing that her tongue had given away her thoughts, added quickly, *"Che si dice in paese?"* a perfunctory way of asking what was new in Torregreca. In a babble of questions and answers it was decided that nothing was: there was still no work. Bianca dismissed the subject with bitter indifference. "That's one thing that'll never change."

"Bah, Torregreca!" Gaetano waved it away in disgust. "Come on, let me show you the house. You know, I actually worked on *this* house. The contractor I work for built all of them out here, so I know every stone, like my hand." He stood up, looking at us. We had settled around the rectangular table, Gaetano at the head, Vincenzo and I on the longer side of the L-shaped bench, with the front window and its full white curtain behind us, Chichella and Bianca on chairs opposite. "And here you don't cheat. Nobody does. If the contract calls for a certain mix on cement—certain proportions of sand—then that's what you put in. No cheating, and the house is solid, the plaster doesn't crumble, the roof doesn't leak. Fit for a human being, that's what it is. And the rooms are big too. Look at this. Big enough to be a sitting room. Fact is, we divided it. Made a separate living room over there." He waved toward a door in the corner of the room, near the one we had used coming into the kitchen from the front hall. "More comfortable. Don't want to sit in a kitchen *all* the time. And see the floors? All wood—every floor in the place. None of that marble chip stuff that's so cold—in here too, underneath," and he pointed to the composition tile floor that may even have been a very superior grade of linoleum. Bianca considered it almost as though it were unfamiliar and murmured to no one in particular,

"So much easier on the feet...." Not too many years ago Southern Italians considered wooden floors a symbol of the basest poverty, of the temporary—concentration camps, refugee housing, army barracks—and my own preference for them, another of my American eccentricities. Only my nationality rescued me from darker suspicions. Against my own instincts I learned to accept certain subjects, among them wooden floors, with their infinite pros and no discernible cons, as beyond discussion. Time, travel, and television have done more than any arguments of mine could. Women's respectability has survived the demonic erosion of smoking, driving, dancing, bikinis, and careers. Husbands and wives are now chosen by preference, not parents. Now even wooden floors have come into their own, which, since "terrazzo" tile floors are suddenly fashionable in America, has a fine retributive logic about it. I have also learned to avoid those "Do you remember my saying . . . ?" remarks, but something about my expression inspired Chichella to wink at me.

". . . Of course there's plenty of heat," Gaetano went on, determined not to be derailed. "Every house has its own, and—" A carillon door chime rang. Vincenzo leapt for the hem of the curtain, lifted it, and peered out toward the doorstep. Gaetano hesitated, then poked a button by the door. "Must be Chiara. What was I saying? Oh, yes, the heat—"

"Don't get off on one of your lectures," Bianca cut in before he could organize his further thoughts about heat. "Let's show them the house." She did not seem surprised at the nonappearance of her daughter, whose footsteps clumped up the stairs, changed their rhythm to cross a landing, and again echoed on stairs higher in the house. The glories of carpeting are not completely understood. "The living room's in here." Bianca stood up and, leaning over the table, urged us, all but lifted us, from our seats and then bustled around behind us, pushing us ever so gently toward the room beyond the kitchen.

We faced a wall of glass and a reflection, ourselves, in the faded luster of a daguerreotype. Until I forced myself to sit with my back to it, whenever I was there that glass had a compelling, almost irresistible effect on me. By day it offered sunstruck expanses of green and a surrealistic back view of whomever I was talking to. By night, even with the coarse beige net curtains drawn, I watched myself or a slide show of private domestic acts projected through the kitchen door and superimposed on the screen of my distant, dreamlike world. In every other way it was, as the impersonal sitting rooms of modern hotels can be, a comfortable room with a thick carpet and deep, soft furniture, upholstered in cinnamon velvet plush—a couch, two armchairs and their square footstools that orbited around a long walnut coffee table. From the top of a low smoked-glass and metal bookcase a futuristic television set glowered at us. All was as the furniture dealer had arranged it in his showroom, except for the books on the shelves and two large jigsaw puzzles that had been mounted, framed in walnut moldings, and hung as pictures.

Bianca glanced about with the pretentious modesty of someone waiting for admiration, waiting to be able to say, "It's really nothing, just a few simple things thrown together." She saw me looking at the jigsaw pictures, which provoked a long explanation of what they were—a German speciality and Gaetano's hobby—followed by a monologue about the convenience of the built-in closet at the end of the tall bookcase. I began to fear that Chichella would burst her verbal seams. Closets are one of my forbidden subjects, something which, in my early years in Italy, I had really missed, and Chichella had watched me put together dozens of jigsaw puzzles. Bianca may have sensed the threat. She led us quickly back through the kitchen, out into the hall, and so to the door of their bedroom, explaining what, from the odd topography, I already suspected: that the house had been divided for two families.

A double bed and two cribs crowded the bedroom. Its bath was at the far end of the hall by the front door. The three older children slept on the third floor in a large room under the eaves. Chiara would be changing her clothes there now, so Bianca would show it to me another time, which she did one warm September Sunday morning, when at eleven o'clock we found Chiara buried under comforters, asleep in her part, and around the corner in a separate alcove the two boys, also buried under comforters, asleep, with the windows closed and the heat sizzling. Isolated on the middle floor was the other family, a German couple and their small child, in what seemed an awkward arrangement for everyone. This had been the only possible solution, Gaetano explained, because there was no plumbing on the third floor. He himself had proposed it, would have accepted any compromise that allowed him to have such a new house. The landlord was content: from two tenants he collected more rent that he could have from one.

There was no way to escape a tour of the basement, all of it— the garage that belonged by agreement to the other tenant, the bathroom the older children used and cluttered with every kind of shaving equipment, cologne, shampoo, and hairdressing, and finally the pride of the family, the laundry-storeroom. Strings of peppers and of round tomatoes no larger than Ping-Pong balls hung from the ceiling. On the shelves Gaetano had spread vegetables to dry in shallow fruit crates. We admired the small heating unit, which was much like any other, including my own, the vacuum cleaner, a waxer, a washing machine, and even the old-fashioned dryer, which was of the same vertical file-drawer variety that I remember having seen as a child in the basements of apartment buildings.

Back in the kitchen we found Chiara wandering from counter

to stove to table eating her dinner and at the same time reading a magazine. Tall and slender, she wore the uniform of Western sixteen-year-olds: very tight blue jeans, a T-shirt, a short denim jacket, and clogs with grotesquely thick soles. What startled me was her face. She was only the first who made this impression. Later I saw many other children, especially those who were born in Germany or had lived there for a number of years, with the same elusive quality. Chiara *looks* German.

Stereotypes, at best, are odious. Mamma Napoli on the box of pizza mix is no more the quintessential Italian than Brunhilde on the box of Spaetzle, the quintessential German, but some general differences between the people are as conspicuous as the differences between the climates of the North Sea and the Mediterranean. One is not easily mistaken for the other. Chiara's blondness is the total blondness of the German child. Her hair is so light it could be spun cotton candy. Her eyebrows are invisible over large, pale blue eyes that are neither deep-set nor popped, but flush in a face without planes. Her pallor is a perfectly healthy lack of pigmentation in smooth, smooth skin that cannot have pores. Fortunately her full wide mouth is very pink, because lipstick, were she to use it, would be a lurid gash. Still, mere blondness is not enough. Her manner is courteous, attentive, and unshakably remote, as though all excesses of enthusiasm or rage have been muted in the octaves of her disposition, leaving no trebles or basses to distort those clean, unshaded middle tones. Like most Anglo-Saxons, her directness is probably not as candid as it appears, nor her detachment as complete. They are the accepted social poses of the world she has been thrown into, not attitudes that come naturally to Italians, who even listen with animation. Some strange amalgam of body and mind has taken place: she looks, she seems German. I wondered then, and still do, if climate, diet, and unconscious imitation could bring about a mutation as unlikely as any alchemist's dream.

The question of coloring is an odd riddle. Any generalization about twenty million people is dangerous, but Southern Italians are notoriously dark—brown or black hair, dark eyes, swarthy skin—not all of them, of course, any more than all Germans are blond, but the Greeks, the Saracens, the wanderers from the Levant have left their mark. So have the Normans, Franks and Lombards, the Crusaders, and other passing armies, including most recently our own, in the form of a golden-blond strain with flushed golden skin and green eyes. Apparently it is not dominant.

Norman Douglas, whose curiosity about Southern Italy led him into the most varied speculations, suggested that the uniform darkness of Southern Italians might be the result of or reaction to malaria. Others have brought forth diet and the semitropical climate as causes. Poverty and the deficiencies that follow from it do produce their own patterns of growth or misgrowth, their problems of alertness, motor control, and development of intelligence, even their own particular kind of hair. Do they also affect coloring? Possibly.

The argument for climate is less likely. Over the ages northern writers have written reams of romantic tripe about the paradise to be found on Mediterranean shores. They were bemused by the "wine-dark sea" before them, the charming, quaint village behind, the sun, the wine, and the limpid summer nights—the *dolce far niente*. They were tourists. On the first of September they went home. The great exceptions—Douglas, Rammage, Lear, and Gissing (who almost died of pneumonia in Taranto)—were also fascinated, but it was no Garden of Eden to them. Italy has a flange of flat land, perhaps ten miles wide, that runs around the entire coast. With the obvious exclusion of the Po Valley and the plains of Foggia, the rest is mountainous and enjoys all the variations and extremes that implies. One winter in Torregreca, at 2,800 feet, would shatter any illusions about the tropics and with it the convenient climate/coloring theory. The Torresi in southern Germany told me that the winters there are no worse than at home and often milder.

So the riddle persists. During the years I had direct contact with the nursery in Torregreca, I saw hundreds of children. They came to us for a year, two years, three years and then passed on into the elementary school where, the teachers told me, they were brighter, more alert (and more demanding, I am sure) than the other children who had gone to more traditional nurseries, or not at all. We always felt that the explanation was fairly simple. We planned the nursery's program around certain deficiencies: manual dexterity and reasoning, verbal facility, and diet.

Toys that require an increase in manual dexterity and reasoning are as easy to use as junk toys and last longer, and by toys I mean toys that are fun to play with, not abstract units arranged into some highly technical, therapeutic whole which must be reproduced by the child, no matter how meaningless to him.

"Verbal facility" sounds as though I expected six-year-olds to be miniature Dantes. The problem was more basic: a child who has never heard or spoken anything except dialect is lost in the school world of Italian. Television has now had its own special influence. Broad dialects are disappearing, or homogenizing into a semiofficial (and barbarous) vernacular, but twenty years ago, even ten years ago, they varied dramatically from town to town, in Torregreca from neighborhood to neighborhood, and were to all intents and purposes separate languages with only a marginal similarity to each other. Precocious ABCs would not have eased the children's transition from dialect to Italian. They might, indeed, have hindered it by giving a preview of the boredom school would impose. What would ease the transition was to substitute Italian for dialect in everyday communication until it was a comfortable habit. When the teacher told a story, she sensed that parts were not clear and had to find ways, examples, symbols, anything to explain it. A child who felt it was his turn on the playground swing insisted, "*U palenzica lu me,*" not "*A me l'altalena,*" words and a construction he had never heard, and while he might understand them, he would not himself use them. To help the teachers resist their own impatience and the temptation to lapse into dialect, ours never taught in their own villages. If the same procedure were true, even today, of elementary teachers in the South, maybe the students who manage to get a certificate would prove to be more than semiliterate. Italian—two different Italians, the spoken and the written—is always the stumbling block. It causes most of the failures in the obligatory eight grades. Many of those who do scrape through and go on to the upper school, to *liceo*, to teacher's training, or the lower professional schools and trade schools will be eliminated, because they still do not know their own language.

The last of the deficiencies, diet, was the easiest to solve. Every day the children had milk in the morning, lunch with a minimum of pasta, which is what they ate at home, and a second course of meat, eggs, or cheese, cooked greens or salad, and fruit. Then, in the afternoon before they left, fruit juice. The effect on children who had lived and tried to grow on a low-protein/no-protein diet was remarkable.

For the years they stayed with us I saw them almost every day and because I worked with their families as well, I continued to see them and their brothers and sisters. Times were hard, food scarce, and pasta cheap. The children had little or no fat in their diets and like stray cats who can only scrounge and never have fish, milk, or luscious leftovers, they had bristly dry hair. I kept no records of their coloring. All I can offer now is an estimate, a cautious one: as children at least 20 percent of them were very blond. Some had blue eyes and stiff, straw hair, others had green or brown eyes and darker, golden hair, just as stiff. No matter where they grow up, the skin and hair, especially the hair, of many blond children darkens, but by the time my Torresi children had finished their obligatory schooling almost all had brown hair or darker, and skin that was compatible. I can think of only six who remain blond to this day. Still the riddle persists.

When Chiara went to Germany she was six years old and blond. At sixteen she is very blond. On my travels in Germany, I found three other Torresi children, two boys and a girl, who were about the same age, had been in Germany for more than nine years, and were strikingly blond. I also met, for the first time, a dozen children between the ages of nine and eleven, who were born in Germany of Torresi parents. They too were blond. Children under six, who were born in Germany and were blond, were legion.

A random sample produces, I suppose, nothing more valuable than random trivia, but I can still speculate. Two facts seem curious: a limited number of Torresi families who have lived in Germany for five years or more have a surprising number of blond children *and* the only drastic change in their lives has been dietary. Curious, and perhaps only that, or perhaps one of the minor consequences of a corrected protein deficiency.

While we stood talking to Chiara, I could feel Bianca moving around behind us, restless, willing us to leave the kitchen for the living room. When Chiara started making herself a cup of coffee, Bianca saw her chance.

"No one else wants coffee, I suppose?" By her phrasing, rather than an invitation, her question became the preamble to another subject. "So we might as well go into ..."

"Me and the signora are going to have a beer," Gaetano mumbled from the other side of the room where he had slumped down in his place at the table and listened to us, shaking his head. Without saying a word his thoughts were clear: women can talk forever about nothing, and all you can do is wait until they get back to Essentials—by which he meant something that interested him. Now his voice sounded defiant, like a small boy who announces his misdemeanor before the fact and dares his mother to scold him. "Maybe even Chichella'll have one," he added in the same tone. To my surprise she nodded. "Come on, then, let's move in there and get comfortable." Gaetano accomplished what Bianca had not. Instead of looking pleased, she frowned crossly at all of us.

As soon as Chichella settled in one of the large armchairs, Lisa climbed up on her knees and they resumed their loving mime. Bianca enthroned me in the near corner of the sofa, which she must have considered the place of honor, so whenever I turned to Gaetano, who sat on one of the large footstools, or to Bianca, almost next to him on the other end of the sofa, I found myself facing that tantalizing window-mirror. Vincenzo never sat down, but cruised around, picking up books and magazines, stopping every so often behind his mother's chair to listen, then ambling off into the kitchen to reappear and lean against the doorjamb. I could not tell whether he was uncomfortable or simply restless. Chiara joined us with her coffee and sat opposite me in the second of the armchairs. As soon as he missed her in the kitchen, Martino came pelting in to look for her and found her. She just managed to slide her cup onto the table before his assault. He threw his arms around her legs and whimpered. A threat was implicit in his whining: there was worse to come unless ... She leaned over, took his face between her hands, and shook it gently, laughing at him. He giggled back at her and tried to pull himself up onto her lap. Still smiling, she whispered to him in German and even though I could not understand, it sounded like the happy nonsense we whisper in any language to fractious children. He insisted. He wanted to get up in her lap. She finally gave in, lifted him up, and wedged him into a corner of her chair with her arm around him. Completely satisfied at last, he looked around at the rest of us to make sure we had seen his victory.

By then I had realized that no one was going to explain these younger children, so with as much sudden discovery and lingering doubt in my voice as I could muster, I turned to Bianca.

"But ... then these younger ones are yours too? The doctors ... didn't they...?" She looked at me, then at the two children, happy and quiet now in the laps of their choice.

"Of course they're mine. Who else's would they be?" She leaned over toward Martino. "Say good evening to the signora." He turned his face into Chiara's ribs.

"Do you go to school, Lisa?" I asked. She nodded. "But the cat's got your tongue," I plodded on with numbing originality. She shook her head no.

Bianca took over for her. "She's in the first grade this year. And Martino's still in kindergarten—his second year—and he's done the same thing she did. He won't speak Italian anymore. Just refuses. Doesn't even hear you."

"That's not fair, Mamma. He's not pretending. He doesn't understand it. Really he doesn't." Chiara gave him a reassuring hug and said something in his ear. "Lisa still does, but she doesn't know how to explain herself. The words—she's lost them, that's all. And why not? Her friends are German. She goes to school in German. What's the difference?" Chiara's answers to our earlier questions had been courteous and brief. This was the first time she had said enough for me to notice the stiffness of her Italian and the slight hesitation that distorted its cadence. She had *learned* the language: it was not natural to her. And if that was true, I wondered, why didn't she speak dialect?

"By God, he'll speak Italian to me," Gaetano suddenly roared. "Martino, come here." Martino looked at him with blank interest. "MARTINO, COME HERE!" This time in German. The little boy crawled out of Chiara's lap and went to his father. For the next few minutes Gaetano yelled at his son in Italian asking him to identify objects, to say good evening to me, to bring his father an ashtray—without the slightest reaction. Two arteries swollen to shafts in Gaetano's thick neck pulsed convulsively. With each command his face was redder. Martino sensed his father's rage. He stood in front of him stiff, pale, and obedient, but silent. Finally two enormous heavy tears trickled down his cheeks, hung trembling from his chin for several seconds, then fell on the front of his T-shirt. Bianca pulled him up into her lap and stuck a handkerchief over his nose.

"Blow! Go on! Blow!"

"Mamma, in German. He really . . ."

"By God I won't have children who can't talk to me. *Lisa*, get me an ashtray." He was bellowing again. Lisa slipped off Chichella's knees reluctantly, went into the kitchen, and came dancing back with an ashtray. "See? That's my girl. Now tell the signora what you're studying in school." Lisa looked at me. I smiled encouragingly, but no words came. She turned and climbed back into Chichella's lap, hoping, I think, to escape her father's inevitable irritation, and in a way she did. He sat staring at his ashtray grumbling, but he did not rage directly at either of the children. I asked Chiara if she had gone to school in Germany.

She and Bianca were relieved to have a subject, relieved to have an excuse to drown out Gaetano's mutterings, so their answers were a choral effort, so confusing for their contradictions, clarifications, and restatements that I could not have it all straight, but would not dare ask again.

When they came to Germany, Nando was eight, Lello, six, both of school age, and Chiara, five, was eligible for the local nursery. Bianca was free to work and did, as a cleaning woman-laundress–baby-sitter for Canadian families at a nearby air base. By Christmas that first year both boys were having a terrible time with school, especially Nando in the third grade. Nothing made sense to him, German least of all. Bianca wanted to keep the children with her. After all, she was their mother. No one else would take care of them as she would. But Gaetano, even then, was rabid on the subject of Italian: their children were Italian, with luck they would be able to live in Italy, they should go to Italian schools—at home in Torregreca. The boys, at least. It made less difference about girls.

Bianca has always been doggedly loyal to Gaetano. The only clues I have to arguments that wracked the family are her overexplanations of his reasoning, repeated again and again in other conversations. He had his own way of seeing things. He was dissatisfied with his job, their housing (no one has ever been willing to discuss where or how they lived those first months in Germany). He only wanted the best for his children. He had his own way of seeing things. She has admitted that faced with his determination, she almost decided to take the children and go back to Torregreca. But she was worried about him. Where would he live? How would he eat? Everything would be worse. They would be separated again. She gave in and sent the boys home with friends who were going to Torregreca for Christmas. They would live with one of her sisters and go to school.

The next years were strange years for all of them, years of children shifting back and forth; of arguments with the relatives who kept them and with Gaetano; of disappointment in the Italian schools and elaborate preparations, a modified Chinese water-torture program, to soften Gaetano's resolve that the boys must go to middle school in Torregreca.

Out working, shopping, riding local country buses Bianca learned efficient, if not perfect German fairly quickly and with it acquired a miscellany of information. She found out that the local provincial government at Lahr runs a middle school designated as "international" because, though there are required courses in German—language, history, civics, et cetera—certain basic subjects, including language and history of the native country, are taught in

Italian. This, she decided, was the perfect compromise. All she had to do was convince Gaetano that Nando should try it for one year, then—well, she would wait and see.

This summary is all the result of a later, laborious reconstruction. That first evening what I heard sounded like an improvised verbal fugue with too many intertangled voices that ended

Chiara: "I always went to school here."

Bianca: "Not the boys—not always—"

Chiara: "... sent them to Torregreca, but they came back."

Bianca: "She went to school with them for a while. ..."

Chiara: "Not before—later. ..."

Chichella: "Where are they?"

Bianca: "You insisted ..."

Chiara: "The teachers said it was a waste of time—remember, Mamma?"

Gaetano: "Wasn't! You needed to learn too. ..."

Chiara: "I already ..."

Bianca: "Gaetano, let her alone. ..."

Chichella: "Where *are* they?"

Bianca: "You'll admit the school here worked out. Gaetano! You'll admit that much?"

Gaetano: "They learned German. ..."

Chiara: "But we knew Italian. You insisted ..."

Gaetano: "... and they got settled, I guess. *Accidenti!* The beer! I forgot the beer!"

Chichella: "Where are they?"

Gaetano: "All right, all right, I'll get them. *Ci vado, ci vado. ...*" (Chichella put her head down on the arm of her chair and started laughing.)

He pulled himself up off the stool and stretched, smiling down at us as though he had never been angry. He had not listened to much of our chatter, only the last part, but however dark his thoughts, the background of the shouts and unfinished sentences had sounded gay. His good humor had returned and with it the vision of the beer that was, for some reason I still did not understand, an illicit treat. As soon as we heard him in the kitchen, Chiara leaned over and spoke quietly, very quickly, as though she had an urgent secret to tell me.

"Mamma'll explain another time about the boys. I went to school here—at the German school, except for two years when they sent me, I mean, forced me to go to the 'international' school. I didn't learn anything there—well, maybe Italian grammar. The teachers talked them into letting me go back to the regular school with my friends, so I finished up right. And now I have a job at the leather factory." She wrinkled her nose in disgust. For the first time she looked like a *very* young girl. She jerked her head toward the other room. "He doesn't like my friends because they're German and he can't talk to them, can't quiz them like he wants to. He—he won't let me go out. He says they can come here and sit with the family, like he *says* they always did at home, but he doesn't understand. . . ." The cry of every frustrated young daughter from Bangladesh to Montana!

She did not believe him. Something must have changed in Torregreca since his day. There was no point in telling her that it had, a bit, that now in the twilight she could walk up and down the road with other girls, even with the young man of the moment, if her family considered his intentions serious. When it was dark, she must be home where he would be given a chair in front of the television with the other children and their mother, or worse, on an off night, would sit, a death's-head like the others in the harsh light of the kitchen, mentally thumbing through his index of gossip for some tidbit generic enough to be inoffensive. It would also be uninteresting, but in a village where everyone is either related or feuding, dull is tactful. Not to be rude, not to stare, he would inspect the tiles of the floor, hoping some appropriate thought would flash across them, like the TILT sign on a pinball machine. He would light a cigarette. The match would growl and hiss in the silence. When he had finished it, he would stand up, mumbling the accepted formula, "*Tolgo il disturbo*" (I'll take away the disturbance), knowing, or perhaps only guessing, that he had been exactly that—a disturbance. Evenings in Torregreca are early—and monotonous.

Chiara wants to do the things her German friends do: go to the cinema, the local *Diskothek*, to a café for a coffee or even the local *Gasthaus* for a beer. Often several girls go together, sometimes by arrangement they meet boys, sometimes not, but for Gaetano no male is to be trusted, and if such places are not of themselves immoral, they encourage immorality in a girl. Faithful to the double standard, he believes that what encourages immorality in a girl does not in a boy. If Lello or Nando goes with her, stays at her side, and brings her home, Gaetano will consider the matter. One or the other must be her dogged chaperone. Lello is "engaged," whatever that term means these days, to a German girl who is not amused by the idea of a threesome that would, in practice, leave her as the odd woman. Lello may understand his father's proscription, but the code that requires it, a genteel fiction, is a relic of another time, another country. He would look foolish to his friends, especially to his girl. He cannot please everyone, so let his sister be disappointed. Later, when I met the girl, I understood better. She is a tall, blond Lorelei with sleepy eyes and flashy clothes, who, even assuming Lello is bewitched by her, is also a symbol of his prowess. To lose her by chaperoning his sister would be more than loss of face. Nando, on the other hand, has never considered the assignment. He must be free to prowl from joint to joint with four or five German boys who are his friends. His sister should stay in her proper place, at home.

I wondered why Chiara was telling me all this in breathless volleys, like shorthand. I never doubted she had a reason. She was cautious, stopping between the rushes of words to listen to the sounds in the next room. She heard her father swear, then waited until he stumped out into the hall and on downstairs to the storeroom. She glanced at Chichella who was mired in the wondrous details of Bianca's last pregnancies and the subsequent deliveries. Without turning I knew that Bianca, enraptured by a new listener, was beyond the reach of curiosity about us. Only birth and death have such absolute, narcotic power. Chiara plunged on until we heard the door from the hall into the kitchen open.

"Well, look who's here," Gaetano called cheerfully. "Come on in, we have a surprise." Another voice we could not quite hear said something. Gaetano's answer was still good-humored. "*Va bene*, you're in a hurry, but you can come in for a few minutes just the same. Here, take the bottles. I'll get the glasses." Chiara leaned even closer to me.

"That's Lello. He promised he'd come back for me tonight, and say he was taking me with him—but, of course, he's not, and he's already cross that we have to fix a certain time to meet so we come home together. That's what I wanted to ask you. You see, now you're here, my father won't want me to leave—and—and, well, I promised, I really promised tonight I'd make it. Could you—I mean, would you stick up for me? I want to go *so* much." Now I knew, and footsteps were approaching from the kitchen. I nodded at her and smiled, I hoped, reassuringly.

"Here's Lello *and* the beer—finally." Gaetano came in carrying glasses. "*Avanti! Avanti!*" He called back over his shoulder. "They've had to wait a long time for this. Do you remember the '*signora Canadese*'? * No, you were probably too young."

The tall, slender boy who appeared behind him, carrying three bottles of beer, smiled uncertainly at me. Then he saw Chichella and whooped with surprise and excitement. If he remembered me at all, I was an aloof figure that stood around in doorways, watching, snooped in cupboards, and had long conversations with his teacher, but Chichella was part of his life.

In the confusion of exclamations, handshakes, and kisses I had a chance to watch Lello. I decided that I had been wrong, that he is neither a boy, nor quite a man, but very handsome in the dark, sharp-featured, flashing-eyed way most of us think of as "Latin." With us he was an eager, laughing boy. Later with his "fiancée" we saw the casual man of the world, quick and absolute in his decisions, something of a dandy, his clothes just so, his straight black hair meticulously combed. Chichella started teasing him, and I was surprised to see him blush. When was he coming back to Torregreca?

"Me?" He put both hands on his chest, as though he could not believe the question was intended for him. "Me? Go back? You're

---

* The money for the construction of the nursery was given by the Canadian Save the Children Fund, the Canadian ambassador came to Torregreca for the opening, therefore I must be Canadian. Although this is the most inaccurate of the many nicknames the Torresi bestowed upon me, it is also the most respectful and the most unshakable. I use it myself now, if I have to leave a message or explain who I am.

kidding. I'm never going back—never. Why should I?"

"What're you doing here that's so great?" she persisted, but with a twinkle.

"Chasing girls," Gaetano sneered, and at the same time preened.

"Nothing new." Chichella smiled. "He was an expert in the nursery. Remember when . . . ?"

"Aw, nobody takes me seriously." He blushed furiously. "That's just a sideline. You wait and see. When I finish this school, I'll have a certificate as a mason. Won't ever be out of work, and I'm going to stay right here and enjoy the good life." And there was no doubt that he meant it. He was in his second and last year of trade school, studying half-day, working half-day and paid a small salary as well. "Say, listen, I didn't know all this was going to happen. I've got a date—I mean . . ." He remembered just in time. "Chiara and me have a date to meet some people tonight—but if you don't come back—aren't you . . . ?"

"I think they should come for dinner Sunday." There must be some block in Bianca's mind: her invitations are always disguised, as though she fears rejection, or what she really dreads may be acceptance. Gaetano's voice roared over our social clucking about too much trouble, another day, and the setting of the actual time for Sunday.

"You're not going anywhere, young lady. Maybe you *had* plans, but you don't anymore, not with company in the house. You're staying right here. *Did you hear me*, Chiara?"

"I promised," she said in a very quiet, firm voice that implied promises were sacred.

"I said NO," he insisted as he might with a naughty puppy. "No, no and NO!" She looked from him to me. I took the cue and charged in with the usual pleas in such situations: we would see her Sunday; she shouldn't let her friends down, besides, after she had worked hard all week, she needed some fun. Chichella settled it, and I decided she would have made a fine psychologist.

"Let her go, Gaetano. Without them in the way we can have a nice quiet visit." This to a man who is longing for a chance to talk!

He relaxed, shrugged, and concentrated on pouring out the beer. Chiara and Lello were as graceful about their hurry as they could be and still escape before their father changed his mind. They tried to take Vincenzo with them, but he professed complete lack of confidence in my ability to get home alone and said he would stay with us. They knew it was an excuse: he had declared himself an adult.

It was more peaceful without them. Martino fell asleep in Chiara's chair, Lisa, in Chichella's lap. Vincenzo took a pile of magazines in the kitchen and soon we heard the intermittent buzz and lisp of a radio turned low. Bianca switched back into her chronicle of births with the precision of someone who has closed her thumb in a book so as not to lose her place, and finally, Gaetano had his chance to talk. He did for two hours. Except for his three trips to the icebox for another beer, which Bianca watched with silent, frowning disapproval, the only interruptions were clipped asides from her, corrections of something he had said, or an occasional question from me.

"You see what they're like," Gaetano said. "Kids today—there's nothing you can do with them. They don't have any sense of the past, of family or duty. It's now, now, *now*. Me, me, *me* and *al diavolo* with the rest. You can't stop them. It was different when I was growing up. You didn't have any choice. You listened to what your father said—even what your mother said. But not now. Not anymore. Maybe in Torregreca it's still that way. Maybe if—that's my fault too. I brought them up here. I ruined them—and myself, and I didn't have any choice. Not really. And you heard Lello. He'll have *a certificate* as a mason. Not like me. He looks down on me already. I'm a bumbler who finagled my way on to a construction crew. Lucky for him I did, is all I can say. But no certificate, so I'm worthless. Sometimes get the feeling he's saying, 'Move over, you old *montone* [billy goat], or we'll kick you out!' "

Gaetano sat, silent for a moment, looking into his beer. I asked if he had ever worked in a factory. He shook his head. Bianca abandoned Chichella to jog his memory. Didn't he remember? she asked. He had for five months, or was it four?

"Shut up! I'll remember what I want to remember and forget

what I want to forget. Anyway, that was in Switzerland. Didn't stay there long. I lived in a barracks with thirty other '*cristiani*' who were starving to death like me. God, it was cold. I'll never forget that, or how hard we worked. The Swiss wouldn't talk to us, if they could help it. Why, there was even a café in that town with a sign—know what it said? No, you'd never guess. It said right out in big letters NO DOGS OR ITALIANS ALLOWED. Some nights I wanted to bash in that window. But I didn't. The work was seasonal, so I left as soon as I could and came up here. Thought I'd find permanent work. And I don't have to remember that either—*so don't remind me, Bianca!* We lived like gypsies—no, worse than gypsies and that's what they called us too. Well, I'm no cursed gypsy. Never been without work in eleven years. Feed my kids, clothe them in the best I can afford. Always want new stuff—this is the 'fashion' is what they say. Can't wear last year's anything. When I grew up, if I had shoes on my feet and a rag on my back, I was right in with the crowd, right in fashion.

"... But it's my fault. I brought them here. I ruined them—and myself, but I didn't have any choice. We'd have starved by now. I'd still be unemployed. Oh, sure, day work, but no pension, no insurance. What if someone got sick? Bianca here—she'd be dead, killed by those same butchers at the hospital, same ones who wanted to cut off my leg. She'd have hemorrhaged to death having Lisa. Didn't have a bit of trouble here. And Martino's glasses. How'd I pay for them? He's got to have them. Hey, Bianca, you make him wear them, even if you have to nail them to his head. You hear me, Bianca?"

"Tell him yourself, if you're so determined," she spat at him. "Not another child in his kindergarten wears them, so he won't either. Smashes them on the floor and refuses to pick them up."

"There, you see what I mean? She can throw that in my face, knowing I can't talk to him. My own son and I can't even *talk* to him. I don't know." He shook his head slowly. It seemed almost too heavy for him to support. "There must be something wrong with my brain. German don't make any sense to me. I try, but I know just enough to get by on the job and no more. Why, she's got friends who come to drink coffee with her. Go shopping together, jabbering all the time—in German—her. *Her!*" He jerked his head toward Bianca, his expression of puzzled wonder and surprise almost comic. "That's how she got this good job, but *really* good job, cleaning an office over in town, through these German neighbors she made friends with. I can't even learn the damned language and she keeps telling me it's so easy. Just listen awhile, she says, and you'll catch on—but I don't." He stood up with his glass in his hand, ready for another trip to the refrigerator. "That's my fault too. Everything is."

Bianca turned away from her conversation to look at his back, frowning more than ever. She shook her head.

"Fault! Fault! FAULT! That's all he talks about these days, as though anybody blamed him for what's wrong with the world." For all that the words were kind enough, her tone matter of fact, something about the remark underlined his insignificance. Intentional or automatic? I could not tell. We heard bottles rattle. She lowered her voice. "Been this way ever since he got sick." When Gaetano came into the room, I was still leaning over toward her. For a few seconds he stood in the doorway, watching us, his eyes narrowed and suspicious.

"Suppose she's been telling you I shouldn't have this beer 'cause I'm sick," he said finally, squaring his shoulders. For the first time since we had come, he was not a slouching, irascible man, fighting little skirmishes he did not expect to win. Defiance leaves no room for self-pity. "That's what the doctors say, all right, but let me tell you something—I feel better now than I did when you came and I expect to feel a whole lot better before the night's over. You know— if doctors knew as much as they claim, they'd be gods. And, Bianca, I heard that crack of yours about nobody blaming *me* for what's wrong with *the world.* Never thought they did. World's too big for me, but this house isn't. I can blame myself for bringing you here, for having kids that sneer at me and my ways. Sure, it's my fault, like it's my fault I can't learn German. It's my fault I wasn't born a lawyer too. Then I could have been one of those lousy, thieving politicians who left us in this mess—all of us—with no choices—so they could get rich riding on my back. Look at the Germans! They

[95]

lost the war and look at them! We're just a bunch of sheep, and if we let the politicians—the same ones, mind you, who've been telling us what to do since the war—with just one result—*they* get richer—if we let them treat us like dung, then we deserve it, but they're to blame for the world, my world, anyway. So, that's sorted out the blame. Nothing's going to change, and if I complain, it's because I know it." He sat down on his stool again, already deflated. He was beginning to mumble, as though these were private thoughts that had leaked out into audible form against his will. "It's my fault if the kids sneer at me—and I've got two I can't even talk to. And it's *my* fault if I just squeeze out a living until I get a pension. What else could I do?" He looked up at us. "Better put that on my tombstone, Bianca. 'What else could he do.' That's pretty good." He seemed to shiver all over. "Let's talk about something else, *per l'amor di Dio.*"

The only subject that offered itself was his health, so I asked. Our own medical adventures always intrigue us. Gaetano led me through his ulcer with harrowing thoroughness. Six months before, when the pain became so acute that he often could not get out of bed in the morning, he had gone to the doctor, who sent him to the local hospital for tests and treatment. He stayed three weeks and, like everyone else in the community, had nothing but praise for the doctors, their skill, the equipment, and even the food. The tests were torture. He thought they made him swallow everything but the ward television set. In compensation they gave him jigsaw puzzles to work and so started his picture gallery. They forced him to take pills and powders and eat a soft diet without the hot *peperoncini* he likes cut up on all his food. He discovered that patients could arrange for weekend "leave," Saturday and Sunday at home, and was so impressed with the earnestness and good intentions of the staff that to prove his good faith he stuck to his diet and even resisted his *peperoncini.* Eventually they showed him his X rays, explained that the ulcer was very deep, close to perforation, and prescribed medication and a diet of bland food, no coffee, no alcohol, no cigarettes. He lit one as he told me that.

They also sent him to the dentist, who found that his remaining teeth (half of them had already disappeared in the usual Torregreca way through abscesses, followed by extraction) were decayed and infected. They must be removed—all of them—and replaced by plates. No sooner had the socket of one pulled tooth healed than another tooth was pulled. In six months of throbbing gums he had almost forgotten the ulcer. For weeks now he had been unable to eat anything but pasta and not much of that. They were finally down to the last three teeth, which were pulled during my stay. He suspected the dentist of being a collector of molds. Every time he went to him, he found himself gagging on a mouthful of plastic, as he described it, plaster and metal forms. Maybe they were needed, like the dentist said, for plates, but Gaetano no longer believed that the swelling of his gums and the infection would subside enough for him to have plates. His one consolation: that the insurance paid all the costs. I forgave him the mumbling, even the self-pity.

The ulcer was still down there: he could feel it, but it was calmer. He took pills with his "meals," what little he could eat. When he woke up and before he went to sleep, he had to dissolve a powder in water, drink it, and then lie ten minutes on his back, ten on his right side, ten on his left side, and ten on his stomach. Lying on his stomach hurt.

"So that's how it is. That's why Bianca doesn't want me to drink anything. From the way she carries on, you'd think I beat her. I don't, you know." He gave his slow, lopsided smile, which I realized for the first time had never exposed his teeth, even when he had some. He sighed. "You asked how it is—and that's about it. I never had any choices, and I still don't, but I'll tell you one thing. The kids can stay here—our little Germans too." He waved another cigarette toward Lisa and Martino who slept, their bodies as defenseless as derelicts. "Those two would never be happy anywhere else. The others, let them stay too. I've got to hold out until I have my pension. Then me and Bianca are going home. Oh, I know, I know." He held up his hand as though to ward off attack. "You don't have to tell me. I haven't forgotten the feuds and the backbiting and the climate and the mess of it all, but you see, the truth is no man wants to die a stranger among strangers. Anything, but not that. Not *still* a stranger...."

We could hear Vincenzo in the kitchen, laughing, then other deeper voices said something in German, and they laughed too. In a moment three young men in blue jeans and denim jackets appeared in the doorway; the dark-haired one in the middle, who smiled in a vague, unfocused way at what he took to be an amphitheater of people, was supported by the other two.

"Oh, Nan-do," Bianca groaned in that descending voice of disapproval mothers use. "Where have you been?" He smiled more witlessly than before, showing two buck, crooked front teeth he had inherited from his mother. She stood up and switched to German for the rest of her lecture, which continued long after she had pushed Nando and his friends back into the kitchen, over the rattle of pans and oven doors.

When we left a few minutes later, Nando was trying to get a forkful of cold macaroni to his mouth, but lost most of it on the way. For several seconds he stared at the plate resentfully, then hunched over and with angry determination began spearing pieces one by one. His two blond German friends stood up and bowed repeatedly as we said good night. Bianca, embarrassed and apologetic, was now determined we must come for Sunday dinner. Gaetano leaned, smiling, against the door of the living room. I think he was finally happy.

We did go for Sunday dinner. All five children were there. The two youngest still ignored everything said in Italian. As soon as we arrived, Martino threw his glasses on the floor. Chiara said not a single word then or at any other time that I saw her. She was carrying out an epic pout. That first night, after we left, Gaetano had been unable to sleep, so he caught Chiara sneaking in alone. She and Lello had argued over so many different places and times to meet that in the end they missed each other altogether. Chiara was confined to the house with a thirty-minute time limit between the close of her shift at the factory and her arrival on the front step.

Nando chugged up on his motor bike just in time to sit down for dinner. He smiled a lot. He answered my only question: after he left "the other factory" because he did not like working with Turks, he found work in Chiara's leather factory. He smiled a lot more and chugged away on his motor bike as soon as dinner was over, leaving me with the impression that he is an amiable adolescent.

Lello brought his "fiancée" in to meet us, then sent her off, arranging to meet her later in the afternoon. Before he disappeared for the day, he helped me make a long-distance call from what was reputed to be the only local telephone that could establish contact with Italy. To reach it we twisted and jounced around through plowed fields until we emerged at the backside of an autobahn service area, and then had to drive through the parking lot in the wrong direction, anathema in Germany. People lined up in front of the booth turned to stare at us. I suggested we try another phone, perhaps the one in the lobby of the post office. No, it seems this particular one has, beyond its mystic liaison with Italy, another appeal: its meter often fails and you win a free call, which Lello considered the ultimate Italo-German vendetta.

We made several false passes at dialing and decided that the prefix was wrong. Lello discussed our problem with the operator. I listened to him stumble along, searching for words, changing them, stammering. Middle school and trade school have given him enough German to read textbooks and write simple compositions. He can talk to his friends, but any contact with the unknown, the outside, formal world leaves him struggling and unsure. My number was busy. I opened the door, ready to cede the booth to a buxom blond who was so belligerent in defense of her position at the head of the line that her breath had left banks of cumulus clouds condensed on the glass.

"Hey, don't go. No German would leave and let *us* have it," Lello objected. I backed out, dragging him by the arm in my wake, and apologized to the woman—in English—for the delay. We stood beside the booth. Each new person who came to the front of the line insisted I try my call again. Before it went through, I had plenty of time to consider the situation. If Germans are less than charmed by their *Gastarbeiter*, the Lellos have only started their basic training to be accepted as anything else.

That afternoon I went back to Bianca and Gaetano's as I did another afternoon when he had had two teeth extracted and another evening. And later too on another trip. After half a bottle of *Schnaps* or a few bottles of beer, he might laugh and tell funny, sour little stories of his misadventures with German, insignificant in themselves, but terribly important to him. And his teeth. He has his new

[*99*]

plates, the ones he never quite believed in, and complains that they are loose. One bright note: the insurance will pay until they are right, a perfect fit. His children have given him the final disappointment. He no longer tries to talk to the little ones. Nando, Lello, and Chiara are looking for a flat of their own where they can be free of him, live their own lives. He talks little about that, but it reminds him of Torregreca, of growing up there, of a past without shadows in soft golden sunlight. And then he shakes his head. No, Torregreca was not like that either. He was cold and hungry there, unemployed and without prospects. He had no choice—and so once more he slips into his soliloquy of defeat. This is no pose, no mood that will pass. This is as much of the truth about his past as he understands and as much of his future as he can plan. Perhaps repetition brought relief. He had spoken. Someone had listened—and I had, dreading what I knew now would be the end.

This man, not yet fifty, would tell me again what he saw as his only reward, his only reasonable hope—that he might "last" until he had his pension and could go home to Torregreca, because, as he said over and over again,

"No man wants to die a stranger among strangers. Anything, but not that. Not *still* a stranger. . . ."

Saturday morning at 9:30 the orgy began. No other word can describe it. My dictionary gives 1) secret ceremonial rites held in honor of an ancient Greek or Roman deity and usually characterized by ecstatic singing and dancing, 2) drunken revelry, 3) an excessive indulgence in an activity. I will admit that ours was not secret and that only little Cristina sang and danced, but we made up for whatever we lacked in the first and second categories by our frenzied perseverance in the third. It was a true orgy, and it was a regular Saturday morning event, a mass delirium that infects all Italians in Germany. By bus, train, car, scooter, bicycle, even on foot if necessary, every man, woman, and child goes shopping.

By the time I arrived at the house, Edda had marshaled her troops. Michele had already been deployed on quartermaster duty to a supermarket near Lahr. Our rendezvous was for 10:30 in the parking lot. Berio was detailed to polish the family shoes, while Edda policed her daughters' toilettes (and later Berio's) starting with a quick bath that she had organized on the line of a sheep dip—for humans. When I came into the kitchen, Vincenzo was sitting at the table, reading a sports paper with a small cup of coffee and a glass of *Schnaps* at his elbow. He did not look up. For a nonreader his concentration was suspect, but not being a jolly, communal breakfast type myself, I sat down opposite him without a word. The paper rustled slightly, then dropped.

"Sorry. I wasn't sure it was you. Want some coffee?" I nodded and was asking what the schedule might be when a howl followed by footsteps hammering down the hall interrupted. Little Cristina, in full rebellion against the bath, had slithered away from her mother's grasp. Edda thundered after her, baying all the way, and caught her just as Berio turned up the volume on his tape recorder. Cristina's shrieks blended into the shrieks of rock, the racket boomed through the house at a level no airport authority would condone, and Vincenzo slammed the coffee pot down hard on the stove.

"This place is driving me nuts! Started at five-thirty this morning. My God, it's Saturday. I could sleep, but not here, not in this asylum. And it's like this ev-e-ry sing-le day. That moron Berio hardly gets out of bed before he's got a tape going. Edda wakes up braying like a donkey—and—Cristina . . ." He lowered his voice almost to a whisper. "I tell you, signò, someday I'll strangle her in cold blood. Why do you think old Michele went off so happy? He can't stand it either, and he's supposed to be deaf in one ear. SHUT UP!" He put a cup down in front of me and stalked to the door. "SHUT UP! TURN IT DOWN, TIBERIO! TURN IT DOWN, DAMMIT! La signora can't hear a thing," he finished softly. The rock retreated into the distance to grumble like a fast-moving summer storm. Suddenly Cristina's snuffles were very clear. Vincenzo slammed the door closed and came back to slide into his place across from me. Very quietly he gave me a resumé of where everyone had gone or would go.

"Where's your mother?" He grinned at me and then turned away to look at his glass of *Schnaps* with a speculative half-smile.

"Think she went to change her . . ." He finished the phrase with a wide gesture around his stomach. "Last thing she said was she was glad you'd stayed in a hotel. I think the noise is getting her too."

I repeated his half-barrel motion. "You mean she's changing her corset?"

He nodded. "Said she couldn't make all those decisions in the one she had on," and he waggled his hand in the air as much as to say you had to be crazy to understand her reasoning. Women and their trappings and the psychological climate they create are still puzzles without answers for Vincenzo. Chichella favors one-piece suits of armor. They vary from downright comfortable flabbiness to a maximum of baling strength that should bring on cardiac occlusion. She buys them secondhand at the market from Neapolitan vendors who dump mounds of clothes on the ground and stand beside them, crowing, "Two pieces, any two pieces five hundred lire [about 60 cents]! Come dig around! Any two pieces five hundred lire!" Depending on her humor, she over- or under-estimates her size, but she always has one iron lung she considers fit for formal occasions. If worn for any period of time, it *would* impair her judgment. The logic was easy to follow. It also gave me a first warning of just how serious this expedition was to be. Vincenzo and I sat in amiable silence until Chichella came in a few minutes later.

"Close the door, Ma."

"Uffa, the noise in this place...." She banged the door shut. "Did you *hear* in there? Vincenzo, can't you give the signora some *Schnaps*—from your bottle? Don't want any trouble," and she jerked her thumb over her shoulder toward the bedlam she had just left.

My protests and Vincenzo's apologies jumbled together to convince Chichella that I did not long for *Schnaps* nor had he been stingy. She abandoned politeness for the more absorbing question of Our Program. Her plans would have stretched well into Sunday. After Vincenzo explained that the stores closed at one, she rushed out in the hall and joined the yelling match. The signora was impatient. We were leaving without them. I am such a convenient dragon!

Assunta was the first to appear, in black slacks and a black turtleneck sweater, her face gray with gloom. She took our cups and heated a pan of milk, which she poured over some crumbled biscuits in a mug. This she placed carefully on the table with a spoon beside it and vanished back down the hall. In a minute Cristina skipped through the door, straight to the table, and began slurping up the gumbo. Vincenzo leaned over to whisper in my ear.

"First time I ever saw her eat anything without complaining it was too hot. I'll get our coats." I was not quite sure of his last re-mark because Berio had lunged into the room, bellowing,

"What's the big hurry? Say, I had an idea. Signora, why don't you take the ones who are ready and then come back for the rest? Two trips, see? Everybody'll be more comfortable." He smiled around at us for approval. "Too bad you don't have an Alfetta. Only car to have. I don't know why you . . ." Just a matter of four million lire! The Alfetta is the most expensive model Alfa Romeo produces. I went to the door and shouted into the emptiness of the hall.

"Chichella, hurry up! I'm leaving." The only answer was the sound of shuffling feet.

"A buyer stopped at the leather factory the other day—I was there to meet a friend—with a new Alfetta." Nothing discourages Berio. He swooped around the room with one hand held out in front of him, planing in imitation of the car. "Never saw anything like it. Zoom and it's gone. Mileage isn't great, but that wouldn't bother you." (Of course not, with gasoline at $2.60 a gallon!) Edda dashed down the hall in stocking feet. She carried high-heeled leather sandals in one hand. With the other she tried to button her dress. Even after she caught her breath the orange, green, yellow, and brown psychedelic pattern of the material seemed to go on pulsating, jumping at us, swirling around, rearranging its molecules to jump out at us again.

Vincenzo came back with an armload of coats and without a word pushed everyone, ready or not, slowly, patiently through the door, down the corridor, and out toward the car. His determination was so obvious, no one objected, but at the gate Edda found her voice.

"Get in—all of you! Get in. We'll be right back." And so I discovered that she, Chichella, and I were to go to the bakery, not, as I realized when they refused to ride there, to buy bread, but to show off the visitors—us.

Edda marched out ahead. We fell in behind her, keeping our distance and our steps regular as troops on parade. The road that had appeared deserted in front of the house now seemed to swarm with people—housewives with shopping bags and children hanging from their arms, some with babies in strollers, boys on bicycles, men chatting in little clusters—and they all stopped whatever they were doing to stare politely at us. In an Italian village strangers, like diamonds, are inspected for flaws. Nothing escapes critical eyes and forked tongues. Only two courses are open to the victim: an attack of galvanic hauteur or ignominious flight. Here, instead, people stared with bashful curiosity and, if our glances met, ducked their heads in apology and murmured, "*Morgen.*" It was *Morgen, Morgen, Morgen* all the way to the bakery, where deep blue and white petunias in the window boxes on either side of the door nodded Morning, Morning, Morning in the same rhythm. Inside, the shop was small, and the warm air, heavy, almost stifling with the sweet smell of fresh bread, icing, spices and nuts, made it seem even smaller. A pink-faced woman in an immaculate white smock smiled and chattered as she doled out rolls and long golden loaves of bread. Somehow she was able to weigh, calculate the cost of each woman's purchases, and wrap them without losing the thread of her customers' gossip. The six or seven women crowded around the glass-fronted counter laughed at her comments and added others of their own. It was all very good-natured. No one was in a hurry, or cross at having to wait.

When finally three women turned away together, ready to leave, and saw us, their faces froze in animation and then slowly, like those electric signs that melt smoothly from one message to another, rearranged themselves into impersonal calm. Silence. The baker looked up, said something, and the others murmured. Edda rushed in with an answer. I was amused: her voice was quiet and mannerly. She tripped along through an explanation of who we were, which I could identify only because she had conferred with Berio about the proper word for sister-in-law. I was "a friend from Tuscany," presumably Italian. The women nodded and clucked and wanted to shake hands with us. We were willing enough, but not having anything we could say was awkward. My one reliable German sentence—Do you have a single room with bath? without bath?—was hardly appropriate. Chichella chose marmoreal serenity. I lapsed into English. One or two of the women looked at me rather closely, confused. They had moved away from the counter in a body, and I saw for the first time that the case was full of neatly displayed meats and cheeses. Two more women came in, and we started again *da capo*.

The mini-reception might have continued through the morning. Edda bought sweet rolls for all of us and two loaves of bread, and slowly we withdrew, smiling and nodding. Outside, our new acquaintances were already explaining who we were to friends they met in the street. Smiling triumphantly Edda led us, still in drill formation, back to the car. We had been properly introduced to local society.

On our way to the superstore, we passed a complex of six, possibly eight white towers of apartments, sitting isolated in the middle of fields. Vincenzo said that during his first tour he had worked on them. Both Chichella and I took second, more careful looks at them. Neither of us had quite expected Vincenzo to be involved in anything so substantial. Just beyond on the opposite side of the road was the main Fiat distribution center in Germany. Rows of parked cars led off in every direction as far as the eye could see, leaving the beguiling impression that with altitude a pointillist masterpiece would emerge. At the center, low, sprawling buildings, factory classics with green corrugated walls and no windows, housed entire armies of scrubbers and mechanics, who clean and carry out the tinkering that should guarantee the delivery of sparkling, perfectly tuned vehicles. A mile farther along we arrived at our store which could have been a twin of the Fiat center, parking lot and all. Instinctively I felt there should have been a sign, like our warning on cigarette packages: "LASCIATE OGNI SPERANZA VOI CH'ENTRATE."

As I was locking the car, Michele came wobbling along our lane, pushing two carts loaded with cardboard cartons. Edda had just discovered a stand under the store's portico, or to eliminate any image of Palladian dignity, the simple extension of the building's flat roof that served as its portico. "Ten kilos of potatoes for 2 DM. Twenty-two pounds of potatoes for [$1.00]!"

"Hey, Chichè! *That's* what you've got to take back," she

crowed, consumer greed overwhelming her more dulcet tones at the bakery. "Look! *Potatoes!* I'll send some back to my mother too." With a squinched, crafty look in her eyes she trotted off toward the pyramid of sacks, dragging Chichella behind her. I had almost forgotten how good potatoes can be (in Italy they are grainy, soggy, and at 60 cents a pound, expensive), but I refused to turn the car into a traveling produce van. I tossed the keys toward Vincenzo and rushed after Chichella and Edda.

"*Mo' commincia,*" he called. "*Vedrà!*" Now it starts. You'll see. And he was right. Potatoes and sugar, which costs perhaps 7 cents a pound less in Germany, became the leitmotifs of my arguments with Edda. Predictably her reaction was a raucous "*Dai! Che fa?*" Come on! What's the difference? and an abrupt jolt on the shoulders that sent me reeling out of the way of her assault on whichever golden commodity she coveted. When we finally escaped to Italy, there were no sacks of potatoes on or in the car, but there were three in her attic storeroom. I had held the line. However, in Turin, Chichella began giving away boxes of sugar. She admitted that some twenty-five kilos of it were slowly trickling out over the clothes in her suitcases. I prefer not to know how many chocolate bars kept them company.

With Chichella's full cooperation I won the first round of the potato war and in convoy, Vincenzo and Michele in the lead, Berio bringing up the rear, we approached the store for our attack on the acres of merchandise.

Inside it was bright, warm, and very still with the unnatural sssh-quiet of a library reading room. Distant polkas tootled over the public address system. If the management thought to ensure maximum concentration, it had calculated without our arrival. We invaded the women's department, just beyond the front door, like a tribe of television Indians swooping down on a wagon train. A large proportion of the female Italian residents (and, no doubt, their relatives and friends) had already staked their claims on whichever of the revolving racks of clothes intrigued them. They set their heels to be shove-resistant and ignored us. Edda tunneled her way from rack to rack, yelling for Chichella to "come and see" what she had found.

Her enthusiasm never waned. For the rest of the morning she searched, she urged, she counseled, she bullied with noisy exuberance. This was Chichella's spree and its success would be measured by her failure to resist temptation. Edda's cries, "Over here! Over here!" or "You missed this," echoed through the department, summoning Chichella. If her way was blocked, she got behind Berio, who was adept at using their cart as a battering ram, and pushed.

Soon I had dropped far behind, more because of obstacles than linear distance—three revolving racks and a dozen frantic shoppers. I stood out in the aisle, considering what the best approach might be. To venture near the racks was tantamount to negotiating a traffic interchange from the wrong direction. Perhaps a flanking operation ... A youngish woman, dressed in gray and pushing a cart, stopped beside me to stare at the melee. Berio chose that moment to argue with a family, father, mother, and two children, who refused to move. Next to me the woman shook her head and said something in German. I smiled. She went on along the aisle. All I understood was "the Italians," but the remark was not complimentary.

Two steps and my sleeve was snagged: a low-lying hanger, I thought. I jerked my arm and an iron-claw grip tightened. I looked down. A wizened peasant woman, wrapped in layers of black, with crackled skin and no teeth, squinted up at me.

"You read that?" She shoved a tag under my chin. I told her the price, wondering what future she planned for a red crepe dress with deep, floppy ruffles at the sleeves and hem, a survivor of the last "*gitane*" craze. "How much is that in *soldi*?" Solemnly I converted the DM to "real" money for her, and asked if she was sure the dress was the right size. "Looks right," she answered and pawed the material, the rough skin of her fingers grating on it. Just behind me a shrill voice ordered,

"Ma, don't talk to strangers." Jugged *r*'s gave them away: Sicilians. An arm reached over my shoulder and snatched the red dress out of my hands. I turned and found myself staring into the malevolent yellow eyes of a dark, worried-looking young woman. "You don't want *that*, Ma. Come on! Housedresses are over here," and she led her mother away, hissing instructions not to talk to Germans.

"It's not like at home where you can talk to everyone. They don't like us, so don't bother them."

"The nice lady spoke Italian," the old woman objected.

"Tell by looking at her she's German," and they folded away into the crowd.

My morning was a series of fleeting encounters. I helped two spare middle-aged women, originally from Caserta, read the tickets on men's sweaters. They were intimidated by the number of people and the quantity of merchandise. It was their first trip to the store. They had heard about it and thought—maybe they were wrong— that the prices were high. Not that the things weren't good, better than anything where they lived, but expensive. They took me with them to the rug department, where we discussed "oriental" rugs and I pulled and yanked and leaned on ranks of carpets hanging full-length from holders until they could see each one and estimate its size. Reading the measurements was no help. They could only judge by eye, and this rug must fit two rooms—the sitting room here and the "dining room," which is the same room, serving the same pur-pose under a different name, "at home." With that settled, we stud-ied the prices. Color was the least vital consideration, which was just as well because they had a choice of two—one fire-engine red, the other beige, brown, mustard, and orange. They rejected the red, and I went in search of someone to lower the mustard-and-orange hor-ror and detach it from its holder. A big man in overalls listened with an odd expression on his face as I tried intensive pantomime with something like, *Tirenzei giù, bitte, il tappeten."* He nodded seriously and motioned me to precede him.

"You speak Italian?" he asked very gently. I admitted that I did. He was from Puglia. I told him I had just come from there, that the grape harvest was almost over, the weather, beautiful, and that work was still scarce. He cocked his head to one side in a lazy half-shrug. "Nothing ever changes down there, does it?"

He rolled the carpet, hoisted it onto his shoulder, and led the way to the cashiers' desks as though he were court chamberlain at the head of a royal procession. He promised to have the rug wrapped in some manageable form, and I am sure he did. After that our paths insisted on crossing until by closing time we were almost friends in the intimate, yet detached way of strangers on trains. I knew, for instance, the house he lived in at home, what kind of furniture he had bought with his savings, what his wife looked like (from a photograph in his wallet), and that he rented a room from a widow who "obliged" in ways we left unspecified. But I do not know his name. He had been in Germany for three years, always with the same job. He was a loader who, except when there was a large crowd, worked in the stockrooms or on the delivery platform. The shopping patterns were distinct: weekdays were German, Saturdays, immigrant with Turks, Yugoslavs, Spaniards, and hordes of Italians. His pay was so-so, not high, not low, but he liked the job and it had one virtue that outweighed any faults: it was the first he had ever had where he never got wet. No cloudburst caught him in the fields, no foreman could make him mix cement in a drizzle.

"We're weak in the lungs—as a family, I mean—so it makes a big difference to me. The only thing wrong is I miss my wife and children, but you can't make it up here on *one* salary, and my oldest boy's only twelve. If I don't find work at home next summer, then I'll have to come back again—alone. It could go on like this another three or four years. But, who knows! Maybe there'll be work at home. What do you think?"

"Who knows, indeed? For your sake, I hope so."

Berio found me in housewares. Chichella needed me to model a coat. She and Vincenzo were surrounded by young Turkish women who wore limp scarves wrapped around their heads and necks. They stroked the material of the coats furtively, slight smiles betraying their pleasure. When they saw me, they pulled their scarves slowly up around their mouths, over their noses, shrinking into non-being. A pudgy dark man, wearing a brown checked suit so unwrinkled it had to be molded plastic, materialized from behind a rack and edged closer.

"They can't all have toothaches," Chichella muttered in my ear as she slipped my arms into the sleeves of a long brown suede coat. In a more normal voice she called to Vincenzo, "See. I told you it was the right size." Their hands pressed seams and smoothed scars.

[*110*]

They twirled me around and stood off to judge the effect, and glitterless black eyes peered out of dusty cocoons, watching my every move. I pretended not to see them so that they would not have to turn away, but that bulky protector would never allow his ladies such an extravagance. Vincenzo decided the coat would do very well for his younger sister, a present from him, as were all the other things they chose that morning. We hung it on the clothespole attached to the cart.

I left them in the lingerie department where dozens of brackets, slanting out from a partition, displayed one-piece corsets with zippers up the front. After a first quick glance, Vincenzo turned his back on them and fixed his gaze, modestly, high on a blank wall.

For a while I held a sleeping baby in the men's department for a tense, emaciated little woman with wide brown eyes and greasy hair. She had three other children to keep track of, a little girl and two boys, all under six, but in the intervals between their jungle fights under the clothes racks, she told me that her husband had lost his job in a factory near Frankfurt. The recession. Ten months he had worked there. Now they had his unemployment and the daywork he could find as an unskilled laborer. They had come south to live with his sister and brother-in-law. One way to save money, share expenses, but their quarters were tight: four adults and seven children in four rooms. They had to go home to Calabria at Christmas—a sister was to be married—and her husband had nothing decent to wear. I understood, didn't I, how it was at home? Can't look like you're dying of hunger, so he said we'd better buy a suit before prices went up again. After that flood of information, she stared at the floor, embarrassed and silent. To distract her I asked if the children went to nursery school. It was a poor choice. She was near tears. Not yet, because *he* still didn't have their papers in order. *He* didn't seem to care either. *He* said she didn't have anything else to do. She could take care of them. A few seconds later *he* joined us, a short fragile man, thinner even than she, with wispy hair and a miserable inch-square scraggle of a moustache. He was disgusted. The suit didn't fit. The jacket came down to his knees. He took the baby from me, thanked me with the flourishes and exaggerations that

Calabrians inherited from their Spanish masters, and ignoring his wife, started toward the front of the store. He assumed she would follow, and she did, dragging the three rambunctious children behind her.

Chichella was deeply engrossed in curtains and table linens.

Outside, I ran into Vincenzo. We had both slipped out to smoke a cigarette. He was worried that his money would not last. I promised him a loan. When I next saw him, he was back in the lingerie aisles, pretending corsets were invisible. Chichella poked him and showed him a price tag. He peeked over his shoulder quickly, as though she were trying to sell him pornographic postcards.

I ran into another group of thin Turkish women wrapped in scarves. It was hard to tell whether the goods that interested them were actually all in dark corners, or whether they had to be interested in the goods in dark corners because better lighted areas would be too public. These had small children with them. A ferrety-looking man who lurked nearby was easy to identify as their warder. Had he been Italian, his clothes—black trousers, black windbreaker and a white shirt—would have identified him as an off-duty waiter. On second thought I gave up the correlation: half the men in Istanbul wear black trousers and white shirts. There were no older Turkish women in the store, or for that matter in Southern Germany. They were all young and thin and looked exhausted, which is reasonable since young men emigrate. On the other hand the men seemed to be of two types: the pudgy, self-satisfied ones in plastic suits; and the wiry ones with scrawny necks and trailing moustaches, whose flickering eyes and gaunt faces reminded me of Neapolitan street urchins, grown up and still hungry.

Michele stopped swirling his fingers through a bin of grass seed to ask if we would ever go home. We agreed that, at the worst, early closing would save us. Berio had returned for the third time to his inventory of the sports equipment. Warmup suits had created their own magnetic field. Edda and Chichella, bodiless behind piles of plates, fussed happily over how many of something to buy. Their cart was already so full that the slightest push sent packages skating off across the floor.

I drifted on, talked to other people, helped them when I could, and listened to them, which seemed to be what they wanted above all else. Their stories were much alike; only their level of discouragement and their loneliness varied. Never before had I appreciated how magic a skill reading is or how lost in a foreign country you are without it.

Convinced that my loitering from counter to counter was conspicuous, I tried to stay near objects too large to vanish into pockets or purse. I lack the bravura and the urge to be a shoplifter, and I did not want to be mistaken for one. Finally an elaborate mechanized meat slicer was about the only item I had not studied. According to the booklet, it was a very versatile appliance. I never knew more because a hearty voice behind me shouted,

"What are *you* doing here, signora?" When I turned around I almost collided with a blowsy woman in a squiggly wool dress and a white sweater. A large mole with whiskers grew on her chin. Either I recognized her physically or the battery of questions established her as the nemesis of my days in Torregreca. I still am not sure, but no one who has ever been on her strike list can wipe her completely out of his memory. No matter who I might be talking to or how busy I was, she never missed a chance to ask me for something, anything that came into her mind: a house, a car, a bicycle for her husband, phonograph records for her daughter, once even a tombstone for her mother-in-law. She never gave up the idea that eventually she would hit my weak spot, or I would collapse, worn down to surrender. She failed, but she would try again. The sight of me would tickle the reflex as surely as the bell prompted Pavlov's dogs to slaver.

Why was I in Germany? Where was I going? To do what? North? Her sister needed a ride to Stuttgart. I was sorry. Her sister could interpret for me. I was sorry. It didn't make any difference *when* her sister left. I was sorry. Were there many Torresi in the area? I asked.

"Some, but of course *I* never bother with them." She eyed me critically, as though I had accused her of consorting with baboons, and then dismissed me with an icy good-bye. Once more I had disappointed her.

Later Michele told me that her husband works as a laborer on

the railroads, considered the most brutal employment Germany offers and without security, and that she no longer speaks to the Torresi because when she proposed to various parents (including Edda
and Michele) an arranged marriage between her daughter and their
son, they had refused. "Only way you'll ever be sure he gets a nice,
clean girl" had been the selling point that offended. Inadvertently she
had insulted the sons. Besides, these days sons do not obey. Michele
smiled.

"Good riddance, I say. She's happy now. The girl married a
waiter from Pistoia. They picked him out. She'd only met him twice
before the ceremony, but that's how it is, signora. With some, old
habits are pretty stubborn."

The crowd had thinned. I looked around for Chichella and
found her—back at the corset racks with Vincenzo. Time was running out and Chichella is immune to doubt. She likes or dislikes.
The price is right, wrong, or she can be tempted, but she decides.
Tastes vary and my presence can inhibit, so I had chosen to wander,
busy about my own affairs. Now we were approaching the level of a
family crisis. Either Vincenzo had some deep-rooted objection to a
corset, which seemed unlikely, or ... Or what? I joined them, Vincenzo still with his back to the racks, Chichella still studying the
price tags.

"Here, can you read this? He says *he* can't." She made a face at
Vincenzo's back. I studied the tag and then put on my glasses. Print-
outs, numerical doodlings from some demented computer, served as
pedigrees for those corsets. The most conspicuous figure was 115—
115 whats were not specified, but Vincenzo had assumed DM. No
wonder he had been worried about money. His mother was determined to buy two corsets for $57.50 apiece! 115, 115, 95 oops, 125. In
every case the model was the same. How could the price vary? I
riffled down the racks. On the third I had different magic numbers:
46–48. My eye told me I could wear the 46–48, roughly the equivalent of our size 14.

I moved on to brassieres, where 115 was appropriate for nothing less than a wet-nurse. Then I knew. These were outsized gar-
ments for stout ladies. By then I was talking to myself. Chichella
volunteered that she needed a 105. She had known that all along! A

quick run produced six in colors from white to fuchsia and black. While she decided she wanted beige and there were none, I recited the figures out loud until I reached DM44. 44! We, even Vincenzo, could afford that, but before I told Chichella, I made her swear, on her honor, that we would leave the very minute I had solved her corset dilemma.

She nodded. Yes, oh yes, if she could get a real corset, a brand new one. I threw two white 105s on top of the cart and prepared to march on the cashiers' lanes. She could convince Edda, by force, if necessary. She did.

As we stood in line, they compared loads with our neighbors', all Italians out for their Saturday orgy. Did you see this? I got three of those. I saw something like that for twice the price in Lahr.... Strangely they agreed. One of the pleasures of the village market is to prove your own shrewdness by outbargaining your neighbors. Perhaps "the enemy" is no longer the Italian next door. At the far end of the counter Vincenzo, his billfold ready, waited with Michele, watching the numbers gallop past the window of the register. Our ransom from this prison of earthly delights would be dear. When the sinister hum of the machine had whined to silence and the tape had skipped its last, we owed almost exactly 1,000 DM. *That* is an orgy.

Once we were home, Edda just had time to retire to the bedroom with Chichella and admire their selections. Then the bus came, tooted its horn, and she rushed out, shouting instructions as she struggled into her jacket. On Saturdays her crew could clean the superstore, the same superstore, in the afternoon. When she came back several hours later—with three roast chickens and a pea-green slip—she was wiping her eyes. We thought something was wrong and rushed to be sympathetic. Not at all. She was laughing.

About a year before, a young Turkish woman, Rea they called her, joined the cleaning crew. At first the Italian women were not friendly. They considered her a warning: their jobs would be taken by Turks who worked for less and never complained. Later one woman had to leave. The store owner accepted their recommendation and hired in her place the sister of a woman already on the crew, an Italian. They relaxed. They even tried to be friendly, as friendly as an absolute lack of common language would allow.

Rea picked up some German. She seemed to be good-natured and she worked hard. The more they could talk to her, the better they liked her. They began teaching her German, their German. Peace returned to the cleaning crew.

Rea had two small children, one about Cristina's age. They do not play together because, Edda says, Rea lives too far away, and it would not be quite . . . well, that is . . . the village would not think it "right." Either Rea understands this bit of gratuitous snobbery or has resigned herself gracefully. She never talks about her children. Instead they discuss how peculiar men are, especially husbands. Rea's family picked hers. He is older than she and kind enough, but very serious about the old ways. He does not approve of fun. Sometimes Rea is very impatient.

That Saturday when they picked her up, Rea said she did not feel well, she was weak, and it was all her husband's fault. He followed, and insisted she follow, the old religion. Silly religion! From sunup to sundown he refused to let her eat. She was weak, dizzy, and still he raged. Maybe she was pregnant? No, nothing but that silly religion. A month she had to fast, *a whole month*.

Once or twice while they were cleaning, the women noticed Rea stop and lean her forehead against the cool wall. They begged her to rest, to sit down. They could do her work too. She refused. They finished, took off their smocks, and collected their coats and bundles. Suddenly Rea seemed very happy. She smiled, but as she climbed into the minibus, she asked the driver to go slow. Afraid she would be carsick, they thought. Why didn't she ride in front? No, no, she wanted the backmost seat, which happened to be next to Edda.

The bus churned off along the road, and Edda leaned back, prepared to doze. A great ripping of paper startled her. She opened her eyes. Rea was tearing apart a roast chicken. She already had a drumstick in her mouth, gobbling, sucking, hardly chewing at all. She shredded the meat off one breast and shoved it into her mouth. With her hands free, she twisted off both wings. She rolled her eyes, smacked her lips, and began gnawing on the second slab of breast. Edda could not help it: she laughed.

"Do not do that." Even muffled by a mouthful of meat, Rea's voice was sharp. "Not nice when you see a friend in pain." She leaned down to look out the window. "Too fast! Too fast, I hurry." She stuffed a wing in her mouth, crunched the bones, then spat them out onto the paper tray that had held the chicken and now held its carcass. She looked down. A wing and a leg. She took the leg, clamped her teeth and jerked. A hunk of flesh came away. She chewed and moaned at the same time.

The women in front had heard the paper rip and the odd little noises, but they were talking. Probably Edda taking another look at her purchases, just to be sure. They all did that. Her laugh made them stop talking and turn toward the back of the bus.

"Hurry, Rea! Hurry!"

"You can chew faster than that!"

They goaded her. They all laughed. The driver stopped at an intersection and twisted around to look and smiled. The woman next to him on the front seat whispered something. He drove slowly down the road, past Rea's corner and on until the street ended in a field. Then he turned left.

One of the women had an inspiration. She had bought two bath towels. She would get them. Rea was covered in grease. Here, Edda! Get her hands clean. The towels sailed back into Edda's lap. Rea was gnashing away at the last wing, spitting the splinters onto the pile of bones. Edda grabbed her hands and scrubbed. Rea folded the paper over the tray, stuck it under her seat, and snatched a towel. Two more left turns had brought the bus to her corner again. She swiped at her face, flipped the towel to Edda, and eased forward past the seat in front of her for the handle of the door.

"You promise me something," she said, looking from woman to woman. "Promise?" They nodded. "You do not tell my husband nothing. Understand? He does not know his religion is silly. Only I do. We must not tell him." They promised. They would not tell him. Rea was safe, if for no other reason than because not a single one of those women had ever spoken to a Turkish man.

[*117*]

After the rigors of our shopping spree and a prodigal lunch of pasta, roast rabbit, salad, various *salame* and cheeses from home, and fruit, I expected a drowsy afternoon. Vincenzo's eyelids were already heavy. Outside the sky had darkened and a gentle but relentless drizzle put an end to vague talk of an excursion. Instead there was an important soccer game on television. The tires of cars passing on the road hissed. Soon the eaves would drip, someone would light the stoves, and we would settle into a digestive torpor, the men in the gloom of the sitting room, the women in the kitchen where they could mend and gossip. Or so I imagined.

I did not know, and no one thought to tell me, that on weekends Michele's house is a general meeting place. From Friday evening to Monday morning "the regulars" wander in to stay a few minutes, a few hours, or whole days. If they leave, it does not mean they will not be back. They have cars. They are very willing to fetch and carry. They always offer rides. Every so often they bring presents—a string of sausages, spaghetti sauce, new apples, maybe a case of beer, and one Sunday when I was there, dozens of ears of corn, which to my consternation Edda boiled for more than two hours. (She was right. It was not sweet corn and with less cooking would have been about as edible as marble chips.) That evening around the kitchen table we had a picnic feast of cold meat, corn on the cob, salad from the garden, and finally, in an aureole of whipped cream, a chocolate cake that Edda had made and then hidden behind the beer bottles in the icebox.

Nonregulars were always welcome. They came and went. As long as they stayed the conversation revolved around *Chefs*, those ubiquitous foremen, the hope of work at home, and the odd mechanics of life in Germany. They appeared and disappeared, leaving me now with a mental album of snapshots: the faces are familiar, but the names are scrambled and the stories have melded into some larger, indefinite understanding.

At times the regulars were restless too, but just as their arrivals were never entirely expected, their exits were never final. Michele's was their clubhouse, the place where they met their friends to drink beer, to gossip, to yarn, to watch soccer games, even to argue or take a nap, if they felt like it. They belonged.

And they assumed that, in some mysterious way, I belonged. Formality ended with the introductions. Conversations, some a week old, were picked up where they had been interrupted—always in the middle, it seemed. Fortunately Chichella was as confused as I: one baffled face might be ignored, two can blight the most promising subject. Someone always took pity on us and explained the cast and plot in a subjective, totally synoptic form that sounded like Verga, slightly modernized, or even certain parts of the Old Testament. With only the dimmest past, very little future, the present too bleak for distractions, the characters seemed to await Judgment in a vacuum. A wakelike quality echoed from these descriptions. He was a good man. Fate was against him. What will become of the children? With true Southern pessimism they mourned what had not yet happened, the Inevitable, and I reminded myself that nothing quickens dramatic instinct like the misfortunes of others. Relieved by their own escape and truly sympathetic, they embellished adversity into premature tragedy. More than once I found the doomed man of yesterday's condensed biography sitting opposite me, if not in riotous good spirits, at least able to drink beer and gossip. Like the others he had stopped by to see what was new. He could forget his worries for an hour, if they would allow him to forget. Sometimes they could, sometimes they could not.

I had come to listen and, as long as strength and mind allowed, I did, trying to determine what pretense or convention had added to a story or pride had left out. We assume that "simple," by which I suppose we mean "unsophisticated," people tell the truth as they see it and see only what they tell us. In other words, "simple" implies simpleminded. Southern Italians are *not* simpleminded. They inherit little more than a will to survive. The techniques they learn quickly, or else are defeated. Self-protection, even at its most elementary level of withdrawal, is a complex skill, almost an art. No statement is entirely direct, no flattery entirely untrue. A reaction can be dogged silence, or a sneer of ferocious wit. They appear to accept conditions and snubs that we would not. But their submission is deceptive: it implies agreement. In fact they have never agreed with anything that has been done to them or, worse, done "for their own good." They submit, but they do not forget. Somewhere in every Southern Italian's mind is a tally of the wrongs done him. He does not brood over them, still they are warnings to caution. About his own kind he can be amusing, vicious, tell all with gloating pleasure. About officials or those "more fortunate," a euphemism which for him covers much of the world's population, he can be wary and cynical. About himself, frank and at the same time obtuse, as though testing his listener, waiting for some magic perception of what has not been said. If your intuition is perfectly synchronized and your guesses close, he will continue: if not, he will sit, stubborn and mute, then change the subject. That we had known each other for twenty years helped avoid stalemates, even encouraged the friends who had not known me, but the hazards of interpretation are obvious and I am certainly fallible.

There was another hazard, an unexpected one: language. Each night when I went back to the hotel, I thought my head would fly apart in neat linguistic segments. Chichella, Vincenzo, and Michele's family all spoke to me in their Torrese dialect. Pasquà, the same Pasquà who fought with the Germans in the bar so many years ago, considers Neapolitan, ever so slightly eased, a lingua franca. (His German wife never came with him. Language again. Pasquà had taught her pure Neapolitan, which we could all have understood more or less, but—and it was a large but—he had not taught her Italian. *She* would not understand *us*. Being a true Neapolitan, rather than translating for her, he thought it proper that she stay at home and more amusing for him if she did. Every few hours he dashed off to see how she was, if she needed anything, and then came back ready for *any* diversion.) The Sicilians in the group were from different towns and could not understand each other's dialect with any ease. A young man from Puglia, married to one of the Sicilians, prided himself on his agility with dialects. By transposing everything into Pugliese, he achieved what he should have expected: nonsense. The only way to carry on a general conversation, which everyone understood, was for each to speak his own private distillation of Italian, a language none had ever managed to learn, much less use. I was the possible exception.

All over Germany I was to hear this new vernacular in one stage or another of its evolution. As a nonexpert the best explanation I can give is that, unlike some dialects, its base is clearly Italian. Conventional verbs do still have some of the common distortions in their conjugations, but the roots are obvious. Many nouns, especially those having to do with the local arrangement of life—food, stores, hospitals, doctors, schools, transportation, government, banks, insurance, unemployment payments—are German words tricked out with Italian endings and arbitrary genders. The results suffer from the same comic ambivalence as *Rigoletto* sung in German, or *The Ring* in Italian. The pronunciations are a bizarre compromise. Other nouns are more or less Italian or specific dialect words that have caught the immigrants' fancy—all welded together with a common solder of Italian conjunctions, adverbs, and prepositions. Eventually it will be almost a language, as distinctive as the Italian spoken in New York, which is one of the many forms of what is called *Italiano all'estero*— Italian abroad or Italian in the foreign manner. Maybe this will be known as *Italiano Germanese, Germanese* being a Southern corruption, an entirely logical one, to form an adjective from the name of the country. (Unfortunately language and logic seldom meet. The proper adjective form is, of course, *tedesco*.) And it may someday, as the "Pidgin Deutsche" spoken by the immigrants already is, be the subject of doctoral theses. Whatever its final form, it is serving one practical purpose: Italian, a shambling, free-style Italian that will not please university professors or scholars of Manzoni, is becoming a comfortable language for Southerners, who, until recently, were only comfortable in their own dialects.

After lunch we sat around the table in Michele's kitchen, drinking coffee. Vincenzo was almost asleep. Still unaware of the weekend cycle of visits, I was thinking of a leisurely afternoon: this might be the time to go to Freiburg, just to see it. Michele was rolling a cigarette, a new, double-edged economy. He smokes less and spends less. Suddenly the outside door banged and footsteps thumped along the corridor. The door banged again.

"Whoever you are," Michele shouted, "close the door." We waited in silence like conspirators. The steps thumped back along the corridor, and we heard the latch forced in place.

"Knew you'd say that," came a man's harsh, nasal voice. "Be right back. I forgot something." Again the door opened and was left open to thud rhythmically against the frame until the man returned to close it.

"Just Raffaele," Vincenzo said, going to the cupboard for a glass and then into the sitting room for a bottle of beer. He put them on the end of the table and went to the hall for another chair. On principle Chichella collected our cups and saucers and motioned to Assunta that she should begin washing the dishes.

From the voice, I had imagined an elderly man, bent and querulous. Instead when Raffaele finally strode into the kitchen, he was tall and lithe, in his late thirties I would guess, with dark blond curls and a long, deeply tanned bony face. He wore blue jeans and a denim jacket with the lanky ease of a cowboy, a manner alien to Italians, who consider clothes, especially such fashionable ones, almost a costume to be worn with flair. He waved at us, pulled out the chair at the head of the table, sat down, and began pouring beer into the glass, all as though he had been with us before and had left to do an errand. After such a play for attention, his self-confidence seemed to fail him. He sat hunched over the glass, frowning slightly.

Time and weather have eroded his face into a network of greater and lesser furrows, like the configuration of foothills on a topographic map. Rather than age him, they give him a permanent expression of wry, almost sardonic doubt.

He moved his glass an inch or two, evidently absorbed in its exact position, but his small blue eyes glanced at me, away, then back again in speculation. They had a metallic glint, hard and opaque. Guessing what went on behind them was impossible; his bristly blond eyebrows that splayed upward at odd angles hinted at private amusement.

His eyes flickered toward me again, and away again as he realized that I was aware of his curiosity and undisturbed by it. Still he hesitated. Somehow I had ruined his entrance, his joke. That was it: he was trapped by his own joke. Surprised at myself for inventing the impossible—a Marlboro man with a sense of humor—I decided to rescue him.

"Do you give up? You'll never guess who I am."

He grinned at me, relieved. "Signora, all I know is that you're *not* this lout's mother!" He pounded Vincenzo on the shoulder. "And *they'll* never help me. If *I* look like a monkey swinging by his tail, they'll enjoy it."

Everyone started talking at once. Berio bellowed at Vincenzo to quit pinching him, which explained his unlikely silence, and Assunta plunged her hands back into her sink of dishes. Chichella chose to ignore everything that had happened and begin again by introducing herself and me. Raffaele listened, nodding seriously, to Chichella's extravagant account of who I was, but as soon as she gave me a name, he jumped to his feet, bowed, even clicked his heels, and shook hands with me.

"*Onoratissimo, signora!* Raffaele . . ." Something. I lost the name forever. "And I must ask your forgiveness. . . ." He did at length. He was determined to continue, to salvage what he could of his joke, which was less than funny and a failure: he should have dropped it. Instead, through his apologies, we understood vaguely that he brought sad news. Chichella pinched her face into the somber frown that she assumes for funerals, but Vincenzo relaxed, leaning back on the bench, his face expressionless, his eyes lowered. Michele was too busy studying the tip of his cigarette, which was not burning well. Only Berio was impatient to know.

"Come on, Raffaele. Tell us! What's happened?" he interrupted over and over again. Raffaele smiled, waving his hand at him: Berio must wait. This was a serious matter, to be approached seriously, and he would turn away to glance at each of us in turn. Finally in a fatal miscalculation he chose Chichella as his target. He had just heard that morning ... from the foreman ... things were bad ... but Vincenzo will have his unemployment ... that's good for a year, after all ... they'll tell him Monday ... they didn't have any choice ... they have to let him go.

Without looking up Vincenzo nodded several times. "Eh." He shrugged. "Another paid vacation! Worse for you—with the kids and ..." His head was still down, but a sly little smile pulled at the corners of his mouth.

"Perfect!" Chichella broke in enthusiastically. "You can come home with us. There's room—"

Raffaele banged the table with his hand palm down. "Damn! DAMN! Cheated again!" He pounded the table still harder. "I fouled up in the beginning." And he turned to me. "That's *your* fault. *She'd* have believed me, if ..."

"Not many people fool Chichella," Michele commented as he leaned over to put out the unsatisfactory cigarette.

We were making too much noise to hear footsteps in the back corridor and so were startled when the door opened and Maria of the afternoon before stuck her head inside. That is, I thought it was she, and then was not sure. This woman was taller and too trim in a silver-and-black-striped pant suit that suggested some tryst more exotic than a visit in a friend's kitchen.

"*Si può?*" she asked in a gentle, arch voice and waited pointedly for Michele's official consent. "Here, love, are your cigarettes." She pitched two packs toward Raffaele. "It didn't work, did it? Admit it! I told you, didn't I? Admit it!" Michele had dragged Assunta's chair toward the table, and Maria sat down, dismissing the subject to rummage in her purse. As she lowered her head long fronds drifted free from her pagoda of hair. She pushed them back, found her cigarettes, and lighted one. "Well, what's new? There *must* be something." And she looked at us expectantly, her face frozen in the archaic smile that convinced me she was, indeed, Maria. Her eyes were fierce, almost accusing, as though we were determined to keep something from her. I peeked at her feet: she wore clogs with six-inch soles.

"Eh, so you were right, but . . ." Raffaele grumbled.

"I knew it! But never mind." She bounced up from her chair. "Assunta, didn't your mother teach you *anything*? Not even how to wash dishes? Here. . . ." And waving at us to talk, she took over the sink.

Chichella has a rigid sense of what is proper: Raffaele had come to call on her.

"You're a friend of Vincenzo's?" she asked and leaned back, her hands crossed in her lap. Formality would be respected.

Raffaele and Vincenzo competed with each other to satisfy her requirements, explaining how they had met. Raffaele was the *ferraiolo*, the construction steelworker, Vincenzo had been assigned to work with so many years ago on his first job in Germany. If Vincenzo is a good carpenter, all credit is due Raffaele's patience, at least according to Raffaele. Berio overcompensated for Michele's deaf ear by relaying the vital points to us at the far end of the table in shouts and gestures that added greatly to the confusion and nothing to the clarity of what we could otherwise have heard. Cristina emerged, from a long-distance crawl under the table, at her father's knee and climbed up in his lap. He smiled and began whispering to her. She nuzzled her chin into his chest, but her beady little eyes never left my lighter on the table. I picked it up and put it in my pocket. Again Berio boomed in my ear. I must have winced. Michele leaned across the table and put his index finger to his lips in a signal that was not to be misunderstood. Berio blushed and ducked his head so low his chin almost touched his chest. For one fleeting moment I felt sorry for him.

Chichella, whose code, once it has been properly initiated, demands reciprocal courtesies from her, was explaining to Raffaele that she had taken advantage of my trip in the car to come with me to see Vincenzo. And, to establish my *serietà*, that all-important quality for a woman in the South, respectability (a woman gadding about Europe in a car for her own amusement is *not seria*), she made a brief, very clear statement about my study. Such strict economy of words meant that she had worked it out beforehand, just in case of need. She was my guarantor. How odd the reversal must have seemed to her!

Raffaele was intrigued by the project, by the idea that anyone would bother to find out how immigrants fared in Germany. Why only the Torresi? He could tell me *his* past very quickly—and did. He was the first of many to rush into an account of his life as he was willing to present it. None would have agreed to answer set questions designed to reveal his moral code, his mode of judgment, his inner secrets. Why should he be bored? Why allow a stranger to pry? But to talk (at times to ramble) about his village, his struggles, even his family quarrels was irresistible. Undoubtedly they edited, shading here, omitting there, exaggerating as we all will—and as the Torresi cannot usually do with me. It made no real difference. Often what they avoided exposed more than all that was said. Sometimes the people with us, who, like most nonreaders, were gripped by a "told story," worried about the gaps and asked questions. The answers, presented as the naked truth, were skillful evasions, and the listeners had to be content. These were autobiographies as the subjects wanted them to be. Some were very moving, others, funny, but what I did not realize at first was that I had an obligation. The teller offered his past: I must now share my questions about emigration. The exchange was entirely in my favor.

Raffaele and Maria grew up in one of the enormous peasant cantonments, too large to be a town, too primitive to be a real city, in central Sicily. As a little boy straight out of fifth grade, Raffaele went to work for an uncle, a small contractor. At first he ran errands, later he mixed cement, hauled it, loaded bricks, whatever needed to be done. He was everyone's apprentice. It was good practical experience. He knew nothing of theory, but in time acquired his specialization as a construction steelworker. He fell in love with Maria. They were married with the approval of both families and all the pomp and expense that implies. They rented a two-room house without water or plumbing, which was what they could afford and better than living with one or the other of their families. They settled down, expecting, if they thought about it, to live happily enough, to work, to have children, and to squabble with their neighbors as their grandfathers had done.

"Do you know towns like that, signora?" Raffaele asked. I nodded. "Where everybody watches everybody else? Your business is theirs, and if you do nothing wrong, a sin is invented for you. But . . ." He shrugged. "We were used to it." Predatory neighbors, like flies and lack of water, are local aggravations. "We meant to stay. We never even talked about leaving until things—well, sort of changed. We wanted to stay." Maria turned away from the sink, drying her hands on a towel, and now stood just behind him, listening, her face serious, almost expressionless, except for the crimps at the corners of her mouth which gave her an air of oracular mystery.

"What he means," she said, putting one hand on his shoulder, "is that I disgraced him—or that's what the town thought. He never . . ."

"I knew better than that." He glanced around at her. "Come sit down. You're giving me a stiff neck." Vincenzo made room for her on the bench. As she slipped in, she was already fumbling for her cigarettes. Her hands are always busy. Either she works or she smokes.

"All right, love. Go ahead. I'll keep quiet." Her voice was less meek than her words.

"I say things began to change—not just one thing, lots of things. That famous Italian Boom was just a whisper in Sicily. We were all waiting for it to happen to us, but by 1965 the signals were running the other way, and there was a building slump. When we finished the last set of apartments, my uncle admitted that he'd have to drop the crew for a while. On unemployment, for what it was worth, but he didn't have anything in sight. I could always find work: that wasn't the problem. I'm good and fast at my trade. No, no." Raffaele waggled a finger at us. "The problem down there is how to get paid. You do the work NOW. *They* pay when it suits them—a month later, a year later, maybe never. *You* get installments—dribbles, promises—next week. And you can forget insurance. You weren't really hired. Why should they insure you? I wouldn't put up with it. Let the blacks work that way, if they want to.* Not me! It was time to leave and we did. *Thank God!* Thank God, we did! So don't listen to Maria and her 'scandal.'" He turned to her. "And you can quit trying to take the credit." Surly as he sounded, the furrows of his face tensed into a wide, puckish grin.

"Wouldn't think of it, *amore.* You'd beat me for less." And to emphasize just how frightened she was, she gave a merry, tinkling little laugh. "Isn't he sweet? He always denies it was my fault."

"I warned you, woman!" His smile was so wide that small, very white teeth showed. "Wait until we get home. You'll see."

"Go on, Valentino. This is your night to dance. Remember? I'll be asleep long before you finish your rounds."

"Ever notice, Michele, that the best way to treat a woman is ignore her?" Michele smiled, but would not be lured into a comment. Marriage in Southern Italy seldom generates much banter, or the closeness and mutual amusement it implies. Rancor, arguments, yes. Total indifference to the extreme of seeming strangers, yes. But banter is unusual, and no matter how cheerful, is a family game

---

* Which is exactly what has happened. North Africans, Somali, and Ethiopians (CENSIS— *Centro Studi Investimenti Sociali*—estimates as many as 350,000) man Sicilian fishing boats, wash dishes in Roman restaurants, are cowherds, gas-station attendants, foundry workers, loaders, and miners. Often they work long, illegal hours without health insurance or social benefits. Theirs are the marginal jobs, unattractive evidently to Italians spoiled by what has proven to be a frail prosperity. A paradox when hundreds of thousands of Italians roam Europe in search of work and 1,650,000 at home are officially unemployed in a work force of 19,500,000 (excluding any consideration of Italian employment quicksands that swallow thousands who are underemployed or moonlighting or staying alive on so-called "black work," the undeclared part-time or piecework.)

with only two players. "Ignore them! They love it," Raffaele repeated, well satisfied with his idea, but he winked at Maria.

"At your own risk. Now, go on, love, and save my honor."

Later, when the men were watching the soccer game, Maria
told us about her "scandal." In a society less bigoted, less self-righteous than Southern Italy's it would have been dismissed as a prank.
Her only crime was poor judgment. At *Carnevale*, just after she and
Raffaele were married, Maria made "Spanish dancers'" dresses for
herself and her little brother. She put lots of makeup on her face,
more on her little brother's, especially rouge, dressed them in their
costumes, settled their masks in place, and swept off to the wineshop
where she knew Raffaele and his friends would be playing cards. She
danced, she flirted with the men, she actually sat on Raffaele's knee.
("And he didn't object either!") One of the men was so captivated
by Maria's brother that he backed him-her into a corner, and Maria
had to rescue him. They rushed back home to change their clothes,
scrub their faces, and be discovered by Raffaele, quietly gossiping. He
arrived soon after, bubbling with the story and lusty details his
imagination had already had time to invent. Maria and her brother
giggled, but said nothing.

They spent the next day planning a second, more titillating
appearance. When it was finally dark and they knew the streets
would be crowded with children, even adults, in costumes and
masks, they set out once more for the shop. This would be a spectacular show and their last, something the town would never forget.
Everyone would speculate: no one would ever know—for sure.

They burst into the shop, expecting the usual customers. Instead the dark little room was crowded with friends and friends of
friends who had heard about the revels of the evening before and
had come, hoping the performance would be repeated, that they
might see for themselves, might pinch the dancing girls' bottoms—
and more, if they could. Maria knew at once that they must escape.
She tried to back out, but the men grabbed her and her little
brother, dragged them inside, and pulled off their masks. So it was
that Maria became a Wanton Woman.

The harder Raffaele and his friends denied their original ver-
sions of the first visit, the bawdier the accounts that circulated

around town. They had danced, slowly stripping off their clothes. No, they had arrived naked, except for cloaks that they threw off. ... Friends avoided Maria in the street. Their unmarried sisters were forbidden to speak to her. Men made remarks as she passed; one or two went further. At first Raffaele laughed, not about the men, but about Maria's joke. As time went on and she was not forgiven, they began to talk of emigration.

A sad little story without guilt. Sadder still to me was Maria's reaction, though I knew she was right. She was so lucky, she repeated over and over again. She had not really known Raffaele then, what kind of a man he was, that he liked fun and did not care what people thought if they were wrong. Another man would have beaten her for shaming him like that—might even have left her, with the people of the town saying he was right. To them she is still a whore.

"...Now, go on, love, and save my honor," she had told Raffaele. "You were going to tell them about that great good friend of yours, remember?"

Raffaele was not apt to forget. It had been the friend who told him there was work, lots of work, in Germany, who had promised to get him a job with his own contractor, any day, any day, just say the word. Raffaele was a real innocent then. He had never even been to "the Continent," as they say in Sicily, and this man was his friend, so he believed him. He quit his job, packed a little handbag, and was off for a lark, like a boy on his first school trip to Palermo—no, farther—to Naples. He asked Maria if she remembered how excited he was? How goddamned stupid? She nodded. He looked at her for several long seconds, blinking his eyes as though they smarted. They were both remembering that innocent young man and perhaps for the first time pitied him. We waited, each embarrassed and surprised too by the insistence of our own memories: like old bruises, they were invisible, but still sore to the touch.

Raffaele sensed our gloom and would have none of it. We were all naïve once. No shame in that. He learned quickly. The trip itself was enough. Already in Palermo his compartment in the train was full: five other men, all emigrants. Their bags and parcels and bottles of olive oil jammed the racks over their heads. Their legs tangled, and elbows were sharp as dibbles. They did not talk much. They smoked and dozed and played cards and stretched and smoked again. Raffaele asked where the others were going. He asked for advice too. They suggested towns he might go to—with strange names—which he discovered they had never been to themselves. Wherever they were going, they insisted, there was no work for a newcomer, and he understood: they were afraid.

When they noticed that the train spent more time on sidings than it did in motion, they began watching for town names. Their geography was uncertain. They argued about exactly where they were, but were all convinced that their route was a zigzag. Raffaele found a ticket conductor: yes, they were off schedule. There was a flood. They might lose twelve hours, twenty-four, who knew?

"What do you care?" he asked. "A day sooner, a day later where you're going—what difference does it make?"

Back in the compartment one of the older men got very drunk and wanted to argue. He finally fell asleep, but when he woke up, he pulled a knife on the man next to him. After that everyone took his turn watching him: one man was always awake. A young boy cried most of the way. He cried himself to sleep and then woke himself up, whimpering. Someone said maybe his mother had died, but the others said no, he was just scared because he did not know exactly where he was going or what he would do when he got there. But then, none of them really knew.

Instead of thirty-six hours, the trip from Palermo to Freiburg took three days. Toward the end food was short. Those who had a heel of bread, a bit of *salame* or cheese, became secretive. They waited until the others slept or took their sacks to the toilet where the stench and filth gagged them. Raffaele had left Sicily prepared for adventure: he would conquer the world. When at last he arrived, he was hallucinating, seeing things that were not there, hearing strange voices. He did not know where he was. He could not understand what people said—and he knew that he was very small.

His friend insisted that all he needed was some sleep. He had a bed for him in the warehouse where he himself lived with half a dozen other men and, Raffaele found, a corps of hungry rats. Michele's loft was the Ritz compared to that warehouse, but for the moment Raffaele had no choice. The men told him what his share of the rent would be. Two months later he realized that he was paying *half* of the total. By then a Neapolitan who was supposed to be a nightwatchman and had been fired for selling bags of cement from the supplies had left, taking with him everything in the warehouse not under lock, including one of Raffaele's two shirts, which he had hung out on the line to dry. Only a Neapolitan would steal from a poor bastard worse off than he, but it was a lesson: trust no one.

At least he had work. His friend had kept his word and taken him to his foreman. They talked a long time. Raffaele could understand nothing, but he poked his friend and whispered in his ear, reminding him that he had his specialization certificate. He was not just a laborer. He was a *ferraiolo*—a construction steelworker. His friend nodded and went back to his conference with the foreman. Raffaele was hired. He was put to work pushing wheelbarrows loaded with sand, up one ramp, across a floor, and up another. By the time he dumped the barrow and trundled it back down, its twin was loaded and ready for him. After eight hours he could hardly stand up, his legs buckled. Tomorrow will be different, he thought. The next day it was wheelbarrows again, and the next and the next. He could talk to no one in authority. The other "muscles" knew no more than he. His friend was evasive. Maybe they did not need a steelworker just then. Maybe this was a trial. Be patient. Raffaele began listening very carefully to all the German he heard. He picked up two or three words, but they hardly made a conversation, so he was patient and listened and pushed the wheelbarrows up one ramp, across the floor, and up another ramp for eight hours a day.

Late the first Friday, when the men were waiting to pour concrete, the foreman came over to Raffaele and ordered him to do something he did not understand. The foreman explained again, then, irritated and impatient, pushed some tools in Raffaele's hands and shoved him toward a column where the *ferraiolo*, who had caused the delay, was trying to finish setting irons. Raffaele helped him, but he only needed a few minutes to understand what the problem was. The man did not know his trade. He was learning on the job and so afraid of making mistakes that he was slow. Slow as death. Raffaele helped him and said nothing. The steel was set, the concrete poured, and finally everyone could go home. Next Monday would be different.

Monday he was back with wheelbarrows of sand. Dummy, learn the jargon, he kept telling himself. Listen and learn so you can talk. The next Friday afternoon work was held up by the same *ferraiolo*. Again the foreman sent Raffaele to help, and he went, but he had made up his mind. As soon as the rods were crimped and set, he led the foreman, almost dragged him, away from the site to a shed where cement was stored. There he spread out his papers, his certificate of qualification, his insurance books, took a deep breath, and threw himself into a frenzied pantomime to explain how fast he was, how experienced, how unwilling he was to push wheelbarrows. The foreman was puzzled. Raffaele did his act again, this time with broader gestures. The foreman nodded, then smiled. *Ja.* He understood. Monday, he promised. Or that was Raffaele thought. He was not absolutely sure, though, until Monday morning.

"That foreman was the first decent man I met in Germany. Ah no, forget my friend! He said I was a laborer, like him. Never told them I was specialized. He didn't want me to make more than him. He'd lose face with his friends here—and worse, back home in the *paese*." Raffaele's voice, always nasal, was almost a snarl now. "Watch out for hometown 'friends.' They're out for their own. Remember, he cheated me on the rent too and tried to fuck me up a dozen other ways—*scusi, signora*, but there's no other word. No, that foreman was the first decent man. When my pay came, I was listed as a steelworker from the first day, and what's more, I was paid as a steelworker—from the first day."

Raffaele stood up and for a moment I thought he was leaving. "And that's how I came to Germany. Still lots to tell, but I can't talk anymore until I have another beer." Perfectly at home he walked off toward the sitting room. An instant later the handle of the icebox door clanged.

Chichella turned to ask Vincenzo. "Is that where you knew him? At work?"

"Sure. He was the first *ferraiolo* I worked with and I wasn't much of a carpenter either." Vincenzo slouched over, propping his chin on one hand. He avoided looking at us. "He cursed me every day for a week. Just to see him coming toward me was enough to make me wet my pants. Then, I don't know . . ." He started pushing a package of cigarettes around with one finger. "He helped me. You know, if I got behind, he'd bang in nails for me, or show me my mistake. All he ever said was 'I'll save your ass, *Paesà*, but make sure you stay around and help when I need it.' I did. I was too scared to do anything else."

"Admit it," Raffaele ordered from the door, a fresh bottle of beer in his hand. "I made a fair carpenter out of you. 'Course that doesn't explain why I'd let myself get stuck with you a second time."

Maria's little laugh rippled into Vincenzo's answer. She was happy now; her smile produced fine crescent wrinkles all over her face, even at the corners of her eyes. "That's easy, love. You're lazy, and he's a good *ferraiolo* now himself."

"I'm a better carpenter." Raffaele made a face at her. "You just *wait* until I get home!"

Suddenly Vincenzo jumped up from the table, shouting for Assunta. He had just remembered a bottle of Chianti that had been his only purchase that morning. Where was it? Assunta! Assunta! Silence while he pawed through one of the closets, found the bottle, and came back to the table crooning to it. Assunta never answered. She is a true fifteen-year-old: like a puppy, after each exertion, no matter how slight, she flops down and goes to sleep. Vincenzo offered his wine, which no one took, then poured himself a glass.

The conversation crumbled into private conferences. Cristina had fallen asleep on Michele's shoulder. Holding her, he leaned over and told me in confidential tones that he was still sorry about Vincenzo's bad time. Michele's foreman had promised a carpenter's job, but when Vincenzo arrived a month later there was no work for him and would be none for at least a couple of months. It was fall. If winter came on hard, he might have to wait until spring. Somehow, Michele felt, it was his fault, but the real mystery to him was Vincenzo's reaction. He had not been in the least worried. He had just shrugged and said he'd talk to his friends. Friends? After eight years, could he think anyone would remember him? would help him?

That sounded very like Vincenzo to me. He has never been gregarious. In a crowd of young men he is anonymous, not the group wit, the dandy, or the irresistible Lothario everyone envies. Still, his friends are friends forever. He is a good, steady soccer player, but listening to shouts from the stands you would decide he is a one-man team. "Go, Giambon! *Dai*, Giam-bon!" (Giambon, pronounced Jambon, is a nickname he acquired as a little boy for reasons unknown. He was always hungry: it may have been the only word he could remember in those torturous French classes that marred sixth, seventh, and eighth grades for him.) "Giam-bon!" "Giam-bon!" they chanted time and time again. Michele need not have worried. Vincenzo's friends are peculiarly loyal. The job that vanished could not discourage him more than being unemployed in Torregreca for a year and a half, or if it did, he would never admit it to his uncle, nor blame him. Each morning he left the house to drift from building site to building site in search of a foreman he had known or men he had worked with in the past, confident that if they could, they would help him.

His luck held. He ran into Raffaele who did recommend him as a friend and a carpenter. Again they were partners, working for a contractor who pays slightly less than others, but makes up for it with hot coffee on cold days, beer on hot, courtesy and understanding for his employees. He also has a reputation for such good work that he is immune to recessions. Michele need not have worried. Vincenzo found his own job and also escaped, tactfully, from his uncle's nervous tyranny.

A glance down the table convinced me that no one was paying the slightest attention to us. Chichella, Raffaele, and Vincenzo were deep in the jungle of national insurance systems, and Maria was murmuring very seriously to Berio who was rosy with delight. This was as good a chance as I might have to ask Michele if *he* disapproved of the village nursery for Cristina.

His eyebrows flew up in surprise, but before he said anything, he shifted her to his other shoulder and swung around in his chair. This was a problem to be faced square on. *He* wanted her to go. *He* knew that it was important, would make school easier for her. It was Edda who objected and had finally refused to send her. She found a dozen excuses. Before Assunta came, she did not like being alone in the house all day. The nursery schedule was wrong—well, if not "wrong" exactly, inconvenient. She would have to take Cristina by 8:30, bring her home for lunch at 12:00, take her back again at 1:30 and then pick her up again late in the afternoon. Four round trips every day in every kind of weather and why? Because they didn't keep the children for lunch. It was less than three city blocks away, but she made it seem ten miles. And I could hear her shriek, *"Eyee, che fa?"* Eh, what's the difference. Next year she goes to school. This year she can play around the house. And there the subject remained, a draw, blocked by her mulish refusal to take the trouble. Please, would I try to reason with her? For Cristina's sake? Maybe, just maybe...

At the mention of her name Cristina's eyes flew open. She stared at us with grumpy suspicion, and we agreed by nods and grimaces to change the subject. Michele reminded me that I had wanted to see the television program especially planned for Italian immigrants. It was about to begin on one of two national channels. To my surprise the others followed us into the sitting room, where we found Assunta asleep on the sofa. She got up, stumbled over to the bed, and flopped down again, but she did not close her eyes. She will watch almost anything on television.

In official comments, German and non-German, this one national TV program for immigrants is cited as proof of the progressiveness of the German government, its conscience, its desire to ease the immigrants' integration into local society and at the same time help them keep contact with their own countries. I would not question the intentions, but it seems a heavy burden to place on one program, particularly if the administrative complexities are considered.

West Germany is a federation of distinct, semi-autonomous regions. Each *Land* elects its own government, which sends representatives to the upper house of parliament, the *Bundesrat*, and which in specific fields (the most obvious, education) carries out completely independent programs. The *Länder* are quite different, one from the other: what North Rhine-Westphalia wants, Bavaria may not. The federal government legislates with the agreement of the *Länder*, and so, in the case of television, the federal government finances the national television channels, but the programming is regulated by "advisory boards."

Such a system makes only the most general statements of

government policy, usually achieving institutional blandness orchestrated to offend no one. Germany might be different. Perhaps television by committee would actually express the progressiveness of the government.

That Saturday afternoon eight of us—Michele, Raffaele, Vincenzo, Chichella, Maria, Berio, Assunta, and myself—lined up in front of the television set as solemn as guests at a Southern wedding. For thirty minutes their expressions did not change, not by so much as an involuntary muscle spasm, while an Italian pianist played such recherché songs as "*O Sole Mio*," "*Arrivederci Roma*," and "*Bella Napoli.*" Between numbers a scrawny German master of ceremonies jumped about nervously, looking, in his skintight jacket and bulgy bib of a tie, like a puppet whose strings were worked by an amateur. If his clothes were intended to be the height of fashion, perhaps his lines were too. They ran the gamut from "How you say 'lovely' in Italian?" to "Ah, only a country so gay and sunny and irresponsible as Italy could invent such joyful music!" To be quite sure that everyone understood and enjoyed these thoughts, he repeated them in both languages: Italian and German. If they were to be taken as a statement of national point of view, they were dazzling, indeed.

When the screen went dark, there was nothing to say. Everyone looked a little sick.

Finally Michele stood up and sighed. "It's not always that bad, but you can see why we don't bother to watch it."

I could, and it is kinder to end the critique right there.

Immigration as a phenomenon-problem varies from *Land* to *Land.* In fairness the quality of additional programs for immigrants and the time given to them on regional television and radio stations might be more apt to reflect local concern and policy.

We were in the *Land* of Baden-Württemberg, one of the most industrialized. Manufacturing complexes, and therefore immigrants, cluster outside its cities, slowly, inexorably forming new cities. In the interim they look like concrete cemeteries for some race of lunar giants. Even when one sees them from a car, flashing past, the rectangular tombstone buildings that sprawl about the landscape without apparent plan can be identified: those windowless, horizontal structures with periscope chimneys are factories; the vertical structures, apartments, storage lockers where the worker can rest and wait for his next shift. The streets are deserted except for thunderous trucks that leave parked cars trembling in their slipstreams, and at night an occasional beer sign gives the only light. In his rush for prosperity the human being has lost his right to ground space. Machinery takes priority now and though the advantages seem dubious, this is progress. Such places spawn work, if not life, for skilled and unskilled workers.

Baden-Württemberg's efficient administration is controlled by the Christian Democratic Party, which in an unusual reversal for a conservative party, has encouraged immigration. The reasons were and are undoubtedly more expedient than magnanimous, but politicians are pragmatic, and there were certain self-evident truths: the Boom that began twenty years ago, the German *Wirtschaftswunder*, or economic miracle, must be kept alive; a shortage of unskilled and semiskilled labor, which the trade unionists predicted, would kill it. Perhaps conservative politicians confer more freely with union leaders than one imagines, cooperate even, or perhaps they were lulled by a deceptively convenient solution. They certainly felt the pressure, understood and reacted to it.

Germany needed then and still needs unskilled labor in factories, in building trades, and in all service fields. Its own citizens were not and are not interested: with basic specialization available through the school system, they could earn more elsewhere. They left holes: foreign workers have filled them, a remedy with immediate advantages and its own natural traps. Housing, already inadequate, was and is more difficult to find and more expensive. Schools and other public services are strained, and then there is always that danger no one mentions out loud: recession. The problems are not evaded, but the optimism of prosperity does blur them, and in those early years there was the reassuring fact that most foreign workers entered Germany on specific contracts from specific firms for one year. If, at the end of that year, they were not needed, they were sent home. After all, who, at the time, imagined 1.1 million Turks swooping down into Germany from the Anatolian highlands? (Who ever thought that Jusef would return to his village with a diesel Mercedes?) Or that, even today after the recent economic convulsions, the foreign population would be 3.5 million?

When, in the early sixties, the Common Market's Council of Ministers did what God and nature had failed to do and created all member nationals equal, no one winced. The guarantees were broad: freedom of movement between the countries, equal social insurances, equal unemployment compensation, equal working conditions, equal opportunity for foreigners (i.e., no citizen was given preference for a job), *and* of course equal taxation. Only Italy had a conspicuous force of unemployed men to enjoy this equality, but since enlightened greed is the secret that binds these unlikely partners together, it was a fair exchange.

After decades of isolation, fifty million Italians had chosen the world. They were becoming consumers and like many converts, they were fanatic: local products, some of superior quality, would not do. They craved German cars, cameras, and electronic gadgets, French milk and meat, Dutch cheese, Danish butter, and other even more obscure objects of desire. Such ravenous goodwill should be encouraged. Italy must be the prime exporter of some commodity, and so she was—of muscle. And Germany acquired its first immigrants who could *not* be sent home.

No one winced. Politicians bustled about, being politicians, explaining the benefits to bewildered voters. Ministers and their undersecretaries and *their* secretaries were officially solicitous about the adjustment of these new equal, but still foreign workers. They called so many meetings all over Europe that their Italian counterparts learned to tolerate the airplane and fly. They agreed eventually that immigrants' problems do not end with equality and cheaper housing, that their greatest frustrations are the result of two factors: lack of language and lack of information. They also agreed that radio and television, especially television, are the most direct, effective means of reaching this mass of foreign residents whose very isolation makes them potentially disruptive. German and Italian officials still meet, and they still agree that the pernicious deficiency of language and information can best be fought by television. They issue joint statements, expressing their mutual satisfaction with their recent discussions and their firm resolve to cooperate with all means at their disposal for the improvement of the quality and extension of programs specifically devoted to matters of interest to immigrants. Then they go home to more pressing matters.

For years bureaucrats met, Italians (and nonequal Turks, Yugoslavs, Greeks, Spaniards, and Portuguese) immigrated, factories produced, and customers bought. With only slight twitches of temperament and occasional slumps, the Boom boomed until 1973, when the unmentionable happened: a recession. No one could be sure how drastic it was or how it would end. One result was immediate and inevitable: many jobs for the unskilled vanished. The recovery now seems consistent, but maddeningly gradual to immigrants who take small comfort from a tenth of a percentage point in an industrial survey. Confused and unable to find work at home or abroad, they come and go, bringing chaos to railway stations and, I think, to the statistics about themselves.

Movement aggravates a congenital weakness of the digestive system in statistics. I offer just one example to prove the dyspepsia is not my own.

The *Istituto Centrale di Statistica*, the agency that collects and processes figures relevant to every conceivable aspect of Italian life, and publishes them in its official *Annuario Statistico Italiano*, states in a note to its emigration figures [1] that the totals shown refer to Italians who have emigrated for the purpose of work (as against, presumably, tourists, students, and businessmen) or repatriated, and continues: "[the data published in this section] is extracted, using as the *sole source*, for both European countries and extra-European countries, the Card Index of Emigrants (i.e., within Italy) and Emigrants for Abroad which exists in the care of the townships." The italics are mine.

Torregreca, then, is an example of this *uniform* system used throughout the country. These figures were given to me by the clerk in charge of the Card Index system flaunted above. He is an old acquaintance and a resident of the housing development that took up so much of my time.

Torregreca: Population 1960   10,185
Population 1976   8,516
Official drop in population   1,669

The decline is more or less considered to be the number of Torresi who have settled in the North. Many have gone, about half have returned. They were well known because at one time or another they changed their residence in order to send their children to school or establish other bureaucratic eligibilities. Half a dozen people whom he swore were living in Torregreca I later saw in Milan and Turin where they have been for years.

Before 1968 there are *no* figures in the town's Index for European emigrants. From 1968 there *are*, but only for Common Market countries. What about Switzerland where 508,712 Italians work, according to the Italian Ministry of Foreign Affairs?

"*Sa, signora*, the Torresi have never had much luck in Switzerland. There can't be many" was my friend's comment.

All right. The Common Market countries. How many emigrants?

"NONE!"

There are, however, 3,500 "seasonal" workers from Torregreca in Common Market countries. They can stay five, ten, twenty years, but as far as the *comune* of Torregreca (and the central government) is concerned, they are seasonal. *No one who has not become a citizen of another country has emigrated.* The question of residence does not come up, as in Northern Italy, because agreements have simplified the procedures. Once the father is legally employed, insured, and paying taxes, an all-in-one step operation, he has a residence permit. The most he or one of his children will ever need from the *comune* of Torregreca is a birth certificate.

And only adults who have somehow come to exist for the *comune* are included in the figures. Michele and Edda, Gaetano and Bianca, and so many others like them are, for the records, non-emigrant residents of Torregreca. Their children's status is more precarious. Berio, his brother Nicola, Gaetano's two grown sons, and Chiara evaporated when they were young. The boys were or will be resuscitated by the army, which holds a pedantic view of life and death. Once a male child is born, at twenty he is either dead or drafted. After eighteen months of military service his body is released to continue its peregrinations, but his papers are reconsigned to the township of origin, which again claims him as resident. So, after eighteen months in Germany, Vincenzo was still listed as living with his mother in Torregreca, Lisa and Martino do not exist, and Chiara, Cristina, and now Assunta have slipped away into an emigrants' Valhalla.

When I looked puzzled, my friend asked me to turn off my tape recorder. He had some private information to give me. The truth of the matter:

Torregreca: Population 1969	10,185
Population 1976	4,500
(estimated)	

5,685 people have gone somewhere and stayed a very long time—years, in fact—as anyone walking up and down the streets realizes, but their absence cannot be shown officially on the books. Why? Because if the population of a town falls below a certain level (5,000), the method by which town council members are elected changes from a proportional allotment by parties to a simple majority, winner take all. *That* would not suit the politicians. They can bear to lose control of the council, but they still want their piece of the pie and logically the pie itself would be smaller, if Torregreca was allowed to slip into the ranks of small townships. The central and regional governments dole out the funds. A demoted Torregreca would not rate a complete school system with all those teachers, janitors, cleaning women, secretaries, and clerks, nor would offices of the health insurance, magistrates, or a Carabinieri command be necessary. Its contributions for welfare funds, public housing, infrastructures (sewers, roads, et cetera), transportation (bus lines), and even tourism would be drastically lowered. With the downgrading and less administrative business, banks would close their branches. Even the number of traffic policemen, garbage collectors, road maintenance men, and midwives appointed would dwindle, and with it, the powerful wedge of patronage to be parceled out to deserving friends. No, no, Torregreca must remain a city of more than 5,000, preferably 10,000 people, so that its politicians have something to administer, a pie to divide. It is not unique.

So with the example of Torregreca always in front of me, I am more than skeptical about statistics. We will *never* know how many Southern Italians have emigrated, for how long, where—nor for that matter will we know when they have come back to stay, nor if they have come back. They never really left.

Assuming that someone wanted to keep track of emigrants rather than confuse the issue, the task was much easier when they were obligingly stationary. That ended with the recession of 1973. However—in 1976, according to the German government, 568,000 Italians were resident in Germany.[2] (A total the Italian Ministry of Foreign Affairs accepts with the comment that Italian embassy figures show the figure closer to 592,205.)[3] Slightly more than one-third of them, 179,172,[4] live in Baden-Württemberg, where they make up approximately 22 percent of the foreign population.[5] They, of course, have children who need language and information just as urgently. The Italian Ministry of Foreign Affairs shows that 75,000 Italian children of school age (three to seventeen years old) live in Germany.[6] After three hundred pages of meticulous nose counts and explanatory footnotes the Ministry abandons us in this particular breakdown. An act of faith is required. Doubt would be uncharitable. We must believe that only 27 Italian children attend German nursery schools (which means that I myself know the *entire* Italian nursery population in local centers. Improbable, but statistics...). In the best actuarial tradition we will assume that the Italian residents of Baden-Württemberg are neither prepubescent nor aged (the young tend to emigrate) and allot them their one-third of the children, 25,000. Our Italian audience is now 204,172 people, who form a relatively stable segment of the population. Like it or not, they cannot be sent home.

Then there are the Turks, Yugoslavs, Greeks, and Spaniards who work in the *Land*, roughly 600,000 of them, if we accept the German statistics, which are based on the premise that the *only* immigration of non–Common Market nationals is through agreements negotiated between Baden-Württemberg and the individual governments. (Again the term contract with all the specifics—salary, housing, insurances, duration—is arranged before the emigrant leaves his country.) German officials deny any appreciable number of illegal immigrants. From the number I met in a relatively short time, that seems willful, if understandable, blindness. The hiring practices of industrial plants can be controlled, but who washes glasses in the back room of a Stuttgart bar or digs a foundation for a small contractor in Pforzheim or picks up stevedore work is another matter. Even Rea, who ate the chicken, is an example. She and her husband make do with what they can scrape together on pickup jobs. *They* do not exist legally, statistically in Germany, and there are hundreds of thousands like them, eking out a living on temporary jobs, drudge work no German wants, no Italian has to take—and they do not expect the going wage with its insurances, and its taxes.

The legal and illegal audience for TV grows. In Baden-Württemberg a realistic estimate might be 900,000 people, more than 16 percent of the area's population, which by any standard is a respectable audience.

Even the most noble administration is chary with radio and television time, and Baden-Württemburg is no exception. Each evening at variable but early hours the *Süddeutscher Rundfunk,* on its third radio channel, broadcasts five special programs for immigrants—one for Turks, one for Greeks, one for Italians, one for Yugoslavs, and one for Spaniards. Each lasts for forty minutes and combines the news of both countries with information considered of special interest to immigrant workers. (RAI, the Italian radio and television authority, frustrated by the German insistence on bilingual programs, also buys time on the powerful Luxembourg radio to broadcast directly to Italian immigrants.) Most of my Torresi have television sets, but few have radios and those who do know·nothing about the programs, so in any discussion about them I am at a disadvantage: I did not hear them. Someone does, because the ambiguous news of how many Italian civil service examinations are to be held spreads from house to house, leaving the impression that Italy bristles with unfilled jobs. Civil service jobs! Application instructions are given for every conceivable career—from second trombone with obligation to fill in on trumpet for the RAI Milan symphony orchestra to lineman for ENEL, the state utility company, or telephone repairman. Parents have dreamt of just such jobs for their sons, and now the dream has come true. They have forgotten, and it is so easy, if one wants to, that thousands upon thousands of men will apply for those jobs with the utilities and that only orphans, preferably disabled in some minor way and armed with at least one cabinet Minister's recommendation, have a chance. The system is not the fault of the *Süddeutscher Rundfunk,* and officials are probably heartened by the news they have to convey: soon, it implies, the Italians will go home.

Television time is valuable and carefully rationed. Germans can learn Italian and French more easily than Italians can learn German. One program, at dinnertime once a week, seemed to be the only language course for immigrants on the regional channel.

I was determined to listen. The men said they were tired, it was useless; grumbling, they disappeared. Edda, who had sent a substitute to the cleaning squad that evening, was not pleased by the idea, but Chichella convinced her to watch—I did not ask how. Assunta is not selective. The cycle had just begun, so the lesson was elementary enough for me to follow.

In the first twenty-five years of my life, teachers led me through five languages as carefully as they might have through minefields. I stumbled after them, hoping that determination would take the place of the "gift" I do not possess. It never did. Occasionally, even now, Italian betrays me and for an entire day I am the victim of aphasia. Every sentence suffers a breech birth. Vowels play hopscotch, genders turn chameleon and verb forms, errant. I take refuge in the subjunctive and pray for sunset, but the muddles can reach bewildering heights of ambiguity. (So far never as disastrous as the *lapsus* of a friend who with an enticing smile suggested to a group of silent young men in a mountain village, "Let's sit awhile and shit together.") Chagrin has etched more grammar on my memory than the caveats of any teacher or text. For me, language is that sort of battle. If my victories have not been spectacular, at least the structural convolutions of European languages are familiar. They are *not* to most Southern Italians, who in their brief scholastic struggles never quite master their own grammar, much less any other. Is there any reason to think that the Turk, Greek, Yugoslav, or Spaniard who emigrates is better off?

All of our televised German lesson was in German. Modern didactics approve the method, and economy recommends it to any television authority with a multilingual audience. The vocabulary was clear, the nouns and verbs even useful, but the explanations of how they were to be used, what rules governed them, were not—to me. I doubt that they were to a Turkish or Sicilian peasant.

Certainly our little study group was not a success. For the first ten minutes Edda sat hunched over, glowering at the screen, her chin propped on one hand, her elbow on her knee. She was motionless except for her eyebrows that wiggled, keeping time with the cadence of the man's voice. Such application seemed a good sign until suddenly she leapt from her chair and waggled her hand at the set.

"*Ma va! va!*" she ordered with ferocious scorn. "Nobody talks that way! *Nobody!* And if *you* think I'm going to listen"—she moved up closer and leaned over, as though our distant teacher might take her more seriously if he could see as well as hear her—"you can just . . ." Her instructions were precise and crude. Then she stalked away to the kitchen, where she seemed to alternate bowling the pots about with riffling plates and silver. Chichella made a face. High German was just as addling to her and less useful, but she would see it through to the end, her eyes wide and innocent, her thoughts elsewhere. At some point Assunta, who needed the lesson more than anyone else, dozed off.

In a strange reversal of images, the scene reminded me of a dark afternoon many years ago in Matera, when I happened to look through the window of an appliance shop and saw an old, stooped peasant woman, wrapped in black shawls, sitting with a little boy, perhaps seven, on her knee. Undoubtedly the proprietor had left his mother to mind the shop, even though her salesmanship was limited to one white lie—"My son will be right back"—and since she had to be there, she could also baby-sit for her grandson. Infuriating as it might be to the gullible customer who believed her and waited, there was nothing unusual in the arrangement and nothing to attract my attention, except their absolute rigidity. They appeared catatonic. They stared straight ahead, hypnotized by some vision of stupefying horror—or beauty—just beyond my range. A few steps back and I too could see the metallic glitter of a television screen where a man, plump and bald, stood in front of a blackboard, talking. Every so often he waved vaguely at the palimpsest of diagrams and figures behind him, but was too weary to be more specific. After one or two false starts, I decoded the basics of trigonometry, sine, cosine, and tangent. For several minutes more I watched. The old woman and the little boy never moved. They sat and stared, unblinking, at this glorious incomprehensible mime. They had not bothered to turn up the sound.

That was long ago when viewers were docile, and television systems all over the world were convalescing from their first attacks of corporate piety. Competition worked miraculous cures for some. For others, monopolies, the course was long and relapses were frequent. In Italy the elitist strain was still dominant. The few judged what was right and proper, what the *popolino* should know. Programs on the lone channel that transmitted a maximum of seven hours a day were based on the estimated understanding of "a shepherd on the Maiella," a much-discussed hypothetical man who lived on a bare, windy mountain in the Abruzzo without the comforts of the modern world, or indeed a television set. By statute RAI was to guard our morals with Messianic devotion. It also prodded our consciences, even strengthening certain traditional prejudices, and because we were intellectually backward, educated us. The level was not ambitious: uniformity of ignorance and spongelike passivity would do. Illiterates must learn to read, students must be tutored in everything from trigonometry to Petrarch and Dante. Nor did the coming of night and "prime time" ease our betterment. Before we could be humored with the trash our low tastes presumably longed for—old American films, primitive quizzes, and variety shows with a stand-up comedian and soubrettes so clumsy they must have been the girlfriends of Important Personages—the news was read to us, at least that part which was suitable, in a language invented to obscure. Then came our civics lesson. Politicians, too recently converted themselves, explained the Meaning of Democracy. They ranted at us—briefly. The rest of the time they ranted at each other. The next night would be the turn of labor leaders, professors of political science, or members of the judiciary, all illuminating in their way and dull, numbingly dull.

The viewers were still docile. The old woman in Matera with her grandson and thousands of other lonely, tired old women like her were intrigued by any movement that shimmered across the screen. Explain trigonometry, if you must. Educate, preach. They watched the picture and not necessarily, as I discovered, with the sound. For their sons and daughters-in-law there were other advantages: everybody could watch; it was cheaper than the cinema and changed, slightly, every night; it was suitable for women and the children would shut up, gape at whatever pasticcio might be on, and slowly, one by one, subside into sleep at the table, their heads cushioned on their arms.

The novelty wore off long before the programs changed, although the public's reaction was clear: for fifteen years the runaway favorite of Italian viewers was a thirty-minute segment of back-to-back commercials between the news and the civics lesson. The advertisers and their agencies, both competitive enterprises, understood what the television authority did not: the viewer will tolerate anything except boredom.

The Italian who emigrates will have been that kind of viewer at home. He likes soccer games, spy movies, mysteries, and if he is Southern, has an insatiable appetite for Neapolitan comedy.

In Germany the external aspects of his life change completely: the climate, his diet, the work schedule, his friends, and even to some extent his language. He learns enough German of the local variety to get by. He conforms, but that does not mean that he checked his mental baggage at the frontier. He still must understand and estimate and judge from his own perceptions. Standards are very personal. Like shoes and toothbrushes, they are almost impossible to borrow. So are tastes. When he turns on the television set, he expects to be entertained, not taught, just as at school he expects to be taught, never entertained.

I do not believe this emblematic "he" will watch the German language course. It is very static, very academic. Herr Professor solemnly holds forth on the screen to the edification of pupils he imagines lined up on stools, obediently taking notes in the dark of a crowded room. Even admitting the complexities, the subtleties of High German, his explanations are impenetrable, in part because they are nonvisual. Why should our immigrant in search of entertainment be bored? He flips the dial—and probably picks up more German of a more useful kind from the adventure films and soccer games that do amuse him than he would from *any* formal lesson.

The German authorities deplore his lack of interest, his inability to learn German and so be integrated into local society. Not to be outdone, the Italian authorities deplore his isolation, the "ghettoization" of his life and imply that all is the fault of Germany. Hypocritical blathering is the essence of diplomacy. Used skillfully it can shove the responsibility for "the situation," whatever situation, onto the other government, while establishing its own innocence and its right, its duty to do nothing. Sovereignty is the key to that set of excuses. In the case of the Italian immigrant versus the German language, the diplomatic laments hide several inconvenient truths:

1) An Italian laborer who finished the *scuola dell'obbligo* (eight years), and that some time ago, is not well enough trained in the structure of language, even his own, for the old-fashioned study of grammar. The terms—defective verbs, dependent clauses, relative adverbs of place, and dozens of others more complicated—mean nothing to him. He could learn by ear, by imitation or practical example, but not from a lecture. The fault is less his than that of the Italian Ministry of Public Instruction.

2) The Italian immigrant is convinced that he will not have to

stay in Germany for long. That is his defense against loneliness, against discouragement: soon he can go home. Italian politicians campaigning in his own village have said that there will be jobs for all those who have had to emigrate, that not one Italian son need ever sweat again in a foreign country to make a foreign industrialist rich. Soon. And too, he understands, he has heard it often enough, that Germany is *not* a country of immigration.* The Italian knows that he is literally a "guest worker," welcome to employment, if he can find it, to taxation, but not to citizenship or the vote. He does not want to stay and is not wanted. Why, then, should he learn a language that will be useless to him?

3) If we take the government at its word and accept that Germany is not a country of immigration, then the *Gastarbeiters'* failure to integrate with local society is hardly a matter for national grief. Their integration is not desirable or logical for either party. The official regrets are just another bit of moral politesse as practiced by diplomats, and the German language program, a token.

---

* A curious position for a country with three million resident immigrant laborers, but no more curious, I suppose, than its arbitrary division of non-German population into an immigrant *Gastarbeiter* (guest worker) category (the three million Turks, Yugoslavs, Italians, Greeks, Spanish, and Portuguese) and a "foreign residents" category (the 440,000 Europeans—Austrians, French, English, Dutch, Swiss, Danish, et cetera).

However limited communication between the German government and its "guest workers" or between the German and his immigrant neighbor, at Michele's a caucus of very verbal Italians was determined to explain Germany and their lives to me—and perhaps to themselves. They dismissed the Italian pianist and the jaunty but tactless German master of ceremonies with a shrug. They had expected no better, and had they been asked, would probably have blamed RAI. Their own government is always their prime suspect: treachery begins at home.

In the confusion of dumping ashtrays and taking empty beer bottles to the storeroom, we all ended up back in the kitchen. Conscious that the soccer game, which later turned out to be film clips of some past game, would soon begin and that if I was to avoid it, I must concoct some alternative activity, I sat down at the foot of the table by the door and took out the book I always carry in my purse against long waits. As I read it a few pages at a time and in uncomfortable places, I never quite remember where the author has led me, but I tried to look intensely interested. My absorption did not fool

Cristina. She wedged herself between me and the door and stuck a hand deep into my purse. I grabbed and came up with her hand, my pen, and a notebook, which gave me an idea: I would look much busier if I wrote up my notes. A landslide of information already threatened to bury me. I flipped through the pages from the night before.

"You want to ask me questions now?" Raffaele asked from the opposite end of the table, leaning forward, half sitting, half supported by his elbows. His smile was expectant and a little shy. He was ready for my part of the exchange. "You know all about me, so ask your questions. About Germany and immigration and—"

At the end of the corridor the outside door banged open and thudded against the wall. Seconds later Pasquà rushed in like a courier changing post horses, a plump and rosy twentieth-century courier corseted by a chocolate-brown suit with wide, furry chalk stripes. The impression was heightened by miniature saddlebags thrown over his shoulder, a recent Italian variation on men's purses, but his abrupt strides around the room, his halts, as abrupt, his turns, his staccato phrases left no doubt that he was in a hurry, impatient to be off and would be—just one more thing.

Had we seen the bargain in potatoes?

Did we know that a new shipment of Italian coffee had arrived in Lahr?

How about the dance? Raffaele was definitely interested, but Pasquà went into a little jig.

Did we like his new shoes? Wing tips of black plastic alligator and gray "suede" with fierce winkle-picker toes were generally admired. I did not have to comment.

Had we heard that the mayor of his village had called a town meeting? Meat had been stolen from the communal deep-freeze locker and his, Pasquà's, drunk neighbor was already hinting that he, Pasquà, was the scum who did it. And when everybody knows he never keeps meat there. Let the Krauteaters have their old leather schnitzels and sides of lard. At his house there was spaghetti and fresh trout and tender scallopini—no frozen crap.

And who . . . ? His large sparkling-sad brown eyes had settled on me. Oh, honored, most honored. His expression softened. He held my hand gently, his eyes searching my face with that frank yet respectful, hopeful yet meek velvety gaze of the consummate Neapolitan. Some psychic recognition of kin led him to award Chichella respect in full measure, but no languid appreciation.

And another thing. If that lazy, good-for-nothing brother of his showed up, we were to ignore him, pretend we didn't know him. He ... Michele had watched Pasquà with a gentle, half-amused smile, waiting for his chance to interrupt.

"Here, why don't you sit down?" He shoved a free chair toward him.

"Thought maybe it was private," Pasquà mumbled not very convincingly. He sat down and to my surprise loosened his tie. A few minutes later, after the details of his brother's perfidy, he asked for a beer and surreptitiously eased the top button of his trousers. He had settled in for the afternoon. The others had known he would. They accept his impetuous arrivals as they would a facial tic or stuttering: they are part of his personality. I accepted them too, in time, but my interpretation is different. Pasquà is a very shrewd little man. He will not allow himself to be bored. He was not really on the wing. He needed time to reconnoiter and, if he always stays at Michele's, there are houses where he has never been known to light.

My first encounter with Pasquà was like sauntering out to play in breakers and discovering, too late, a treacherous undertow. It had seemed a mild surf, rollers of unknown names, troughs of despond, an occasional wave of real force and rage, but he enticed me out over my head with Do-you-knows? and What-would-you-dos?

Did I know what it was like to be shipped off to Germany at eighteen, away from home, your mother, Naples? Away from the sun! You were the eldest of eight. At home you would starve. So *you* were sent off. Not a year and your mother dies, electrocuted—a defective heater. And a year after that your father dies, and you're head of the family. So what do you do? You support them all. You pay their board with relatives and you fight with them and bully them to school and get them married off. Then you make the sisters keep their little brothers. And what do you get? Ingratitude, that's all. *Ingratitude!*

He'd warned his children—five to judge from the parade of names. They did what *he* said or they were whipped. They had to finish school, every one of them and then—then they were all going back to Naples—the children, his German wife, himself—and the children were going to support them. Like it or not, that's how it was to be. *No* ingratitude! *No* rebellion! *No* insults! WAS HE NOT MAN ENOUGH TO DO IT? Is that what I thought? Speak up! By all the gods, by all the blood of all the saints that protected him, and there seemed to be a great many who were quasi-members of the family, he would not put up with it. He had thrown his brother out, refused him the house! No brother could sponge off him and refuse to abide by his rules. All right, so he had lost a brother. All the more reason he would make sure that no child of his defied him, and if I thought otherwise . . .

It was a relief to hear the back door bang again. With new arrivals I could catch my breath and make sure that except for a few abrasions I was back, unharmed, on the beach. Raffaele winked at me.

"Don't worry. The worst is over," he hissed down the table. "You'll get used to him—after a while. When he first comes in, he's like a fire siren that's stuck. Then later . . ." Maria made a sly remark to Chichella and they both giggled.

A young couple stood tentatively just inside the door at the end of the table, watching us, bemused by the noise. They were both exceptionally small. He was dark and his face had the oddly flattened look so common to boxers even before their noses are squashed. His name was Marco, he told me in a light, aggressive voice. He worked for Fiat, came originally from Puglia, near Lecce, and didn't care if he never went back. He wore a dark suit, which served as conservative background to show off the rest of his finery: an expensive-looking white jacquard shirt with a collar so high and stiff that it threatened to engulf his chin and a red and blue satin tie, which with each breath flashed messages in a private semaphore, the sort of challenge that might eventually have become hypnotic if his pronouncements had not been just as gaudy.

He treated our most casual remarks as new enemies to be slain. Dauntless he charged from the lists, his opinion at the ready, his eyes narrowed on his victim. So we learned that: more Fiats are sold in the United States than any American make of car; England is oppressed by the feudal system, which explains its decline—half of every workingman's salary goes in the Queen's pocket; if the Germans had finished the job they started, Israel would not exist to cause us so much trouble; too bad more Northern Italians—arrogant bastards—had not been hauled off to Auschwitz; Richard Nixon's disgrace was the punishment *all* the other *liberal* crook-politicians in the world deserved; Italy's national soccer team would never win because the referees are anti-Italian. And on and on it went.

I took up the defense of the United States, which included clarification of the phrase "The Invasion of France"—that it was long past, not imminent. Raffaele and Michele joined me for the "Battle of Britain." We did not deign to answer Israel and Auschwitz, and Vincenzo, single-handed, forced him to admit that the Italian national soccer team did not win because it did not play well. Richard Nixon inspired a shouting match, which left me free for the moment to consider Marco. He had not expected our attacks. He was apologetic, hardly able or willing to defend his edicts, and now listening more closely, I realized that every explanation involved a foreman at the Fiat plant, a German he had met, a man who worked with him, a man in the personnel office, or an insurance clerk. His international syllabus had been borrowed piecemeal from others. Raffaele's voice boomed through a sudden lull.

"For Christ's sake, Marco, what's got *into* you?" From their various shouts and nods, the others agreed. Marco hunched his shoulders and looked at them sadly, one by one.

"I don't know," he admitted finally. "I guess I just heard people saying things like that and—well, I ought to have opinions. Sometimes I feel like I don't know *anything* and then, the signora was here..." His voice dwindled away, and I understood better. The cocky little man had been reduced to his normal state of doubt and confusion. He had not impressed the foreign signora, his friends thought he was crazy, and he felt rather silly. After his inauspicious debut, Marco relaxed. He was kind, interested in few things, educated in almost none, stubborn, hard-working, and at times very funny. He was, of course, a natural-born butt, which kept him on highs and lows between bantam rooster and mouse.

In my mind his wife, Gina, shall forever remain the "Child Bride." Chronologically she must have been twenty-three or -four. Physically she might have been fourteen. Her bones were slight. In the jumpers she wore, she looked flat-chested, and her round face, what you could see of it behind enormous glasses that tried to slide down her nose, was lightly spotted with acne, not the last vestiges of adolescence, but a temporary disruption: she was pregnant. She could sit for hours, smiling sweetly into space. If she noticed that she was bored, she went to a mirror and experimented with possible up-sweeps and pompadours for her long, sepia-brown hair. She flirted gently with any man, giggling her comments in a thin baby-voice. Alone with women she was very matter of fact and surprisingly practical. At the moment much of her energy was devoted to the exploitation of pre- and post-natal benefits. She and her doctor had agreed that first pregnancies are fraught with unknowns: she was enjoying three weeks' leave from work to "rest."

What seemed at first a pose, one that could easily cloy, turned out to be Gina's real disposition. She is childlike, easily enthusiastic, easily discouraged, not interested for long in anything, but always ready to be amused. Germany holds no surprises for her. She finished school there, and when her family returned to Sicily, she elected to stay. She was having such fun! She had lived with relatives and worked—and this time I was almost prepared for it—at the *grand magasin* in Lahr as a sales clerk. She and Marco met and married in Germany, and while he hoped never to see Puglia again, she suddenly longed for Sicily. Each summer, there had been three so far, he had taken her back. The first few days she is ecstatic. Another few days and reality is in such violent contradiction to memory that she begs to leave. Marco is neither cross nor surprised. He knows that by next spring the same irrational nostalgia will reach the compulsive level, that he will take her again to Sicily and again it will be found wanting. The baby might change all that.

In fact the baby was one of *his* major accomplishments. For all his strut and swagger, he was overwhelmed by his own, apparently unexpected, virtuosity. It was amazing, this feat of his, didn't we agree? Raffaele offered some salty comments about virgin birth, which, obedient to the rules of Southern propriety, I pretended not to hear. Pasquà, after solemn consideration, delivered a father-to-son lecture on the true art of the situation, i.e., nonconception. We kept our faces straight.

For a long time afterward Marco sat, muttering to himself, waving his hands first to one side, then the other, as though he were presenting an argument to a ghostly opponent. Once he tried to question Pasquà and was waved away. Our conversation had slipped off to German mores, and from there, who knew where it would end? Almost anywhere.

These, then—Raffaele and Maria, Pasquà, Marco and Gina—were the core of the group who from Friday evening to Monday morning wandered in and out of the house at even the most unconventional hours. Often one or another turned up for breakfast, and there was an evening when, on our return from a visit to a nearby family, Chichella and I found Raffaele, Marco, and Gina sitting, talking around the kitchen table. Michele and Edda had given up and gone to bed. A household of five adults and little Cristina that absorbs five more adults and when we were there, Chichella and me, is not restful. Weekends required a certain stamina and seemed an unlikely time for confidences or semiprivate conversations, but the confusion almost encouraged them. Each person was too busy about his own amusement—television, argument, whatever—to notice who slipped out or be curious about what he was doing.

My perch, chosen so casually, was ideal for an observer and sometime participant. At the end of the table I was out of the way *and* on the only route to the back door and the toilet. Everyone passed me. They stopped to talk, some for a few seconds, others for long, sit-down conferences. The kitchen was also the retreat of the women who were not drawn to the soccer games and cigarette smoke of the sitting room. While Chichella and Edda gossiped about their relatives, I worked on my notes, but I also listened. Edda's voice, already subdued for her, slipped gradually, almost imperceptibly into a whisper. I could imagine her glances toward me, her eye signals. She wanted to discuss a secret, but Chichella, who no longer worries about what I hear or know, would not cooperate.

"Speak up, Edda! I can hardly hear you." Her order, a novelty for Edda, was followed by silence and probably more eye language. "*La signora?* She doesn't care. Probably wasn't even listening. Eh, *signò?*" I looked up, smiled, and went back to my notes. "She hears all sorts of things, don't worry." This bit of flimflam slipped by Edda, and so I heard about Berio's "problem." He has one undescended testicle. When he had first told her five or six years ago, Edda had said he could wait to go to a doctor. (I could almost hear her—"*Che fa?*") When nothing happened, Berio was frightened and modest and unwilling to discuss it with his mother. Michele was away in Germany. Years drifted by. Now the army had rejected him for military service. Berio wanted to go to a doctor, but at the same time was terrified. Edda was afraid he would never have children. What should she do? What could a doctor do? A question Chichella could not answer. She was sure I could.

I am her all-purpose expert and more often than she realizes have to depend on common sense. This time I was luckier than usual. From some biology course I remembered that Berio could have children and even managed to explain why. She need not worry: he could, he would have children. And I tried to convince her that he must see a doctor, although I thought it was too late to remedy the condition. As I finished, Maria came into the room and stood very still, listening to my advice about a doctor. I was careful to leave the exact problem nebulous.

"Berio?" she asked Edda, who nodded. "I talked to him a bit this afternoon about that nice doctor, the one who's so patient. He half promised. Don't worry. I'll ask him again in a few days. I said I'd go with him, if he wanted." She gave us her quarter-moon smile and then, taking out her cigarettes, changed the subject. "Gina's going to be alone when the baby comes."

Innocent as it sounded, that was the starting gun for a competition between the three women. Which of them had suffered the most in childbirth? Which had survived the most perilous complications? Which could prove that her doctor or midwife was the most inept of butchers? With its elements of fear and danger and absolute naturalness the subject allows infinite variations, all satisfactory. The stages of the same delivery can be told and retold and will be listened to with the same enthusiasm. Then what happened? What did you do next? The friends live through each new horror themselves. They feel again the pain, the anguish, and the slow warm flood of relief. The seance is reversed. The audience is the medium, and when the spell is finally broken, each woman has triumphed and is at peace.

Optimism is not part of their nature. They see a gray world in which success is negative, a disaster avoided. "Things" happen *to* them. They act or react *against* events, they do not initiate them. To survive is to win. Even in such a world birth is positive and no less miraculous because it is common. With each they prevail again and survival is confirmed. What to an outsider is harrowing and ghoulish in their trancelike reevocations of their labors may be a celebration of victory. I have listened to their litanies dozens of times and know only that what upsets and angers me about their trials gives them a pleasure beyond their definition.

That afternoon I could not listen to all their tales because Marco joined me at the table. Still I heard enough to be anxious the next day when they started discussing childbirth with Gina. If they had dredged up more atrocities to explore and enjoy, they would frighten her. Not intentionally. They are not cruel women. They can be brutal, when angered, and caustic, when amused, and to expose a fool is a temptation they cannot resist, but they would not see fun in taunting Gina. They might, though, forget that what was familiar to them was not to her.

At first I could not tell where they were headed. Then I realized I was watching the subtlest kind of teamwork. They twitted her gently about not being a cat who could drop her kittens just anywhere—in an old tree stump or the corner of a barn. She had to plan. Had she thought about the layette? It was more than diapers and a blanket. For instance, bellybands. Did she know about them? Chichella brought up swaddling and, without a glance in my direction, delivered my lecture against it. Gina fussed. If she went to Sicily to have the baby, her mother would insist on swaddling. A baby's legs would not grow straight and strong without it, that's what her mother always said. Why should she go to Sicily? Maria asked. Not to be alone, she answered in a whisper. Maria was very firm. Travel is dangerous. Sicilian hospitals are vile. (Maria, another Sicilian, dared to be so open.) German hospitals, on the other hand, are amazing: they are clean and efficient, and the doctors know what they are doing. Besides Gina must be fair to Marco. This was his baby too. He had a right to see it. They were a family now, and she could not be a little girl running home to mother. Edda promised that she and Maria would do anything she needed. One or the other would always be free. They could help her or take care of her. She would not be alone. Every day when Marco went to work, Gina objected stubbornly, she would be alone. What would she do if the baby started to come and he was not there to help her?

"*Uffa,* he'll be more scared than you are," Edda shouted gleefully. "Listen, a healthy girl like you could have the baby without help from anyone. It's simple. You can tie off the cord . . ." Gina's face turned to putty. A chorus of voices reassured her and soothed her and teased her about her lack of courage. They were very gentle with her, but they forced her to admit what they undoubtedly suspected all along: she knew little about her body and nothing about childbirth except the grim, half-understood whispers she had overheard as a girl.

They all leaned back. Now, this was better: they could explain it straight out to her. They told her what to expect after the waters broke, how to time the contractions. They warned against her first milk. She must wait. (I kept my doubts to myself.) They suggested weaning times and cures for sore nipples and advised her not to believe, as women used to (including the three who were talking to her, I am sure), that she could not conceive as long as she nursed the baby. She could.

And then *da capo* with the breaking of the waters. This time I was brought in for a technical explanation of how the placenta and umbilical cord function. She watched me with wide, startled eyes and understood nothing. How did I know? she asked. I took to drawings. After a first involuntary shudder, she followed the end of my pen, nodding. Chichella, Edda, and Maria watched just as closely. They nodded wisely too without saying anything. My non-medical description may have been the first clear idea they ever had of the process they know so well from experience.

When I finished, Gina was bewildered and embarrassed, as though her body, by its changes, had submitted to some furtive debauchery and disgraced her. I withdrew to my notes and my formal detachment, leaving the women to continue their campaign. They seemed to know when to be brusque with her, when to be gentle, when to explain or dismiss, and she was reassured. Later she trailed around behind them, murmuring her questions. If she could, she sat close to one or the other of them, and often after that weekend, we found her, sitting in the kitchen of an afternoon, waiting for our return. The women had appointed themselves auxiliary mothers. They were kind, casual, bossy, and even tender as they might have been with a child of their own, and in a way that Gina understood. She felt safer.

(By chance, six months later I was sitting in the kitchen early one morning, having coffee with Michele and Edda, when Marco burst into the house, shouting "It's a boy! A BOY! Yippee! It's A BOY!" He was too excited to sit down. He waved a bottle of champagne, which in spite of the hour he eventually forced us to drink. The baby's name was David, not the Italian Davide. David without the *e*, like in the Bible, he said. Gina did have a hard time. During the pregnancy she was in the hospital twice for brief periods, and her actual labor was long and exhausting. Marco was convinced that now everything was all right. He was in a terrible rush to get home. It was his turn, their turn to sweep and wash the building stairway and front stoop.)

Whether or not Marco was aware of the cabal's tactics was hard to tell. He is a ditherer by nature. He fussed and worried over Gina's pregnancy as a matter of course, the slightest symptom or chance remark of the doctor's, but he was just as nervous about job assignments at the plant, his landlord's intentions, or the interior mechanisms of his camera, his lighter, his television set, or his car. What works today will not tomorrow, or so he reasons because he expects only betrayal from inanimate objects. They, as is their way, accept the challenge and go berserk.

He lavishes so much free time on worry that his friends call it his hobby. True to form, that first Saturday we met he had been victimized by yet another mechanical device. At least he sensed that he had been. Such is the German reputation for efficiency that he hesitated. Maybe he was wrong: maybe he had misunderstood. He started watching the soccer film, but the problem nagged at him, poked its way between him and the screen until he had to be sure. He needed light, so he came to the kitchen. With hardly a glance at the women, who, anyway, were deep in their catalogue of childbed woes, or at me, he sat down at the table, spread out a strip of paper, perhaps a foot long and five inches wide, and huddled over to study it line by line, pressing his index finger determinedly under each word. When, as nearly as I could tell, he had worked his way to the bottom of the strip, he turned it over and, frowning, ran his finger down a list of headings. He flipped back and forth, back and forth several times. Then he muttered to himself and flipped the strip again. I asked if anything was wrong. At my voice he started. My physical presence could have been no surprise. He must have as-sumed that I was as enmeshed in my problem as he, in his. He needed a few seconds to rearrange his ideas.

"I don't know," he said finally, looking at me. "Maybe you can figure it out." Two noisy jackrabbit hops with his chair brought him far enough along the table for me to read the slip, which turned out to be a statement of all the deductions his salary had suffered on the perilous road between gross and net. A computer had printed its crabbed secrets on the front. On the back was the item/letter code it was thought to prefer.

We studied and flipped, studied and flipped for a long time. My mind is slow at computer language. It looks like what the tele-phone operators of my youth might have written had they followed their own pronunciations. Even the time lag in comprehension is maintained. We sorted out the taxes withheld, and the union fees were clear enough: two debits were not. Marco could explain the reason for one, not for both.

Before he is hired, each man answers a number of questions for the personnel office, among them to which church does he belong? Deductions from his salary are based on his answers: one, a fixed percentage of his salary, is an automatic contribution to his church. This month Marco had contributed, automatically, to the Catholic church, his—and if the key was to be believed, he had also contributed just as automatically to the Protestant church. This was the puzzle that brought him stumping in and out all afternoon, each time more angry, more determined to straighten it out with Fiat, even if he had to take a day off and spend it at the accounting office (which, in the end, he did).

"*Maledetto contributo!* Gina pays at the store. I pay at Fiat. I WON'T pay a third time, and *not* to the Protestants." By Sunday evening his paroxysms of rage and doubt had brought him close to prostration.

The others were patient with him. In relays they listened to the entire, detailed explanation of the slipup, but once they had done their duty, the sight of Marco fumbling in his pockets for the strip, now pleated and a little grimy, launched them into animated discussions that he never could quite interrupt. The vagaries of the computer aside, they accepted the church contribution as just another German pecularity. Theirs were also deducted, automatically, from their paychecks. So? When I asked if they could refuse the deduction, they stared at me as though I had said something blasphemous. They had no choice: they *must* contribute. Odd. At home these same people resent the priest's requests for money and avoid them with considerable ingenuity. He asks too often, for too much. They ignore him. If he is young and persistent and unmoved by the indigence they claim has suddenly overtaken them, he may shame them into giving, but never very much and always grudgingly. Germany could not have changed them that much. I tried another tack.

Rather than refuse, what would happen if they said they were atheists? Then no one could force them to contribute. No, no! They shook their heads at me. I did not understand. They could not do

[*164*]

that. They had to be some sort of Christian—Protestant or Catholic. *That* was the regulation. (1.1 million Turks seemed to march across my tired brain, but I resisted the temptation to mention them.) And a certain percentage of their wages would be withheld for that church. *That* was the regulation—and in Germany everyone abides by the regulations.

That was the point and a lesson in civics far broader than any they learned by rote in school, or heard chanted on television. It was also the absolute reversal of the system familiar to them. No matter what the church or textbooks or politicians tell them, Southern Italians recognize their government as their enemy. They must outwit it, twist its laws, circumvent them in some way to live, not to be the victims of government. They do not expect equity from its bureaucrats, those great modern snobs, who before they perform their duty and consider your rights, must be sure of your connections and, too often, your generosity. Laws are invented to punish and equality before the law is a slogan. For Southern Italian peasants to believe anything else—in Southern Italy—is suicide. Germany is a shock.

My Torresi could not reverse their concepts overnight. They did not understand laws, suddenly, as the individual's protection against others, nor were they impressed by the justice of the laws themselves, but by the justice of their administration. That each law applied equally to everyone and was respected by most convinced them that The Law was right. They must obey it, blindly, literally without question.

We each grow up in a certain tradition, and each country has its own, which stamps our minds with invisible hallmarks. No one is better than any other, but as different as the history, society, and thought fused in the alloy. The German is different from the Italian, and mine, different again. I believe in the total separation of church and state. My church and the contribution I choose to make to it are no affair of my government. It does not regulate my conscience—yet. Each citizen still has a private inner realm, and I would fight to protect his right to it. If I, as foreign as the Southern Italian, lived and worked in Germany, I would not accept the tithe, not because it is an invasion of my private realm, which I firmly believe, but because I am asked to pay my share for comforts and services I cannot enjoy: my church does not function there in my language. I am forced to live as an atheist. For fiscal purposes I must be treated as one and exempted from the tithe. Southern Italians are much more anarchic than I, innately so, yet Michele and Raffaele and Vincenzo and Berio and Gina and Marco and Pasquà and all the others in small communities pay the tithe without a thought of mutiny, even though they have no Italian priest, no mass in Italian, no confession in Italian, no advice, and no comfort.* What they receive in Italy and refuse to pay for, they pay for in Germany and do not receive. Were they reasoning in their normal way, they would have evaded the tithe as instinctively as bats bank away from walls. Instead they are in Germany. They are proud that they have abided by the regulations.

Their reactions to law and government have already been reversed—in a country not their own. In time their concepts may also be, bringing a clearer sense of rights, which we all grasp with instant acumen, and of obligations, which are less immediately attractive. But it will only happen if Southern Italians stay out of Italy. Their distrust of their own government, viewed from a distance and compared to another, has turned to contempt. In Germany they have seen that a modicum of honesty and equality is possible. Politicians can enjoy reasonable graft without converting bureaucracy into a legalized Mafia, and citizens can still enjoy the normal services, for which, indeed, they have paid, without recommendations, threats of blackmail, or more Machiavellian expedients. Southern Italians feel betrayed. They are ashamed, too, of the cheapness of the corruption practiced on them. At home grand international swindles do not

---

* The situation is very different in large cities. There are Italian priests and missionary orders, most notably the Scalabriniani Fathers, who work entirely with immigrants, care for their spiritual being, and try, as well, to advise and help them. My impression is that most Southern Italians, especially the men, are even less inclined to attend mass there than at home, but they take full advantage of the children's centers, the catechism classes, the special films and after-school groups. And in adversity they always turn to the church. Obviously I would not suggest that they rebel against the tithe. They are offered the comforts of the church, and as always they take from it only what they want. For once they have contributed.

bother them. They expect their politicians to have their own share in them, to sack government-held industries, to speculate with public land and buy swamps from themselves for airports. But the greediness of the five-thousand-, ten-thousand-, the fifty-thousand-lire bribe that has gnawed through all the ranks paralyzes the country and demeans them. And they are ashamed of the mores of survival that they were taught are right. But in Italy they will continue their payoffs, be they in money or kind, to teachers, social insurance doctors, communal clerks, provincial clerks, regional clerks, and in desperation, nabobs of the central government, if they can reach them. As I said before, to do anything else would be suicide. Whatever else may change, they are convinced that the morality of Italian politicians will not. Government remains their enemy and law, their punishment.

Italian men revel in politics and corruption, as their wives do in childbirth, but not all our conversations at Michele's kitchen table tread that mill of frustration. There were some dreams—Berio told me about the car he longs to buy someday, although he does not have a license or know how to drive. And Vincenzo slumped down beside me every so often to vamp idly back and forth over possible sources of work at home. Even Edda came over one afternoon to hiss in my ear that Michele had lied to me—out of pride. When he was unemployed—did I remember?—he said that with 80 percent of his salary paid by unemployment compensation and the extra work he could find, he was better off than with a job. Remember? Well, it wasn't that way! He found work all right, and he was careful never, never to exceed the twenty-two-hour limit for work in one week. They had enough money. But, signò, he was so worried he couldn't eat. "*Non mi va! Non mi va!*" is all he'd say and push his plate away. Nicola begged him. Even Berio, but there was nothing to do. He wouldn't eat. And when he finished whatever little repair job he'd found, he came straight back home. He was ashamed to be out of work. If people saw him around, it'd look like he was lazy, didn't want to work. And he wouldn't have a beer with his friends. Didn't want them to come to the house, because he was ashamed. Oh, now he puts a good face on it, but he worried himself almost sick. Without a real job, without insurances, he had no security and no pension. Believe me, we've lived through some nightmares. Everything's all right now, but there have been black times, plenty of them.

They all talked of vacations at home, speculating on which was the best time. The consensus was that no trip in the winter was worth the trouble and the money. The weather is bad. Nothing happens at home. If they went at Christmas, the presents had to be elaborate and for all the relatives, not just parents. No, better to stay in Germany. Maybe in the spring, or next summer. Some of the children did not want to go, and in a way they were not wrong: there is nothing for them to do in Torregreca. There never was. And those trips are expensive because you have to put on a good front, show you're making it. No one actually said so, but they suspect that they are outsiders at home too.

Raffaele was uncharacteristically gloomy at the prospect of a trip to Sicily the next summer. He had every reason to be, he insisted. Last July he and Maria had planned to drive down with the children. He had the car serviced and bought new tires. The night before they were to leave, he packed everything—their bags, their food, their presents—in the car ready for an early start. He left it in its usual place at the side of the house. He wanted to be off just before dawn, so they were in bed by eleven o'clock. Hours later, it seemed, though it was only a bit after eleven, a friend pounded on his door, yelling for him to get up, something had happened. When he stumbled to the door, his friend pointed at the car: all four new tires had been slashed. They never left. Raffaele could not afford another set of tires *and* the trip.

He knew who did it, he was sure he knew. One of his German neighbors! The one who always complained that the kids made too much noise. No question! *He* did it, all right, but the police just shrugged. No proof. Raffaele had none, but he knew, he knew and would spend hours planning his revenge, even planning traps. What if he packed the car again, pretended he was going home for Christmas, and then waited and watched at the window? Would his neighbor try again? If he did, Raffaele would catch him. All he asked was ten minutes in the dark without witnesses. Just ten minutes!

On those several weekends, because I sat by the back door, I saw a lot of Pasquà. His supervisory visits to his wife brought him back and forth with predictable regularity. He left in an irritable flurry, but when he returned, he was ready once more for any kind of amusement, preferably discussions.

They are Pasquà's favorite sport. He plays by eccentric rules: you defend the goal; he ranges around the field and off into the trees, if he chooses, shooting from any position, any angle that appeals to him. Spectators have the best of it, and I was careful to remain one, but my reaction to one subject, offered before I understood the wisdom of nonparticipation, tantalized him. If he found me alone at the table, he had to stop and try again. As he saw it, sooner or later I must change my mind.

His plan, as soon as his children finished the German secondary schools (the equivalent of our high school plus two years), was that the entire family should leave for Naples. There the children would find appropriate jobs and support their parents. Naturally everyone was to live happily ever after. I did not speculate on the children's willingness to follow this order. I also avoided any mention of the staggering unemployment of the young in Italy, which, since the palmy days of Pompeii has been endemic in Naples and is now, at 200,000, close to a national disaster. A more basic problem worried me. How were these children, trained to be clerks or possibly bookkeepers, to find jobs when they do not speak, read, or write Italian? Neapolitan is not enough. Street argot will get them around the streets. Nowhere else. *If* they find work, *if* by tears and threats Pasquà rounds up enough recommendations for them to be hired, they will be day laborers. They can be nothing else. Why do they have to leave Germany? Why, when they can find decent work there, should they become illiterate exiles? They have an advantage none of the other children has: their mother is German, they are German citizens. If they cannot read, write and speak Italian . .?

Pasquà never admitted the impediment, but the idea worried him. Each time he tried a new approach. He must persuade me, coax me, bully me if need be to agree with him. Each time he failed. I countered with more examples of their helplessness. No physical disability could be more crippling, I insisted, than their lack of language. Finally silent and frustrated, he would sit, glaring at me in hypnotic despair, as though his eyes could siphon the thoughts from my mind, one by one. He was shaken by my intractability. He knew I had nothing to gain and that the world of offices was more familiar to me than to him. The doubt, never expressed, was there and it grew. Someday, perhaps, I will know whether it grew enough.

That was the serious Pasquà of private worries. We saw him seldom. The more normal Pasquà was the one who burst into the kitchen one afternoon, breathless from an inspection trip at home. Anything happen? Anything happen? No, well, shut up then. He'd just remembered what he'd forgotten. He bounced up and down on the balls of his feet in sheer enthusiasm. About the stolen meat. From the communal freezer. He'd just remembered—he'd never told us the grand finale. Too bad we missed the whole scene. It was wonderful, gorgeous!

"Now listen to this," he shouted as though we had a choice. "Listen now. Just imagine that Hans lives here," and he pointed to the hall door. Ludwig lived in the closet and filthy Johann, hateful, drunken Johann lived, for that afternoon at least, in the cupboard.

He would have us imagine how he had felt on coming home one afternoon to find his wife in tears. Filthy Johann had told everyone in the neighborhood that *he* knew who had stolen the meat from the communal freezer. Who was sly and a thief? Who made passes at their women, corrupted them? Who was the scum of the neighborhood? Who would steal their meat? Obvious, no? said Johann. That Neapolitan maggot, Pasquà, that's who.

Pasquà charged out of his house (across the kitchen, that is) and over to Hans's. He knocked on the hall door. Had filthy Johann said those things? With an elfin leap he placed himself in the doorway, sagged against the frame, and looked sleepily at us. "*Ja, ja.* Johann said that, but we do not believe, Pasquà. *We* do not believe. I promise."

Pasquà hopped back to the middle of the room and then with

his usual stride approached the second door, the closet, now Ludwig's house, knocked, and reversed to play not only the man but his wife. "*Ja, ja*. Filthy Johann said those things," they both confirmed. "We know better, Pasquà. Go home. Do not worry."

But Pasquà was not to be pacified. He threw out his chest, walked up to Johann's door, the cupboard, and pounded on it. The door flew open and Pasquà started shouting. Had Johann said those things? Had he dared to say that *he*, Pasquà, had stolen the meat? Had he?

Pasquà slipped into the doorway and his new part of the belligerent drunk struggling to get away from his wife and fight his Italian neighbor. His arms flailing, his voice more and more threatening, he twisted and strained to escape. Dancing around, Pasquà dared him to come out and fight. Each time after the wife managed to pull her husband back inside and slam the door, there was a moment of silence. Then the door would fly open and Johann would lunge out snarling. The neighbors, as Pasquà was careful to show us, stayed, watching from their doorsteps, eager to witness the battle they knew could not take place until Johann actually stepped outside his house onto neutral ground. To hit a man in his own house is trespassing and assault. He must be forced, or lured, to the sidewalk.

Three separate times after Johann's wife had turned the key in the door and pacified her husband, Pasquà went home. And three times, a little drunker and more crazed by the insults, Pasquà roared out of his house to storm Johann's, and the neighbors came to watch, shouting encouragement, egging drunken Johann on to fight. Pasquà repeated his heroic monologue three different times. On the fourth try he almost wrestled Johann from the door, almost dragged him to the street where he could hit him, but at the last minute Johann's wife yanked him back inside, turned the lock, shot the bolt, something thudded on the floor, and Pasquà, lying on the floor by then himself, decided Johann had passed out. He went home to more drink and finally to bed.

"And two days later, guess what happened," he challenged us as he bounded to his feet. "The police came to my house. At night. They asked me questions. They went to Ludwig's house and they asked questions. Then they went to Hans's house. *There* they didn't ask questions. They arrested *him*. HIM! That swine! He watched me all that night. He baited me to fight Johann—HIM, they arrest, and all he says is '*Ja, ja*, I took the meat, but you have no proof. We ate it all!' And they've let him go. He's FREE! Do you think they'd have turned *me* loose? No! No proof! *He ate it all!*" He threw back his head and laughed with pure, childish joy at the idea, then turned to us very seriously. "And that's not all. The other night Johann came and knocked on my door. His wife had sent him to apologize. To APOLOGIZE to me!" he shouted. "How do you like that? The neighbors were all out again, listening, so—I refused. I told old Johann that I wouldn't accept his apology unless he made it in front of everybody at the next town meeting. I said, 'My honor is at stake!' " Pasquà rolled his eyes skyward in Neapolitan anguish and innocence.

"And what did *he* say?" Raffaele asked on cue. Someone had to or Pasquà would have held the pose.

" '*Ja, ja*, I understand. Next meeting,' " Pasquà imitated him in a deep slurry voice. " '*Ja*, I do!' Then he shuffled off home, got another beer, and beat his wife. Pig!"

Those weekends were confused, freestyle affairs. People came and went, fitting in as they could. The regulars did as they pleased. No one ever knew exactly what would happen next. We ate a lot and talked more. For hours we talked—and laughed. Without warning serious conversations turned into farce, or, as easily, farce into drama, but the farces were comic, not cruel, and the dramas, usually from the past, left only a slight bitter aftertaste. Mutual tolerance bestowed its own mysterious equilibrium. They were friends, which was no longer as surprising to them as it was to me.

At home the poverty that isolated them from modern society had been shared with their neighbors, twenty million of them. Much as they might hate it, much as they might aspire to something better, theirs was a "normal" life in that world. Each person competed with every other, friend, enemy, or relative, for every job, every welfare handout, every recommendation. Each was the natural enemy of every other and guile was a cardinal virtue.

In Germany they were aware of real isolation for the first time, that it was not, had never been purely economic. It was physical and social. An anomaly perceived has a strange effect on lives.

At home Michele and the other men might have played cards in the back room of a café, or they might have discussed politics over a glass of wine in a shop, but they would have remained lifelong acquaintances, who did not trust each other, seldom talked of personal matters, and if they did, never exposed the whole truth. Their wives might know each other well enough to stop for a gossip when they met on the road or to wrangle over who had arrived first at the baker's. Probably at some time they would have gone with the other women of their parish on an excursion to a religious sanctuary. It is unlikely that they would have visited each other's houses just for a chat, unthinkable that they would if the husband was home.

Every society has its customs. In Southern Italy, for better or worse, marriage is a union against the outside world. Only relatives appear on the doorstep without invitation. They demand deference, loyalty, favors, endless favors, money, and sometimes worse. They receive never less than a patient hearing. Each with a family to satisfy, two pressure groups inevitably at loggerheads themselves, a husband and wife must choose total immersion or total war. Either will indoctrinate them in human wiles, consuming their time, energy, and, tragically, their last few calories of trustful optimism. Outside friendships no longer seem feasible or desirable. Sociologists tout the joys of what they will call "the extended family," but I wonder if they have considered the bitterness, the impositions, the outright exploitation and moral blackmail inherent in them. Southerners learn quickly and painfully that altruism is a vocal exercise, not a universal truth. Hardly surprising then that cooperatives do not flourish there, and that voluntary organizations, like reform committees, die aborning. Life is a battle best fought alone.

In the South. But for the last few years Michele and his friends have lived in Germany. They are secure for the first time in their lives. They have work and decent housing and money in the bank. Prosperity is upon them, and they are ready to enjoy it. They are settled. They will stay a few more years or many, always working for their pensions, saving to go "home," but as *signori*. Yes, *signori*, men who have made a success. Nothing less will do. They want the pensions, the nice clothes, the money to buy new furniture that proves their sacrifices were worth it. The sprouts of self-respect, so frail at first, are growing sturdy: they must resist the Southern climate.

All this from the dread expedient—emigration—and more. Michele and his friends have relaxed. They have not noticed that Germany has changed something else for them and probably thousands of other Southern Italians who came to ground, as they did, in small rural communities there. They are not besieged; the world does not teem with enemies. In fact there seem to be very few. The other Italians cannot harm them, might even help them. The Germans do not love them, or they, the Germans. Theirs is an armed neutrality, part mutual need, part benign antipathy, but neutrality it is with some resentment and no envy.

Michele and company seemed to thrive on their freedom, and the discovery that they could like some people and, for no reason that has to be explained, not like others was almost as exhilarating as the power to buy something, not because they *needed* it, but because they wanted it. All had relatives nearby, often no more than a mile or two away: they never saw them. They no longer had to pretend there was a bond beyond the accident of birth or marriage. Some more elusive affinity governed the choice of real friends. I would not attempt to define it. All I know is that the regulars came and went, bringing confusion and noise and laughter and problems that seemed a liberation to me. For once the men were not off in some dank café together, bored and restless. The women were not at home with wailing babies and drying laundry. Sometimes the babies wailed at us. *Pazienza!* We were all bunched in together, the women as much a part of the discussions and the jokes as the men were a part of the preparation of meals. They were together simply because they were friends and that was enough for the moment.

Less than six months later I was in Germany again, and again I was sitting in Edda and Michele's kitchen. Winter had taken its toll. Flu and bad weather had left everyone pale. Enormous jigsaw puzzles in various stages of being mounted were evidence of long days spent in the house. Two were enthroned on the sitting-room couch and another, already varnished and fixed to its piece of plywood, took up most of the kitchen table. Berio measured the sides with slow precision, then remeasured. Frames had become his specialty. The moldings must be just so. All over Germany in the houses of the Torresi I would find myself banked in puzzles, now almost ready to be hung, their antidote for boredom in a bleak climate, the symbols of another winter endured.

Little had changed. Edda's hair had grown long and scraggly, but one of the traditions of Easter is a permanent. Dinner had slipped back, as I had known it would, to six o'clock, and Cristina had not gone to the nursery. Edda said, "After Easter! Now that good weather has come, I'll take her. After Easter!" Neither Michele nor I said anything: we did not believe her. One Sunday afternoon, when the men had gone to a soccer game, she and I lit the stove in the sitting room and stood over it, talking as we turned the shirts and shorts and sweaters we were determined to dry. Hangers draped with socks dangled from the corners of the buffet and a pair of corduroy trousers hitched to a nail on the molding made a backdrop for the stove. It was a steamy operation. A wintry one.

Winter had discouraged them all. A particularly lingering strain of flu had kept Michele in bed for more than a week with a high fever. Construction had slowed and men were being laid off. He was afraid to stay away too long. Finally, still with a fever, he went back to work. She said that for the last month he seemed to be walking in his sleep.

Before Christmas Assunta had two months' temporary work at the leather factory. Three thousand DM ($1,500), the promise of the first opening, and two or three new friends had reconciled her to Germany. Greed, Edda muttered, could cure most longings.

Their elder son, Nicola, a slight, quiet young man with wavy brown hair and silver eyes, was back from his military service. The garage owner, who had promised to keep his place for him, claimed there was a slump, that he did not have enough work for the men already on the payroll, that he could take him on soon—maybe. In the more halcyon days when he was eager for a relatively cheap mechanic, he had filed a formal claim on Nicola with the labor office. Now that he wanted to renege, he was subject to a fine. If and when he paid it, Nicola would have something, not, however, the only thing he wanted, a job. He had planned to buy a car. He had looked forward to it all through those months in the army. Cars have always been his passion. It was to have been a small secondhand Fiat. Later, when he trusted his driving further, he would buy a brand-new one. Now that the dream had vanished, he was silent, almost morose. Each evening he studied the bus schedules and the want ads in the local newspaper. Each morning he left early, saying he did not know when he would be back. He was always in his place for dinner, scrubbed and uncommunicative. No, nothing today. He never said more than that. Shortly after I left, he found a garage near Lahr that took him on for 1,200 DM ($600) a month.

He is looking for his secondhand Fiat, but it must be just the way he wants it.

Berio was the surprise of the household. He no longer shouts. He no longer offers the authoritative word on any and all subjects. For long periods he is in the house without making a sound, which could never have happened before and is apparently a reaction to Nicola's return. Berio feels no obligation to supply the male presence. He has also given up the soccer team, says it took up too much time. He went to Torregreca for Christmas and about that he is laconic too. "It was all right"—hardly an effusion. Recently he was promoted on the painting squad to *stuccatore*—plasterer—which means he mends cracks, makes ornamental moldings and the casts for them. His salary has been increased to 1,200 DM. Father and two sons now bring home slightly more than $1,700 a month. Edda may have another $200 from the store—and her bargains.

Cristina does not change. From under her bangs she still watches everything with her shrewd, beady brown eyes. She touches and hums and capers and disappears on her own secret errands. Next year her freedom comes to an end.

I am never prepared for the Southern Italian's non sequiturs of behavior. The decision, if any is actually taken, is so without logic that it surprises and irritates me. That it should be Vincenzo who surprised me, irritates me still more. He went home for Christmas, which seemed an indulgence after the month he spent there in the summer while his thumb healed, but Christmas has a special pull for anyone away from home. New Year's came and went. It snowed in Torregreca. Then billows of thick, bitter fog tumbled down the mountains and the sodden, unechoing silence of winter settled over the town. At some point between New Year's and Epiphany, January the sixth, Vincenzo discovered his dread of going back. He was to be in Germany to start work on January the ninth. Berio left, taking with him a medical certificate that implied, without saying so, that Vincenzo had had an attack of appendicitis. Two weeks' reprieve, which he stretched into four and then out of inertia to six. The doctor obligingly issued a second certificate and then more obligingly still, a third. Armed with these illegible and meaningless scraps of paper, Vincenzo presented himself to his employer at the end of February—and was fired. The contractor felt he had been taken advantage of and who would blame him? Not Vincenzo. He hardly bothers to offer an excuse. If pushed, he says he had to go home in the spring for his sister's wedding anyway, so . . . ? So what? The groom's father works in Germany too. He asked for and was given ten days' leave. Vincenzo could have done the same had he returned on time. He knew, as Michele knew, that construction had dropped off more than usual for the winter season and that another job would not exist.

Like most strong medicines, emigration has toxic side effects. Doctors are familiar with the psychosomatic reactions to mild disorientation, the ulcers that heal by magic on the long train trip back to Sicily, the migraines that vanish in the Abruzzo, and the gall bladder that would not suffer the leanest diet in Switzerland yet thrives on Calabrian sausages. The pains are as real as the cures; the only deception is in the cause, which rather than physical is probably a combination of tension, rampant nostalgia, and a desire, often subconscious, to retreat from a hostile world.

Another toxic reaction that frustrates social workers and enrages employers is the sudden shriveling of will. One morning a man cannot make himself get up and go to work, or he is startled to hear himself announce at breakfast, "It's time for me to go home." And twenty-four hours later he has gone, unsure of quite why. It happens to men alone, to men whose families are with them: no one is immune. Others, like Vincenzo, fail for no particular reason to go back. They can never explain why and in time this suspension of will passes, leaving them to wonder at themselves.

Occasionally when I lived in Torregreca I had brief seizures. A nameless depression settled over me. Nothing was right, though nothing was obviously wrong. I could not point my finger at one specific discomfort or defeat that had been the final too-much, but my mind and with it my power to force myself to do what must be done, my will, receded into some distant, hermetic limbo. Decisions were beyond me. They came about by my lack of action: things just happened, as though I were in mild shock, standing off to one side, puzzled, watching what I myself had done. Vincenzo did not describe it exactly that way. At best he is not loquacious. He repeated, with a resignation I found frightening, "I just couldn't, signora. I don't know why. I just couldn't."

From my own experience, I think that among the mind's many protective devices, there is one autonomous little fuse for involuntary failure. After long gray periods of frustration and loneliness in a situation that seems futile, it blows, isolating part of the mechanism. The failure that we could not excuse by reason becomes inevitable, and so escape. No permanent aberration is caused. Once the current is normal again, the fuse slips back into place, connection is reestablished, and life continues.

Emigration has all the elements to blow that fuse. None of the men wants to fail. Many have gone home with certifiable illnesses. Many others have gone home for no reason that they could ever explain: the job came to an end, there was illness in the family (a great-aunt, a third cousin), the climate was vicious—these are acceptable pretexts that can be offered in public—but the real answer is more often that mumbled "I just couldn't, signora. I don't know why. I couldn't."

Since World War II emigration within Europe has meant a temporary absence from home, or at least the men had to think of it as such. They were not and are not encouraged to stay. They are not to become permanent residents: they expect to go home. On the other hand Italian emigration to the United States in the first years of the century was, we and many of the immigrants thought, a permanent transfer. We expected them to settle and become citizens. Some may have planned to stay five years, ten years, make money, and go home. Some did just that. Some waited until they had their pensions and returned to Italy only to find it unchanged and backward. Once more they went to Hartford or Philadelphia, but this time they knew they were going home.

The variations have obscured one element of that emigration: it had the same quality of rotation that is the pattern of the more recent European emigration. Men went to the States, stayed six months, a year, and returned to Italy. They might try again, even half a dozen times. Entire families shunted back and forth before they finally came to rest in one country, probably from sheer travel fatigue. If that sounds like an exaggeration, between 1902 and 1914, 3,211,293 Italians went to the United States. And 50 percent of them, 1,161,713, returned to Italy in the same period.[7] Those trips, in accommodations they could barely afford, were not pleasure cruises or annual vacations. They had given up; they were leaving, and unlike political or war refugees they *could* go back.

Over the years in Italy I have met hundreds of old men in the piazzas of mountain villages who wanted to tell me about the year they spent in Boston or Cleveland or Chicago. Why had they come back? The climate was bad, or the pace of life too fast, or there was no peace in that country, or the excuse I heard most often, which has its own naïve appeal—*l'acqua non mi andava*—the water didn't suit me. I have never quite decoded the real meaning of those phrases, but they must be symbols for something more that happened, perhaps that same shriveling of will that overcame Vincenzo.

Vincenzo was fired because instead of taking a three-week vacation he disappeared for nine, and too, because he thought he could bluff his way through with false medical certificates. He had to try it. If it worked, fine. He would keep the job at least until he went home for his sister's wedding. If not, which was more likely, he had a plan. He is very proud of it. He thought it all out and decided that, given the situation, he should turn it to his own advantage, which, though he does not know it, is exactly why German employers have learned to prefer Turks, Yugoslavs, Greeks, and Spaniards. The Italian is less hungry now. He knows he is privileged, that he is fully covered by the same insurances as any German worker. He has studied the system and the ways to beat it, if something goes wrong and he is on the defensive. When Vincenzo realized exactly what he had done, that he had trapped himself, and what the probable consequences would be, he reverted to his Southern Italian ethos. It was natural, even logical: he was at home in Torregreca.

At the end of February he returned to Germany. In the six weeks before his sister's wedding, if he was fired, he would file the necessary applications for unemployment compensation. There would be time for the payments to come through, for him to notify the board that he was leaving to look for work in Italy. On his arrival in Torregreca all he had to do was show the German documentation of his status at the employment office, file another set of applications, and begin collecting his three months' unemployment, which in Italy would pay him 12,000 lire a day ($13.95) or $278.40 a month, free of taxes and withholdings.

He would spend April, May, and June, the only months he *might* find work there, comfortably at home in Torregreca. If the unexpected happened and he found a permanent job, well and good. If not, there was an alternative. By the end of June his unemployment payments would stop—unless he returned to Germany and stayed there ostensibly looking for work and collecting his payments. His intention was to be in Germany by mid-June, after most of the summer hiring, especially of skilled workers, was over. July, August, and September, the pleasanter months in a northern climate, the time of wine *Fests* and beer busts, he would enjoy there. After all— something would happen. Either the employment office would find him a job, and he would be forced to take it, or—well, something.

I am in the unhappy position of sympathizing with everyone. The German contractor cannot keep to any reasonable schedule with workmen who come and go as the whim takes them. The German workers on the building crew will know that Vincenzo does not want work and is simply taking a free ride. Already they think that Italians who come to Germany work the minimum six months, then get themselves fired, or if that fails, quit, to enjoy the maximum of unemployment before they look for work again and repeat the cycle. They resent it. In every country where the system exists, some people manipulate unemployment compensation into a fixed source of income. "Take what's going" is today's cry, and "Everybody does it," the justification, one that suggests an advanced case of arrested development. Vincenzo returned to Germany, a two-thousand-mile trip, for the sole purpose of collecting a second three months of compensation, which he was not otherwise entitled to, at twice the rate he was paid in Italy and at a time when he could be fairly sure *not* to find work, which in any event he did not want. He had planned another of those modern fraudlets for which there is, seemingly, no charge.

Vincenzo has only one defense, which is very close to the root of last winter's trouble: he is determined to find a permanent job at home. He is not lazy. He wants to work, to marry, and live near people he knows who know him. In Germany he is not apt to meet young women. His work there can never be permanent. He tried the industrial cities of Northern Italy where he shared a room with three young men and worked like so many others for good pay, but without all the social insurances required by law. His eventual pension suffers, which may seem an odd concern for a man his age, but it is all he will ever have. He must worry about it *now*. The local girls despise Southerners. He had no way of meeting Southern girls who were kept carefully at home and met only young men introduced by family friends. Custom and the local bucks excluded him from certain places. His accent gave him away. People pretended not to understand him. If he insisted, they sneered, *"Terrone!"* * at him. He would not go back there, and this once the recession has helped him: there are no jobs.

The Torresi are clannish people. They move in bunches. Once they are settled, if they find that extra workers are needed, they "call" their relatives. Fifteen years ago the smaller cities of central Italy attracted them, even though they were not as glamorous as the North and "The Miracle" had not quite touched them. It never did, but there was work, lots of work. The Torresi prospered there. They "called" more and more relatives, built houses, spread out until now they form regular colonies on the fringes of the cities, or even on the fringes of nearby towns. Vincenzo has friends in two of these, one outside Pistoia, one outside Empoli. He has been to see both and is now negotiating for his room and board. Work is no problem. Accommodations are. The price he will pay for a bed is to become engaged to (and in a few years marry) a girl he scarcely knows. He

---

* The *Cambridge Italian Dictionary* gives "(Northern Italy) Southerner (a derogatory term denoting all Southern Italians, especially those who emigrate to the North)." That definition is too bland to convey the voltage of scorn generated by the abuser or the shame and rage of the abused. It is a vicious word used only as an insult—and often.

can stay at her brother's: not by chance he is a contractor. I do not know how it will all end. Vincenzo grew up hearing about the grandiose projects for the South, politicians still promise them, about the Italian Miracle of the North. He has learned not to believe in such notions, but a job, a permanent job, in his own country hardly seems too much for him to ask.

On my second visit to Germany I saw as much, if not more, of "the regulars" as I had on my first. They shook their heads over Vincenzo. It was accepted that he had been foolish. What else was there to say.

Raffaele's brother, Guido, a plump, cocky young man, came in one morning, raging mad, and I had a feeling, about to cry. He had been in Germany for three months, looking for work without success. The tanning factory had taken him on for a month's temporary work. When it was over, he was promised the first job that fell open. He had been careful to call on the supervisor every week or ten days, just to remind him, to assure him that he still wanted the place. He had gone that morning and found that his "friend" Roberto, another Sicilian who had come to Germany with him, had gone to the supervisor the week before, had told him that Guido no longer needed the job, and had sent him, Roberto, in his stead. Three days later Roberto had a job at the tanning factory. Guido stumped around the house, drank a couple of glasses of *Schnaps*, banged his fist into the woodwork several times, and left.

Everyone worried about what could happen by evening. They dread fights. Late, about eleven, he stumbled in with a flashy German girl, who understood little Italian. He shouted and railed against Roberto, drank more *Schnaps*, this time followed by beer, and then succumbed to the German girl's gentle strokings and purrings. After they left the silence was heavy. The men looked away into space, but from their grunted remarks I knew that they suspected any German girl of fair attractions who bothered to seduce an unemployed Sicilian of being up to no good. She was better than the alternative they had feared.

The next morning I found Michele alone in the house, sitting, reading a sports magazine at the kitchen table. We talked some about nothing and everything, random bits that interested us. Neither of us felt obliged to keep up a conversation, which was a relief. Once, after a silence and without reference to anything, he said he hoped Nicola could get his car soon. That way they could all be away from home sometimes, and the friends wouldn't find them. Flu seemed to have exhausted him. What he couldn't take was always, always having someone sitting in the kitchen, eternally talking. They never go home. Like last night. They had stayed two hours after I left. They don't understand that you don't always want them here. He never went to their houses unless they invited him. Maybe, if he weren't home always, he could make them understand ... and so he had learned what we all learn sooner or later. Friends add a unique dimension to our lives, are a joy and a support, but not *all* the time. Their enthusiasm had set them off on a binge. Once they recover from the aftereffects, they will be more cautious and enjoy their tipple more.

This was my first chance to ask Michele what he thought of our prodigal, Vincenzo. He considered the question with the detached fairness that tempers most of his opinions, at least those he is willing to express. I will never know the progression that led to his answer.

"Well, I guess you'd have to say he's young and the young are given to *capricci.*"

"Young at twenty-seven?" He nodded.

"Yes, he's still young. If he'd had a family, a wife, he wouldn't have done it." Judgment, then, along with responsibility, strikes at the altar.

"Would you have done it—assuming you were twenty-seven and not married?"

"No," he said slowly, smiling. "But that's different. Vincenzo has a profession. He's a construction carpenter. He can start again. I never could. I'm just a laborer, and there are too many of us. We can't quit a job. There may never be another. We just have to stay where we are—unless we line up something first—and plod along, keeping our resentments to ourselves and our tongues in our heads.

[*184*]

But—we can think whatever we like. Our thoughts—they're our *capricci*." Though he still smiled, it was at something distant, invisible to me, that amused and at the same time saddened him. He decided that we should have a beer.

While he was away in the sitting room, I placed what that smile reminded me of, what it was that I had seen one night and had never been able to forget.

Late one afternoon we were all in the sitting room—the regulars, Michele, Berio, Chichella, and I. Vincenzo, who had gone to take a nap, never reappeared until the next day. For some reason, beyond the smoke of our cigarettes the light in the room was very dim. Everyone talked at once, so, of course, we heard nothing. Suddenly the door flew open and an enormously tall, thin, bony man's figure, a black shadow against the light from the hall, stood in the doorway, casting a still longer, gray spidery shadow across the linoleum.

I may have been the only one who was startled and a little frightened. I half expected him to raise his hands high over his head and lunge at us. Instead Michele jumped up and went over to take his arm, urging him to join us. Someone switched on another light and the man bent his head very carefully to clear the doorway, but would come no farther. Now that we could see him, in twill trousers and a striped shirt he was a mild-looking, very thin young man whose legs had continued to grow long after his head and body stopped. He had a very large nose, seconded by a large and very active Adam's apple, and he whispered quietly, earnestly at Michele not to disturb us. Raffaele leaned over to explain that this was Rudi who owned a bar-café and often asked Michele to play with him for dances he organized there. He played the accordion himself and also owned a battery of drums, Michele's favorite instrument. Their conversation seemed good-natured, if complicated, almost an auction with two auctioneers, except that the figures had to do with times and meeting places rather than money. A beer celebrated their agreement. Rudi would still not sit down, but stood, grinning, as Michele told me that he spoke English.

"*Ja*, I speak very good," Rudi said carefully. "After ten, twelve beers." When I had translated, everyone laughed. He seemed pleased, bobbed his head up and down several times, and left.

The dance was that evening. I asked if Chichella and I might go too for just a little while. Chichella frowned at me, but said nothing. Raffaele volunteered to be *cavalier servente*. Berio immediately claimed equal right. He would go too. After all Chichella was *his* aunt: he must protect her. She left the room rather hurriedly, careful not to look at me.

Michele met Rudi and his truck at eight. We waited an hour or so to avoid the warm-up squawks and thumps of our out-of-practice musicians and those self-conscious, faltering first dancers. I wondered what Berio's costume might be, but the prospect of two older women and no *Disko* did not inspire any extravagance beyond a clean white shirt and blue jeans.

Raffaele directed me along narrow roads that seemed to go nowhere across flat misty fields. One last sharp curve and a long, well-lighted building came into sight. An odd place for a bar-café, I said. Raffaele stammered a bit. He hadn't told me, but the dance was at the sports club, the sponsor of Berio's soccer team. This was the members' annual party. I stopped the car and began maneuvering to turn it around. It was a private party, and we had not been invited. At home they had treated the idea of the dance coolly, a whim of mine to be humored. Time and anticipation had whetted their appetites. They were determined to go. Raffaele swore that Michele had asked if we might come, that there would be a table set aside for us. He hopped out of the car and went in to see. In a few minutes he came back, smiling: we had a table. I was outvoted.

Inside the clubhouse was a huge, rectangular room, paneled in light varnished wood. The roof, its rafters and purlins also varnished, formed the ceiling. One long wall was entirely eaves-to-floor windows, protected, when the club was closed, by shutters of the building's outer siding which could be lifted outward and up out of sight. Opposite, a bench ran the length of the back wall with just enough room left in one corner for a bar and behind it a service kitchen. A few derelict Formica and chrome tables with their complement of chairs piled on top had been shoved against the windows, leaving a prairie of empty space for the dance floor. Near them, in the corner diagonally across from the bar, Rudi and Michele wheezed and thumped in lonely quarantine. No one was dancing. Off on the other side of the room, in front of the bench and as far from the music as possible, a single long table had been improvised from the smaller Formica tables. Fifty or more people sat at it, facing each other—in absolute silence.

It was not difficult to identify the table arranged for us. Only one was set up with its chairs neatly in attendance and it was right next to Rudi and Michele. The fifty silent people turned to watch us cross the floor. No walk was ever longer. Chichella, as she always does in a strange public place, tried to pretend she was not there by sitting with her back to the room. Berio, blushing furiously, sat next to her, and Raffaele at the end of the table with his back to our hosts, faced Michele and Rudi. Not two feet from Michele and on a line with him, I was the only one who could see everything that happened.

For a while, not wanting to appear too curious, I concentrated on the musicians. Rudi had a loose-leaf notebook of sheet music propped on a stand in front of him. Each page, and there were not more than twenty, encased in their own individual plastic envelopes, had room enough for the melodies of two songs on the front and two more on the back. He worked through them quite methodically, pausing between numbers to study the next for a moment before attacking it in his precise, but placid style. Michele, who had no music, cocked his head to one side, listened to the first bar or two, and then fluttered off into the exact rhythm he wanted. I had expected an accordion and drums to sound like the lumbering accompaniments of my dancing-school days, when the musicians reduced every piece to groups of heavily accented beats so that we could hear the one-two-three-fours we mouthed with such determination and move our feet accordingly. Michele saved us from that. He played extremely well and his instinct and skill infected the songs with some of his own verve, creating a not wholly accurate impression of professionalism.

Still no one danced. The members lost interest in us and turned back to their table and each other. Now that I could watch, I saw that little conversations did flicker up, only to be snuffed out by the silence that greeted them. The members were youngish, in their thirties and very early forties, and all well dressed. The men favored suede or velvet jackets, but there were some tweeds. Several wore ascots, the rest ties. Recently they had had good haircuts, which gave them a uniform look of "mod" conservative, almost an absence of style, as though they had instructed their barbers to find a decorous compromise between GI and hippie. Silk dresses or skirts and sweaters and solid low-heeled shoes more suitable for walking than dancing had been the choices of most of the women. Two wore pants and transparent blouses. They were also the only women with garish makeup. A more experienced palmist of the neighborhood would have recognized instantly where they fit in the local scheme. All I am sure of—and that from what I saw later in the evening—is that the men treated them courteously, yet more casually than they did the other women. At the moment everyone seemed to find the bottom of his own glass the most bewitching thing in sight.

Two stout, cheerful women rushed around with four heavy glass mugs of beer clutched in each hand. They served us our four liters before we ordered, collecting our money on the fly. As hard as they pounded back and forth to the bar, they never caught up. Someone was always impatient for another. Rudi and Michele churned on with their music. An argument started at one end of the table between two women and a sullen-looking young man. Friends down the way shouted him down and silence returned. A pretty young woman, not a girl and not quite a woman, with silky brown hair and large wistful brown eyes leaned across the table to talk very seriously at a woman I could not see. The servingwomen pounded back and forth, and two pairs of men began to talk over the women between them. Finally—at last—

One man, very slender in his beige trousers and velvet coat, stood up, bowed, and asked one of the women sitting near him to dance. These were his first words of the evening. While the woman slipped out around the end of the table, he straightened his jacket, buttoned it, smoothed his ascot and then his hair. When she arrived in front of him, he struck a position, left arm out, right arm crooked, head thrown back, and she was to fit herself into it. He waited until she did, then waited a beat for the music and skimmed off across the floor. Almost immediately there was a shuffling of feet: the woman had guessed wrong. She continued to trip about halfway through every figure. His steps were too complicated, but he neither simplified them nor complained. He ignored the mistakes, his head high. He danced with a second lady and a third, who fared no better, stumbling and lurching after him, before two other couples joined them to pace gravely around the floor, trying to stay out of the way more than dance. For as long as his consumption of beer and his legs allowed, Prince Charming danced. During the intermissions he downed a mug or more of beer. Then, when the music started, he continued his progress around the table, absolutely impartial, dancing with the lady whose turn it was, in total, joyless silence. Just before we left at 11:15 his career suffered the first of several setbacks. Without warning he lunged facedown across the table into a snoring coma. He did not hear the roar of laughter.

The gloom had lifted. Conversation did not thrive, but there was a lot of shouting. Still no one seemed inclined to dance. A slight older man in a gray suit and silver tie appeared in the doorway and stood, surveying the scene. Obviously he did not approve. There was an aura of success about him and, judging from the way the younger men rushed to smile and joke with him, if he did not approve, something had to be done. He pushed through the group around him and approached the table, where he stood, looking over the women as he might cows at a market. He did not attempt to be impartial: he chose the handsomest and wheeled her around the floor, talking all the while. He returned her to her place, picked another attractive woman in a rather *droit du seigneur* manner, and wheeled off again. When the set ended, he made an announcement, which was greeted with cheers, and left. Raffaele reported that the man had promised to liven up the party by bringing back more beautiful girls!

A furor of shouts and laughs subsided into dragging rhythmic song, and I looked up to find that the men and women at the table, asleep or awake, had linked arms and were swaying, slowly, back and forth, back and forth. Even the semiconscious tried to sing. Watching them swaying, swaying, made me seasick. I wondered how they felt, besides drunk. The servingwomen trotted from the table to the bar, frantic to fill orders, and the members sang on, rocking themselves into oblivion.

The next round of music from Michele and Rudi was greeted by bleary squints from the members, and Chichella had had enough. Several times Raffaele had asked both of us to dance, and we had refused, reluctant to attract attention. Now Chichella had decided. Would Raffaele dance with her? He sprang up from his chair. As they swung away from the table, Berio whispered that he hoped I did not want to dance, that he did not know how to do "this kind." But he danced at the *Disko*? Oh, that's easy. All you do is wiggle a lot.

Chichella and Raffaele twirled madly around the floor, laughing and talking. At fifty-three, fat and prolapsed, she is no painted beauty, but she leaned away from him, twinkling up at him with the kind of flirtatious brio that flatters any man. And her feet flicked over the floor. Raffaele did a basic four-step square, his steps ever smaller until he only pivoted while she flew, reeling around and around and around. The Germans stomped and clapped. Michele was his sister's accomplice, speeding up, and Raffaele spun her faster and faster and faster. They blurred before our eyes. They reeled and they reeled, talking, joking, enjoying themselves, spinning, spinning until at the end of the piece they spun back to our table and collapsed in their chairs. A burst of applause, shouts of *"Evviva l'Italia!"* and couples swarmed on the floor to dance. Raffaele and Chichella, both breathless, congratulated each other on breaking the log jam. Beer and schnitzels arrived at the table, compliments of persons unknown, and Chichella's eyes sparkled as I had never seen them. "I guess we showed them," she said more than once and then exploded into tearful giggles.

They were still fanning themselves when the important little man returned herding five women whose claims to charm were limited to their evident good spirits. He dragooned five sleepy-eyed

men from the table into dancing with them, chose a decorative partner for himself, and pushed his way onto the floor, where couples
bounced up and down, shouting, laughing. One or two couples
leaned heavily together, resting, or maybe even semi-asleep. The
noise was unbearable.

Soon afterward we left, which was just as well. The party went
on until after two o'clock. Riding home in the truck Michele, Rudi,
and Raffaele, who had stayed behind, found three women, part of
the little man's troop, asleep in the middle of the road. They got out
and dragged them off onto the verge. The women begged inco-
herently to be taken home, but not one was sure at that moment
where she lived. The men had no choice. They wrapped the wom-
en's coats tightly around them and abandoned them to the sobering
effects of the cold dew.

Before we could leave the dance, Raffaele insisted, out of deference to Chichella and me, on a quick inspection of the parking lot.
We were not to encounter men peeing against the tires of cars. As
we waited by the door for his "all clear," I watched Michele, gazing
off over the heads of the dancers, playing automatically. Suddenly he
seemed alone, isolated. He had divorced himself from that clubhouse
and those stumbling, drunken people. Perhaps the drums influenced
me. I imagined him withdrawn into his measured thoughts, for he is
a man of measures—of himself, of the world around him, and of
himself in that world. They guarantee his pride. A woman on the
dance floor slipped and fell. Michele glanced down at her and then
quickly away, up again, above the dancers' heads. His expression, his
mouth curled in a gentle smile, his eyes focused on some distant
vision of his own, was a curious mixture of amusement and sad confidence. I am different. I am above this display, his look said.
Michele, the inferior immigrant, was enjoying a mild flush of superiority.

His smile that Sunday morning in the kitchen was much the
same smile, and I understood better. He *is* a man of measures and of
measured thoughts. He is also an unskilled laborer, so his thoughts
are his freedom and, sadly, his only *capricci*.

IO

Offenbach is an industrial city (chemicals, machinery, and leather) of 120,000 people, which, though it sprawls about in Topsy-ish disorder, is wedged between Frankfurt on the northwest and the viaducts that braid back and forth over what must be one of the largest rail yards still in existence on the southeast. Several autobahns and the Main River impose the other boundaries. After announcing an exit, the highway authorities take a rather laissez-faire attitude toward Offenbach. Presumably anyone who wants to go there knows how. The outlander is left two choices: he can hurtle on into Frankfurt, or resign himself to the more exotic pleasures of the freight yards, the wholesale markets, their various loading platforms, and the battalions of TIR trucks that gambol and snort around them in impromptu games of Chicken. After trial runs at both the alternatives, if his supply of adrenaline lasts, he will sense that he must stay to his left, away from the river.

Off over there is Offenbach with its factories and its long, wide, bare avenues, which are slightly gritty as though the shabby nineteenth-century blocks of flats that line them were sloughing off, granule by granule, their skimpy cornices and window pediments, their very ensigns of gentility. Buses barrel along, but there are few cars and no pedestrians, not even children. Day and night such streets are deserted. Only for an hour in the morning do figures scurry along the sidewalks to bus stops and again for an hour in the evening, more slowly now, tired, the figures drag back to their doorways and disappear into the labyrinths behind the dowdy façades.

Closer to the center of town a few dusty trees break the linear bleakness. Then on a boulevard, divided in the middle by a row of trees that meet overhead with trees on either curb to form two leafy tunnels, the traffic begins to swirl, dragging you mercilessly on, past a park into the unfinished glass and chrome and concrete world of the city. Modest skyscrapers act as bookends for lower structures, furniture showrooms and stores of electronic equipment. Vast windowless walls of concrete, some studded, some quilted for texture, loom over garages, amusement arcades, record shops, restaurants, and potbellied trucks dribbling their premixed concrete near the hoardings of a would-be skyscraper. At the end of a short street, drab with two-story buildings, rooming houses, and dejected shops, squats a miniature station, its newly painted gingerbread bangs and gingerbread eyebrows giving it a sullen expression. Half-defiant, half-apologetic, a remnant of the past, it looks out on the wrong century.

Offenbach was the first German city I saw and in retrospect I am glad. Others, more elegant, more confusing, depressing, or charming, were also too large and complex. Sheer space and the number of people in it dilute and confuse impressions. Offenbach was small enough that the many facets of a day's activities, any day's, were visible almost simultaneously.

The first afternoon we were there I took a long walk, alone. Chichella refused to come. She preferred to sit in our hotel room, stiff and suspicious, guarding our luggage. Beyond the chaos of the traffic, the blank walls, and the construction sites, I found a shopping plaza, reserved for pedestrians, with stone walks and benches and unexpected little fountains, spraying gently, trying to be cheerful, but adding somehow to the first chill of fall. Shops, glittering with glass and chrome, offered every imaginable luxury. Inside, the sultry silence of ultrathick carpeting and the gently modulated voices of handsome salesclerks were planned to impress the customer, simply by his presence there, with his own grace and good taste. Outside, as well as in, everything had been carefully arranged. Flower beds and benches and flagged walks—peace, order, and temptation. But another day. A stiff breeze that swept across the plaza sent people hurrying off down the ramps, into the protection of narrower streets and milling crowds. A forest of electric signs added to the closeness. There were sales in the department stores. I watched women lay siege to the bargain counters and then ducked around them on the sidewalks when, with their shopping bags crammed, they met friends and stopped to compare purchases. A few blocks away somber women, all in gray, sipped hot chocolate in a pastry shop, and still farther on four women, small packages tucked under their arms (clean pajamas? a couple of apples?), waited outside a hospital for visiting hours to begin.

I wandered, taking whatever turn attracted me, watching the neighborhoods change in some secret ebb and flow of their own. In one street where the low apartment buildings, neither old nor new, wore stains from faulty gutters like bedraggled pennants, little girls in dresses with slacks underneath played on the sidewalk. Their mothers watched from the windows above and chattered at each other in a language that was not German. An unmarked panel truck rolled to a stop. The women left their perches and the driver got out to open the back doors and expose his wares, Turkish specialties. His customers had expected him. He was their mobile grocer. Later I would see others like him all over Germany, and once in the Ruhr, even a Turkish bus, its blue paint whitened by time and weather, its windows held together with tape and trimmed with rainbow fringes, set up on bricks at the edge of a vacant lot to serve as grocery store-cum-residence.

Deep in a maze of narrow streets and narrow sooty houses children played, in pairs, on the sidewalks. The wash that hung on wires looped from window to window looked familiar, and the game they played was *Morra*, a simple gambling game that Mussolini tried without success to outlaw.* They were Sicilians, dark and chubby, dressed in random combinations of mended (and unmended) clothes and not very clean. I talked to them for a few minutes. They had been in Germany two, three years, some more. It was all right, they shrugged. They were all waiting for their mothers to come home from work. No one trusted them with the house keys. That was all right too, if it didn't rain. Did I speak German? They did. Listen! I listened, but it sounded very much like Sicilian with guttural additives to me. Somewhere nearby a bus had arrived. Six or seven women turned into the street. The children ran toward them, shouting complaints. In answer the mothers screeched threats, and I went on, struck by how much noisier they were—the children and the women—than the Turks I had just seen, but scarcely heard.

By dusk women had vanished from the department stores and the shopping plaza. Office workers trotted past, hurrying to get their buses. Well-tailored businessmen sauntered through, stopping to look in shop windows, then went on, out the other side into the traffic jam. The stoplights released flight waves of cars that swooped along in tight formation, beating back cars that would eddy up from underground garages.

The sidewalks teemed with men, workmen in windbreakers and blue jeans, carrying plastic sacks. They milled around, silent, aimless. Some crowded at the window of a newspaper kiosk. One by one as the men came away, each would ripple quickly through the pages of his magazine. A slight nod, a quick roll of the paper, and it was shoved into a pocket. When my turn came and I was finally square in front of the counter, three naked, contorted women leered at me from three stacks, all different publications. The weekly supply of pornography had arrived. The vendor was very courteous: he regretted that he did not have the *Corriere della Sera*. I moved aside,

---

* Only two can play in a game. Each shows several fingers of one hand and at the same time shouts a number under ten. If one calls the exact number of fingers shown by both players, he wins.

but was still standing there, looking at the magazines, when an Italian asked for *La Gazetta dello Sport*. He was waved away without a word.

From a distance, people coming along the block saw the knot of men and deviated from their course, skirting wide around them. A few ventured into the traffic, cutting diagonally across the avenue to disappear in the dark on the other side. So many still, dark young men, so very much alike and so very un-German made them uneasy. Better to avoid them. The men did nothing. They just stood, glum and uncertain. For the first time their smallness, the underfed, almost stunted kind of smallness, seemed pathetic. I had always seen them at home. To people who did not know them, their anonymous sameness would be alarming—their swarthy complexions, their droopy, pirate moustaches that varied only in length and bushiness, and their shared aversion to shaving. Stubble masked their faces, making them hard to see and so, furtive, just as their nervous eyes, shifting, slipping away, careful to look at no one, seemed furtive. I felt sorry for all of us: for the men—Italian, Greek, Spaniard, Yugoslav, or Turk—who knew they were unwanted and somehow inferior; for the Germans who were alarmed and sensed an ill-will that might or might not be real; and for myself, only because I could not explain that what each of the others understood as hostility, aimed directly, malevolently at them, was three parts anxiety and one part confused resentment.

The men dissolved into little groups and headed toward the corner and the stoplight. I followed, thinking how strange it was that they did not talk, at least among themselves. Nor did they bother to look back at the new busloads of men, who had already lined up in front of the kiosk, and try to find friends there. When the light changed, we marched across together like a group of tourists and on along the street under the dark, leafy tunnel of trees. In ones and twos they dropped out, stepping aside and then, leaning up against a wall or standing in a doorway, lit cigarettes. They still did not talk. They lounged in the invisible safety of shadows, staring at nothing, thinking their own thoughts, which, like Michele's, are their *capricci*. When Chichella and I left the hotel half an hour later, they were still there, leaning against the walls, smoking in the most private place they knew—a dim street.

For more than twenty years now Chichella and her children have lived in a four-room apartment on the top floor of a building in one of Torregreca's earliest postwar housing developments. The peasants were restless, which frightens politicians, so it was built in a hurry, on the cheap and badly, and then left sitting in its own field of rubble, weeds, and mounting garbage. The peasants were still restless, and the politicians still worried: these fractious people might do more than threaten, they might do the unthinkable and revolt. Pacify them. That was the best policy. So in time other buildings, just as gimcrack and eventually just as squalid, joined Chichella's and began accumulating the quota of weeds and garbage necessary to qualify for full membership in the new neighborhood. It was in mid-decomposition when Chichella moved out, I moved in, and my adventures in frustration began.

Summer with its cool nights, its dry, searing heat and railing cicadas by day gave only minor hints of future discomforts. The fleas were voracious. Chickens and pigs browsed through the dust bowl searching for snippets of garbage that might still be edible. They were not too particular. Teething babies screamed in their beds, their cranky brothers and sisters screamed in the courtyard, and on into the night the babble of human voices picked away at my nerves. The sense of too much human life, too crowded together, too meagerly lived and yet so raucous, was an irritant and a comfort. Then quite suddenly winter closed in on us like a gray, furry pall.

Dawn did not brighten. Dull and heavy with fog, it hung over us until darkness and another night came. Only clocks could tell the hours apart. The old town slipped from sight, veiled in sodden mystery. Rain and wind lashed at the buildings, prizing off whatever might be loose—chunks of plaster, roof tiles, rusty stovepipes, and once even a balcony railing that plunged three stories into the gumbo below. Each morning the neighbors collected there to grumble and make an inventory of the debris. The housing development that on some Roman architect's drawing board may have looked like a masterpiece of modern skill and comfort was a leaky vessel apt to break up in the next storm and sink gently into its own flotsam. But the poor, so the myth went, were better off than ever before.

I grumbled too. We paid a fixed monthly amount for maintenance. The service was a fable. A piglet had been brought in from the cold to live under the stairs in the front entrance, and a flock of diseased, half-starved chickens pecked at my feet on the stairway or flew up, spraying me with excrement and feathers. Should I take out my rage on the architect who planned peasant housing without stalls or on my peasant neighbors, who faced a meatless year if they could not raise their animals? My neighbors had no choice. The average income for the district was between three and four hundred dollars a year, but they had never even reached that starvation average. A family of small children on the first floor used the two steps just above their door as a latrine. And they had no choice either. Each morning at dawn they were locked out by their parents who had to leave for the fields. The pig grew and developed alarmingly carnivorous tastes. When a short circuit extinguished the hall lights, only a blind acrobat could reach my apartment without some disaster. No one dared touch government property, so for the next four years, except when I was in residence and strung a bulb out from my front door, the darkness remained, though the obstacles changed. Winters were long and harrowing. Food and hope and patience were short, but the myth continued to grow: the poor were better off than ever before.

Little has changed. Several years ago the rubble was asphalted over, garbage is collected more regularly, but the trees on the architect's plan were never planted, and we still have fine stands of weeds. Rain and mildew have collaborated to decorate the walls with an atlas of lost continents, but the stencil "D.D.T. 1961" has not washed off, nor does water, the perennial promise, gush through the pipes more than a few hours a day, except, of course, in August: the emigrants are home then. They are not fooled. The average income I mentioned was, in 1959, half the national *average*. Along with everything else, the *average* income in Lucania has galloped upward and today is still only slightly more than half the national *average*, which, without mincing words, is why four out of the six apartments in Chichella's building are empty—except in the month of August. (Naturally the neighbor who stayed is the one who plays her radio so loud the windowpanes on the staircase rattle and who, when my brain rattles in unison and I ask that she lower the volume, always gives me a half-dazed, half-demented little smile and says, "Oh, it could be *much* louder, you know.")

Years before they left, the tenants of both first-floor apartments had heavy galvanized mesh put up around their balconies as a protection against thieves, of which, at that time, there were none. What exactly they were protecting was also hard to say. They had little or no furniture and few clothes beyond those on their backs. Nevertheless these cages of mesh, supported by metal poles and anchored by irons to the wall, were installed, and, if they served no discernible purpose, they did add a touch of distinction to the building's appearance: it looked like the monkey house at a zoo.

Two years ago, in August, when the Festa lured people home to Torregreca, I arrived to find a disconcerting *novità*. In the cage to the left of the front door sat two dark-haired girls, one slightly behind the other, both rigid, staring off well over the head of anyone who might pass right beneath them. With their astonishingly regular profiles, which they seemed to present for admiration, and large, unfocused brown eyes, they might have been off-duty caryatids. Torresi etiquette is very specific: each time you come face to face with neighbors, known or unknown, you must wish them good morning, good afternoon, or good evening. Repetition makes you feel like a gabbling hen, but that is the custom, so I said good afternoon in the general direction of the cage. They neither saw nor heard me. Chastened, I went upstairs.

I came to feel that Madame Defarge would be a jollier concierge than those two who, as far as I could tell, did not even knit. No matter how early in the morning I went out, they were already in their cage, sitting one slightly behind the other. At lunch they disappeared and were invisible through the hottest hours, but by late afternoon they were back again to stay until well after dark. Daunting as I found them, there was so much else going on that it was several days before I remembered to ask Chichella who they were. She looked startled, and I knew that I should have recognized them.

"Lucetta's girls," she said. "And the boys arrive this afternoon."

When I had last seen them, "Lucetta's girls" were two and three years old, and the three boys—who arrived that afternoon in two large, hoarse German sports cars with seat covers of long, shaggy white fur, an uncomfortable bit of swank in a Mediterranean August—had been five, seven, and nine. These were the same children who years ago were locked out when their parents went to the fields and who used the steps as their latrine.

And Lucetta, their mother, was the owner of the pig that had skulked in the entrance, waiting to nibble on innocent visitors. We had some violent scenes over that pig. I complained to the *Vigile Sanitario*, who dutifully came and issued a fine, though he explained with some sympathy that it would be useless, that no Torrese thought a pig safe unless he were *sotto casa*, right under the house. Lucetta accepted the fine with a shrug, saying The State owed her a stall, and of course never paid it, any more than she paid the second or the third. We had reached an impasse, and the pig, who was by then enormous and had a deep baritone voice, was no longer satisfied to nibble: nothing less than an arm or a leg would do.

Once Lucetta chose civil disobedience, I was helpless. Chichella would never accept defeat so easily, I told myself. She would find a way to bring pressure. She would ... And then I had an idea. Late that afternoon I warned Chichella, who needed every lira I paid her, that either the pig left, or I would be forced to leave. She argued patience. He would be gone by Christmas, or at the latest January. No. I was adamant. I would leave if he was not removed from the front hall. She nodded, looked at the floor thoughtfully for several seconds, and went away, closing the door unusually quietly. I was amused that she, of all people, who knew that I had nowhere I could move, had accepted my statement. For the next hour doors banged and voices echoed up and down the stairway, but it could have been the normal homecoming cacophony. I waited.

After an eerie thirty-minute intermission of hisses and shushes, the hall exploded. Women screamed. Someone clubbing the iron banister had set it twanging. Footsteps thundered down the stairs, the children's quick and scraping, the grown-ups' slower, but just as urgent. I could not ignore such a fracas. By peering out from my landing all I saw was a broom flailing about in midair. I went down the stairs until, just above the first floor, I caught up with the laggers in the crowd. Below us women and children, seconded by dogs, chickens, and two rather bemused older men, had Lucetta jammed against her own front door. Her big brown eyes rolled in what could have been a parody of fear, but was not: she was terrified. She had every reason to be with Chichella, red in the face, screaming just under her chin, a loutish fifteen-year-old boy swinging a broom around and around barely clearing the top of her head, and in front of her the pack of women who howled and threatened as though their hearts were set on a lynching.

The pig! The pig! The pig! Dangerous for the children! The stench! Unfair! We should all have pigs! Each followed her own line of reasoning and at the top of her lungs, waving her arms and pounding her neighbor's back with her fists. On one of the boy's more feeble swings with the broom, I caught the handle and wrested it from him. At least no one would be hurt that way. He wheeled around, furious, but before he could grab for his broom, one of the old men slapped him and shoved him toward the street. The women were distracted. For as long as it took to drive the boy away, they directed their venom at him, and I knew that we had reached the turning point. There is one vital moment when a slight incident, often fortuitous, settles whether such brawls build to mayhem or subside to a seasonal, spleen-cleansing physic enjoyed by all concerned. Not that the noise level drops, but the tension does.

This one roared on for another ten minutes and then broke up into rump groups that continued to snort and moan *pro forma* rehashes of the affair. Everyone was happy, purged. Soon euphoria would creep over them. It had been agreed that each morning Lucetta would tie her pig behind the building, up under her own back balcony, which brought it within speaking distance of her kitchen, and at night she would find somewhere else for it, in her apartment if she chose. She chose. She had her revenge, though she never mentioned it and I never complained. Each night she drove the pig around the building, through the front door, up the steps into her apartment, and settled him *on* the back balcony below my bedroom window. He slept in fits and starts. The rest of the time he heaved himself up, flopped down again, and rutted around trying to get comfortable, grunting and baying his complaints all the while in a serenade I shall never forget. Each morning I woke convinced that I was sharing my bed with an irascible, smelly old man.

Lucetta bore no grudge. As she saw it, her quarrel was with the government that had deprived her of a stall. She was abject in her apologies for the long process of toilet training her children, which she sensed was another subject of rancor. Each afternoon, when she came home, her first chore was to swab down the stairs and then slosh them liberally with a particularly putrid disinfectant. Her life in Torregreca and my memories of her there seem to center around the front hall. We met there, if at all, but also it was there one year that she sawed and then split the family's winter supply of wood. It was raining. She had to be inside: she was sorry. *Scusate.* I'll finish as fast as I can.

For ten days the entrance was blocked by the special sawhorse, two sturdy wooden **X**'s connected by a heavy pole, that held each piece of wood firmly in place to be cut, and a large tree stump, a sort of woodchopper's anvil, for splitting her stove lengths. Sawdust and chips littered the floor and were tracked on into her apartment by the children, who played around in the mess, waiting to carry wood, a piece at a time, to wherever she was stacking it. The operation seemed endless and one that depressed me for reasons in no way connected with the confusion of the hallway. All morning and all afternoon her husband, Paolo, lounged against the front door, a battered felt hat pulled down over his face, a toothpick sticking out of his mouth. Whenever I came in sight, he shooed the children out of my way, snarled at Lucetta to hurry, to get on with it, and then led me by the hand, like a partner he had invited to waltz, over and around the treacherous mounds of litter.

The public performances were bad enough, but when he thought no one was listening, and I often did, stopping on my way down, just out of sight, at the turn of the stairway, he cursed her in a quiet, sneering voice for a bitch, a whore, a sluggard, a woman who had married for a warm bed, an incompetent, a bitch, a whore. And over and over and over again. He might have been saying his beads. Lucetta never answered back. She went right on sawing and splitting and when I came down the last flight, not even a sidelong glance at Paolo suggested I had interrupted a diatribe. She always smiled wanly and shuffled aside, saying *"Scusate, signò! Scusate!"* I never saw him touch a piece of that wood, but all morning and all afternoon, every day for ten days, he slouched there against the door, carping at her for her slowness when anyone could hear, chanting his insults when he thought he was safely alone with her. I came to loathe the sight of him, a man I did not know, to loathe his face, dark under his hat, dark with whiskers and the little toothbrush moustache still fashionable then with Southern peasants, and to loathe his civility to me almost as much as I loathed his churlishness to her. As far as I know she has never complained of Paolo to anyone. I have never mentioned him to her, but after the wood-cutting episode, I was more patient about her children, their racket, and their messes.

Lucetta wanted to stay on good terms with all of her neighbors, though she hardly ever saw us. Most mornings at daybreak she and Paolo left for the fields. They owned several small pieces of land themselves and were, what had already become rare, a couple who would work on the land of others, if they were sure that they would be paid in cash. Coming back at dusk with the shopping still to do, dinner to prepare, children to scold and spank and clean up, a whole day's worth of each, and a husband, who relished his glass of wine and his nightly argument, to pacify, she had no time to stand around gossiping. But if we saw them seldom, we heard them. Promiscuous intimacy with your neighbors is an inescapable fringe benefit of public housing.

That summer two years ago I heard Lucetta before I saw her. The evening the boys arrived was unusually hot and still, even with the windows open. Most of our neighbors were out, probably calling on

[*203*]

half-forgotten relatives, which is a vacation ritual, but a general rumble of voices and clicking of silverware drifted up from Lucetta's kitchen to ours. At a certain point a man's voice, not Paolo's, shouted, *"No, non così!"* Objections interrupted him. Than an abrupt silence and we heard the doorbell. Chairs scraped, a confusion of greetings, and more chairs scraped as they were dragged from the kitchen. Over it all Lucetta's voice rang out clear and angry, but distant, apparently from the sitting room.

"All right. Now that you're all here, sit down and shut up. This . . ."

"Eeeh, she's off." Chichella smiled, waving one hand in a windmill motion. "Just like years ago."

We waited, almost looking forward to her performance and a return to the familiar pattern of the past, which, so irrevocably gone, can seem more intriguing than the banal present. Downstairs the kitchen doors banged shut.

"Hmm, must be serious," Chichella said, her eyebrows raised in surprise. Resigned, we talked of other things.

Next morning I met Lucetta at her front door, her head wrapped in a clean white cloth, a broom propped against the wall. She had just finished her morning sweep of the stairs and hall and was ready to unfurl her doormat once more. Twenty years have changed her little. Not tall, she was and still is slender with a quick deftness about her movements that disguises her physical strength. Only her hands give that secret away, I thought, watching her reach behind her head to untie the knot that held the cloth. Her hair is still dark, cut short and stiffly waved in honor of the trip home, and the brown eyes that I remembered flittering constantly back and forth over everything around her still sparkle with restless curiosity. And yet her face *has* changed. There is a different look about it. In some way her small features have spread, as though a tissue-thin layer of bone had worn away under the skin, allowing them to sink ever so slightly. That morning she looked tired, or perhaps the shadow, the light cutting across her face . . . I am not sure now. At the sight of me the expression vanished into a broad, flashing smile. We had not seen each other for seventeen years, and if at times I had been a snappish neighbor, I was an old friend, now almost dear. Her enthusiasm was contagious. She had so much to tell me, so much had happened, and in a torrent of words and truncated phrases she tried. Seventeen years and so much had happened, she said, and I believed her. As I listened, I noticed that whatever the trials of those years, she enjoyed one blessing at least, a very non-Torrese blessing: she not only had all of her teeth, but neat gold inlays proved the skill and attention of some German dentist.

Did I remember the day she left? I did. When she packed her clothes and the children's in that bare apartment, Paolo had already been in Germany for a year. He had worked off his contract with "The Company" and had found a way to stay, an independent job, and a place to live. He needed Lucetta to care for him. This was her duty. He ordered her to come up and bring the children, five of them, the eldest nine, the youngest barely two. Lucetta would never have asked, and he would never have offered to come back and help her with the trip. Oh yes, I remembered her standing at the door, crying, her bundles around her feet, her children clinging to her legs, crying too. People crowded in the hall, giving her advice about where to change and the times of trains here, there, and yon, details left in their minds from schedules of God only knows what year. Why must they confuse her? Frighten her? She would lose her way soon enough. She would miss her train and misunderstand and be hungry and angry and scared, all soon enough. The children wailed, and I marveled at her courage, praying that the friends and relatives, who on such a trip would already be lost at the station in Potenza, might leave her in peace. I could do nothing except kiss her on each cheek and wish her *buon viaggio*, but I seldom passed her door without remembering how alone she looked and how desperate in the midst of those tearful, yelling people.

For Lucetta, years of such trips have brought experience and a certain sophistication. The first odyssey has dimmed. Yes, it was long, terribly long and something *did* go wrong, but ... well, so much has happened since. She has forgotten: they got there somehow, and Paolo had a place for them to live and a job. At first, because she had to take the baby wherever she went, she could only clean for neighbors by the hour. The boys were in school, the girl went half-days to a nursery. In the mornings she was free, and every little bit helped. Food was expensive in Germany, so expensive, she thought—and clothes too. Two years after she arrived, she took her first full-time job.

But—and her face lit up—in the end it was worth it. All those sacrifices had paid off. Her children never did well in school, just not cut out for it. Except the little one. Now, *she* has a knack—for languages, Lucetta added with a mother's proud, uncritical bravado. They wanted her to go on in school and be a translator in an office, or maybe even an interpreter. After all, she knows three languages already: Italian, German, and English. Next year she might begin French.* The boys were settled with jobs. One was married, all three were headed toward *"una buona posizione"*—a good position, an expression that implies "a good position *in the world*," and so refers to their work only to the extent that it could affect this elusive change in social position. Two of her sons are mechanics, one is a waiter. Had I seen their cars? *"Belle, no?"* she asked, rolling her eyes and lifting her shoulders in sensuous appreciation. "Oh yes, all those years in Germany were worth it."

Almost every morning we had a tête-à-tête on the stairs and some days a second in the afternoon, still on the stairs, she holding her door closed at her back. I suspect that she watched for me, but she did not ask me inside, which was strange. Nor did she apologize beyond nodding toward her door and turning her eyes to the ceiling, from which I was to draw my own conclusions: there was trouble at home. Once she finished that little mime, she was in no hurry, and so I heard about the garage they had bought in Torregreca—for the boys—with an apartment above and about the land next to it, only a sliver, that they were buying to expand the garage an-

---

*Eventually I forced both girls to talk to me. The younger one, the would-be interpreter, is fluent in the Torrese dialect, ungrammatical and hesitant in Italian, mute in English, and judging from her school record—she has repeated three classes—no more than adequate in German. She has one year to finish for her secondary certificate and said flatly that she would not go back to school. Poor Lucetta. She wanted one child who was *istruita*, that mystical, often useless state that is every peasant's ambition for his children.

other ten feet or so on the ground floor and add a second apartment above, two or three small rooms for the bachelor mechanic. (The waiter-son never figured in these housing arrangements. I wondered if he were declassé now that we thought in terms of *buona posizione*.)

She urged me to go and see the garage, which, I knew, was an invitation to admire. It was easy to find on the main road, at the edge of town, the middle garage of three in that particular stretch, separated from each other by two or three narrow little shops. Twenty years ago there were few cars in town. More social emblems than means of transportation, they were kept in garages, ex-donkey stalls, and brought out for an airing on Sundays. The three garages of those days were forced to specialize in motor bikes, scooters, even bicycles to stay open. Now cars jam the Piazza and all the streets leading to it, and some eleven garages vie for the honor of tinkering with their insides. Many of the mechanics were trained in Germany and all complain that there is little business. A twelfth garage hardly seems a good investment, but there it was with a new coat of white paint and next to it the shallow excavation for the annex.

Lucetta was sure they would make their fortune. Those other mechanics are not trained, just half-trained. *Her* boys had been to *school* in Germany. They knew what they were about. Give them five years, and they'll be the richest men in town. A change of subject seemed wise: when would all this take place? In a year, two years! Just think of it! Two years at the most and they would be quit of Germany. With the money they had saved and their pensions, they would equip the garage, finish the addition, and settle down to live out their old age in comfort. I could imagine Paolo strolling around the Piazza, showing off his leisure, but Lucetta, ten years younger than he, in her early fifties, is a strong and active woman, not one who has ever spent days sitting on her balcony playing the signora. For her this "early retirement," with the minimum pension that twenty years of contributions provide, would be an early abdication from life. Maybe they were going to farm their land?

"*Who, me?*" She stiffened in indignation and for emphasis splayed both hands out on her breastbone. "Never! I'll *never* go to the fields again, ever. Besides he sold part of it—and the rest—*he* doesn't intend to work it, why should *I*?" Why, indeed? Since the subject of Paolo had come up, I asked about him. For all those days he had been invisible, never even coming to the door to see why she lingered so long. He does not condone time wasted—by her.

"Not good. Not good at all!" she whispered, shaking her head, her eyes closed in a most graphic imitation of pain. "The Trouble, you know! This isn't a good time in our house. He won't go out. Wants to see no one. He just sits and worries—and then at night"— she shrugged as much as to say, "You know what he does." This seemed the end of another meeting. I started upstairs, and she called after me, as she did each time, "Tomorrow I'll give you our address in Offenbach. You must come and see us. Then we can talk *con calma*—not like this."

"*Si, si, Domani,*" I always agreed. "There's plenty of time." But, as it turned out, there really was not.

"The Trouble" had been the subject of inspired speculation and was reconstituted, just as dried eggs, powdered milk, and dried mushrooms might be to make an omelet, from tidbits of information known or panned from gossip by Chichella and her friends.

Rosa, the elder of the caryatids in the cage, had quit her job in a factory and announced to her parents that she wanted to marry a boy she had met the summer before, during their annual pilgrimage to Torregreca. No one knew exactly what contact they might have had in the following eleven months, but Rosa was determined that her mother and father accept their engagement and proceed with the marriage negotiations. Lucetta and Paolo were far from satisfied with the boy who was "nothing but a peasant," i.e., he had not finished the eighth grade, did not have a trade, and would, therefore, be forced to eke out a living on the land or as an unskilled laborer (as Paolo had). There were two other embarrassing impediments: years before they had argued with the boy's family and worse, they were already negotiating themselves what they felt would be a more desirable match for Rosa. Their overtures had been well received, but the would-be groom's parents were now reluctant to discuss the terms of the settlement. They too had heard rumors: no one wants to pay a high price for secondhand goods (and no one wants to be played for a fool in front of the whole town). It added up to enough trouble for one vacation.

Lucetta and Paolo could not leave Rosa in Germany. They had agreed to bring her down with them on one condition: she must understand that she was not to leave the house, was not to parade with her friends up and down the road, incidentally discussing the affair with them, and was to be at all times chaperoned by her younger sister. Rosa, as determined as they, agreed, but insisted she must have fresh air, which was the explanation for their extraordinary daily vigils in the monkey cage. Evenings were devoted to acrimonious fights.

Rosa's choice was inconsistent in his stand. Some evenings he came to face her brothers' challenges and her father's accusations; others, he sent word that he was "too tired," a dubious show of ardor (although who knows what pressures were applied at home). He professed his intention to marry her, but admitted that his parents refused to call on Lucetta and Paolo, that they would never make this required gesture of acceptance, that he had no steady job and would have no home to offer her, other than the cot in the corner of his parents' room where he now slept. They jeered at him and certainly his prospects were not brilliant. They were probably also right that he expected, he pretended, they should cede their apartment, which stood empty most of the year. They jeered at Rosa too for dreaming of such a misalliance, for daring to suggest it. Her groom would be another. Her father demanded her obedience, and so at sunset the first lines of the evening's scene would be heard: the doors banged to; on the neighbors' balconies and at their dinner tables the harvest of the day's rumors began. As regular as sunrise, next morning Rosa with her duenna took her place on the balcony and settled down, waxen and aloof, to take the air. If nothing else, her stamina was awesome.

The Festa was building slowly to its climax. The bishop had blessed the cars, the Madonna had accomplished her shaky progress to the cathedral, her annual visit, by truck, the peanut stands and shooting galleries were ready in place, white shoes were appearing all over town, and the sun, not to be forgotten in the excitement, blazed with a withering, caustic heat. Outside even the shadows were incandescent. Inside the heat billowed in steamy clouds. At midnight, with luck, a frail breeze would rise, and we could fall asleep, exhausted, to wake at sunrise already bathed in perspiration. Doors were never closed now.

One evening after a dinner which no one had felt like eating, we sat on Chichella's balcony, too stupefied to talk or fan ourselves, waiting for the first rustle that might mean relief. We noticed the sudden flare of light, a long rectangle across the weeds, that came from Lucetta's kitchen, but were so apathetic that it was a jarring change, not an intimation of exciting activity. We heard heavy footsteps. A shadow cut back and forth across the light, across the weeds as far as we were concerned, then there were lighter footsteps and more heavy ones. The room must have been crowded, but no one spoke, which was ominous. Apparently someone in a hurry to set out glasses snatched them from a cupboard in a bunch, one to a finger. They clanked together, and a second later bumped down on the table. One rolled and crashed to the floor.

"Leave it," came Paolo's surly voice. "Here, take the wine and help yourselves. We're going to settle this—*tonight*." He raised his voice, calling "Rosa! ROSA! Come in here." Footsteps. "Send that donkey home. He's got no place here tonight. OUT! And you . . ." he shouted as an afterthought. "Come right back in here."

For several minutes no one spoke. A glass tinkled against another, a match rasped along the emery paper of a matchbox, and Chichella shook her head. Pursing her lips, she turned away, far to her right, and stared at the floor, which is always a sign of a decision in the making. She shook her head again and stood up, motioning with one hand that she was going inside. When she repeated the gesture, I knew she would not be back. Curious and eager as she had been, almost dogged, in her search for details, she could not eavesdrop on the scene that had to be the denouement. I followed her, relieved for all those conventional reasons—one does not eavesdrop, read the mail of others, or borrow without asking—and too because the shouts and screams, the savage accusations, the recriminations, the brutality of those scenes leave me, the outsider, demolished. I have no stomach for them.

It was early and too hot to go to bed. Television offered little, so we gave up and sat in the kitchen, talking in a desultory way, always with the muffled shouts and exclamations from below rumbling behind us. We were both depressed. Subjects wilted almost as fast as we picked them, leaving us engulfed in the yowlings of a quarrel we could not hear well enough to understand. Paolo's voice rose in his usual, growling abuse of Lucetta and dropped, only to rise again. He would soon be drunk; in the old days that meant stumbling, crazed violence. The boys shouted him down. Over them all Rosa shrilled, unable to stop herself, "I won't! I WON'T!"

And then Lucetta screamed, shrieked really, high, piercingly over all the other voices. There was a crash of furniture and a thud, the thud without echo that only dead weight can make, followed by silence so thick that we, upstairs, could feel their surprise and fear without knowing what had caused it. Chichella propped her forehead against one hand and with the other began tracing the pattern of the oilcloth table-cover. Seconds later voices hissed accusingly. They were too quiet. Chairs scraped, but quietly too. There was a feeling of conspiracy about the unnatural hush, until Rosa wailed, "Mamma! Oh Mamma!" and burst into tears.

A few minutes later we heard steps on the stairs and our doorbell rang. Chichella answered it, coming back in a moment to say she had to go out. She was needed—urgently. For more than an hour I sat in the kitchen, reading, fighting the dizzy sleepiness that was my reaction to the return of peace, and wondering who had called her. So urgently. Lucetta? Someone else? Part of her own enormous family? About something quite different? When she let herself in, careful not to bash the door, which is the only sure way to close it, she looked tired and sad. She was surprised that I was still up, had hoped I would not be. She did not feel like talking and all she did say was,

"Lucetta had one of her fits. Those awful fights—they always do it to her. And Paolo gets scared and calls me. Ought to get scared before, not after—and I told him so just now." She shook her head. "Poor Lucetta. If they get her worked up, she goes into a fit—don't know what else to call it. Faints. Always has." She went into the bathroom, got her night clothes, and went to bed.

From what little she told me the next day, it must be some form of epilepsy. Chichella is the only nurse Lucetta will accept. She knows how to bring her around. She makes the others obey her, get what she needs. She undresses Lucetta, puts her to bed, and cleans any cuts she may have gotten in the inevitable fall. After an attack Lucetta is weak and exhausted. She stays in bed for two, sometimes three days, and when she reappears she makes no reference to what happened, not even to her nurse, Chichella. I had lived through the cycle dozens of times before, convinced that Chichella's ministrations and Lucetta's convalescences were the results of Paolo's brutality. No one had ever so much as hinted at "fits."

I did not see Lucetta again that summer, but the morning I left, she sent up a slip of paper with her address and instructions for Chichella: she must extract a promise from me that I would visit them in Offenbach.

Lucetta lives on one of those wide, bare gritty avenues in Offenbach where every structure and side street follows a strict geometric order. Each block is a square of equal area. Streets cross at right angles. Every building is four or five stories high, has the same frontage, and is connected to its neighbor by a short wall with a "carriage gate," leading into a courtyard that is never quite visible. Even the stairs up to large respectable front doors are similar and the decorative mold-ings have been worn away by time and weather, melted as though they were of soap, to uniform modesty.

Twilight comes more slowly in treeless streets, a lingering dull-ness, but in this one, so deserted, it might have been a winter dawn. We walked along, looking for our number and talking again about Rosa. After Lucetta's "fit," everyone had been careful not to upset her, so careful that in the end nothing was settled. Lucetta and Paolo had to leave for Germany. So did the boys. Rosa refused. She would not go with them. When Chichella and I left Torregreca more than a month later on our trip to Germany, Rosa and her sister were still at their posts in the monkey cage. Cold weather would soon drive them inside, but that hardly seemed an answer. Rosa thought she could come to an agreement with the boy's family, if not her own. They ignored her, and she waited, ever present, ever in sight, and I wondered, what else—ever amenable, ever obliging? As we walked along, I reminded Chichella how, the night before we left, coming into the building I had heard a man's voice in the apartment. She told me I was wrong, that there couldn't have been a man inside with them. I was not wrong, but just then we found our number and the subject was abandoned, unresolved.

Lucetta and Paolo were not among the two dozen names listed in the front vestibule. When I came out, Chichella had sauntered through the carriage gate into the courtyard and was pointing at something ahead of her. Behind the wall, in a canyon formed by the apartment buildings that rose high on all sides, was a secret neighborhood within a neighborhood. A large, squat structure with a flat roof and rows of metal doors—they must be car stalls—was a central island separated from an amphitheater of two-story buildings that surrounded it by a narrow, circular alley-street, just wide enough for cars to be maneuvered in and out of their garages. The turrets and gables of three minute houses, prisoners in this sea of vanilla cement, presented a giddy profusion of windows that was absurd and slightly pathetic in the midst of so much blankness. Italian names were tacked up next to all three doorbells, but they were not the right ones. We went on around the circle, peering into open doorways, most of which led into empty garages. The others, exactly like them, gave onto stairways that led upward into impenetrable darkness.

A full tour and we were back at the gate where we found rows of mailboxes and names. One, Franco Manzoni, was on my list. Looking for Lucetta's address, I had not noticed that his address was the same. Now, at least, we could see *them*, I told Chichella. She twitched her eyebrows at me, and I was reminded, yet again, that I try her patience. Had I forgotten that Franco is Lucetta's brother? I am not sure that I had ever known it, but never mind. We went in search of Franco.

We stumbled up stairways, strained, with the help of my lighter, to make out nameplates on the doors, and then stumbled back down again. Mazes of unlighted interior hallways dead-ended into walls. Light switches, even when I found them, produced the dimmest, far-off glow. Finally, somehow, we ended up on a peculiar catwalk, on one side a blank wall, on the other the slope of a roof that hid all below it except a wedge of daylight, blinding it seemed, and an unidentifiable section of the alley. A short flight of stairs led up to what could only be a mezzanine floor and on each step was a pot of leggy geraniums. Chichella froze, leaning toward them like a bird-dog on point. We exchanged nods. While she tiptoed up the stairs, across the landing, and stopped at each of three doors to bend over and listen, I watched, thinking how suspicious, and how silly, we would look if someone materialized suddenly from the dark. At the last door she straightened up, shouted *"Lucè! Lucè!"* and began pounding on the door, which, for reasons that were self-evident later, was opened immediately.

Lucetta, wiping her hands on her apron, looked out in disbelief. We had come! We were actually there! She called Paolo and someone named Antonietta. Look! Look who's standing on the doorstep! Paolo did exactly that, noncommittal and sullen. Lucetta urged us to come in, but thought better of the invitation and had us wait until she could move something behind the door. In the process her feet got wet. Paolo backed off, and we squeezed into a diminutive hall that doubled as a kitchen with a small sink, a two-ring burner on top of a cabinet, a dish-draining rack fixed to the wall, and all manner of things that hung from the ceiling—pots and pans, strainers, ladles—lowering it to dwarf proportions. We stepped over a large plastic tub full of clothes put to soak, the source of Lucetta's wet slippers, straight into a very small windowless room, so small in fact that a two-seat sofa, only slightly larger than a love seat, just fit against one of the longer walls with a coffee table in front of it. I would see the same table all over Germany, awkwardly high when you sat talking, too low when, covered with a cloth, it became a dinner table. Opposite the little sofa was a television set of almost equal size, guarded by two straight chairs, which barely left room for a stool, apparently Paolo's place because he retreated to it at once. Even so little furniture prohibited movement and the ceiling was too low for me to stand up straight.

On the sofa sat a little girl of seven or eight with tow hair and violet-blue eyes who stared at us, undecided between mild interest and mild irritation. A notebook was open on the table in front of her, and I could see rows of shaky letters wiggling off across the pages. She let out a very grown-up sigh, picked up her pencil, and went back to work. If we were going to pay no attention to her, she would, at least, be ready for television.

"That's a good girl, Antonietta. Dinner's almost ready," Lucetta said to her, pushing Paolo's knees aside so that she could take us into their bedroom, which, equally small, held a single bed, a chest of drawers, and one straight chair. A window at the end looked out over a roof, a stretch of perhaps ten feet before it joined another wall. To the left a glow of light was the only hint that there might be earth down below. The linoleum by the bed and in front of the chest was worn through to the floorboards. It was scrupulously neat, looked and smelled clean.

Faint praise? No. On the contrary, Lucetta performs miracles to keep what is no more than a human kennel in such order. When the girls are there (and they have been since Easter—Rosa's scheme came to nothing), the sofa is dismantled, extended, and made up as a bed every night. One puzzle I have not been able to solve is where the coffee table goes in such an arrangement. On top of the television? They rent a room for the boys along one of the nearby corridors. Paolo and Lucetta sleep in the bedroom on the single bed, something I have rarely seen. Even in the poorest households, the judicious arrangement of planks and supports usually provides more room. (I said that to Chichella, and she was not impressed. "They did it before—we've all slept that way when we were really poor. Head to foot's not so bad unless you're a restless sleeper" was her comment. She knows better than I.) When I asked for the bathroom, Lucetta was embarrassed. She began apologizing and then maybe she remembered how many houses I had seen in my life without water or plumbing of any kind. It was a closet, more the shape for brooms than human beings, just off the "kitchen," which in this case meant right beyond the two gas burners. A toilet and a basin the size of a chamber pot, plus all the cleaning equipment and the door, made for a lot of squirming and sidling and ducking mop handles that snapped away from the wall aimed at my head, but there was running water, which is more than we can be sure of in Torregreca. In such tight quarters where four people sleep, "take care of their bodily functions," as the euphemism has it, bathe(?), sponge(?), argue, and in theory live, Lucetta also gives six adults breakfast and dinner and manages by what legerdemain I will never know to wash, dry, and iron their clothes as well. That it was scrupulously neat, looked and smelled clean—under those circumstances—is *not* faint praise.

I was consigned to Paolo and Antonietta. They were to amuse me while Chichella and Lucetta fussed and gossiped just beyond us in the "kitchen." Lucetta dithered because there was *past'e ceci* (macaroni and chick-peas). She would send out for meat. Chichella hissed back at her, insisting that I did not care about meat, that if there were any changes, I would leave that she was not to worry. It was all quite audible, but we pretended it was not. Paolo, a figure of dejection with his elbows on his knees, sat slumped over, staring at me. His face was pale, his eyes watery and opaque, and deep grooves ran from his cheekbones to his chin, leaving folds of skin to wobble at the slightest movement of his head. What I had taken for his habitual surliness was, instead, exhaustion and defeat. Suddenly he was an old man. We started the only way we could: how many years had it been . . . ? When I asked how Germany had treated him, he looked at me for a long time before he answered.

"*Così.*" He waved, his arm stretched out to indicate the apartment. "You've seen for yourself. Why ask?" I had also seen the garage in Torregreca, the addition they were building. That too had come from his years in Germany. He nodded. The boys were working. They had professions. "And we can go to our graves knowing that, at least. Do you think that's enough?" He expected no answer to his question, which bitter as it sounds, was asked with resignation.

[*216*]

He went on almost immediately. "We have one bottle of beer in the house. That's my nightly ration. Would you share it with me now or later—with dinner?"

"Whichever you prefer." Before he could stand up, Lucetta handed the bottle and two glasses around the corner.

With the beer talking seemed easier for him. He remembered that first year in Germany, so long ago now, when he had worked under contract in a factory and lived in the factory barracks. That was the worst year. The loneliest, away from home. He was still young then, had *needs*—did I understand? Not so strange. Instead, alone, he was a slave in a foreign country, almost imprisoned. A slave. A slave! Slavery would be his ritornello through every conversation we had. Bitterness and exhaustion had left only that in his mind. He had worked in factories—it made no difference what kind—he was always a laborer. Wherever he was, he did the heavy work. Some years, when the weather was good, he had been able to stick to construction. At least he was outside. The Torresi must work, but they are happier outside. They understand that better, he insisted, away from the fumes and the noise and those glaring lights. They can breathe. Then there had been years when the only places were in factories—that was his slavery. He had even been a night-watchman. He hated that, alone and cold, but the pay was good. Days upside down and lonely. And now? What was he doing now? Nothing, signora. Sitting at home, enjoying unemployment benefits. *Enjoying!* He sneered, looking around the little room. Antonietta came in after school in the afternoons to keep him company. They did her homework together—that was his enjoyment. He smiled at the little girl with a sweetness that was touching because it was so tentative. She did not look up. Realizing that I did not understand, he explained that he had returned in the fall to be told he was no longer needed. His job did not exist. Some jobs he'd quit, some, he'd lost. This one he'd liked, planned to keep it until he left for good. They didn't need him. No fault of his, so he was on full unemployment. He would wait. In the spring he'd look for work. That way his arthritis ... It wouldn't make any difference to his pension. No, he would *enjoy* the winter at home. Spring was soon enough.

He turned the television set on for the news. Antonietta interpreted for me. Politics were not her strongest subject, but the weather and such simpler matters were given to me in clear, cantering Italian. Like Paolo's. He had not spoken dialect, nor did Lucetta. They too had converted to that improvised Italian *all'estero*, and I had not noticed. Antonietta wanted to show me her homework. She went to a school where some of her classes were taught in Italian, some in German. Her mother said she must learn Italian, to *write* it, but she liked the German classes better. She had a nice teacher. Perhaps she did not know it, but soon all of her classes would be in German. She looked at me very carefully, seriously, deciding for herself whether I could be right, and then smiled. She liked her German teacher.

Lucetta ducked around the partition with a tablecloth, napkins, and silver. Domenico would be home any minute now. On cue the door opened, but instead of her son, a tall, blond woman with blunt features, especially her nose, which was large and also humped, stuck her head inside, announcing that she was back. When she saw me, she stopped, turned to look at Lucetta questioningly, and finally convinced, came and threw her arms around me.

Twenty years have added a few dry, shallow lines to Anna's face, nothing more. She could be the bride I first met on a house visit with the housing committee of the town council. For one entire summer every Sunday morning we went from house to house, working our way through the list of families who had applied for the new houses in the "Villaggio." To qualify they had to be *nullatenènte*, that is, owners of nothing and therefore poor, and live in unsanitary conditions. And probably, if they were to have any hope, they had to "know" someone of influence: my best efforts never frustrated the system. Anna had only been married a few months and lived in a small house without running water or plumbing—a room and a half, the only window naturally in the back half-room—which she shared with her mother and father-in-law, two brothers-in-law, and of course her husband. She and Franco had applied. They qualified in every way and were what I wanted most in the "Villaggio"—young, active, willing to change, and not yet burdened with too many children. (That they had *none* was against them.) I doubt that I effected their assignment of a house, but I was delighted when their names were on the official list.

Eventually her first child, a boy, came to the nursery, and I found that Anna was as energetic as I had guessed. She was always better dressed than the other women, in simple clothes that I would see her buying from the secondhand dealer who came to the market. She had a sense of what suited her and she never deluded herself that she could wear a dress two sizes too small. More important she was not afraid of work, nor was she afraid of complaining against injustice or suggesting changes, and the women listened to her. She was a social worker's dream: a woman who was still convinced that the system could function, could be forced to function. If bureaucrats only understood threats, she would threaten. If more effort, more responsibility were required of her, she was willing to do her part and she was willing to urge on others: for her nothing was yet impossible. But Franco did not have enough work and so we lost them to Germany. It is said that the best emigrate, the most skilled, the most energetic. I do not entirely agree. In spite of the implications of timidity, to stay and fight takes courage. To stay and wait, complaining, takes none. To leave and go where work is guaranteed? Courage, yes and no. Still, we lost Anna and Franco.

It was natural for me to wonder what she would be like now had she stayed. Also futile, for here she was, almost elegant in a well-made skirt and sweater, busy, just back from work, about to collect her child and cook dinner for Franco. Antonietta wanted to stay with us. No, Anna was patient but firm. She must leave us in peace. Later, when we had all eaten, we would come to their house for coffee, and Antonietta could talk to us again. Yes, said Anna, beginning to collect notebook, pencil, and books, she could stay up— just this once. Still not satisfied, the little girl insisted on showing her mother the grades on yesterday's work. Together they looked over the corrections very carefully, agreed that, *tutto sommato*, she had done quite well, but tonight she would get everything right. Antonietta bobbled her head up and down, smiling a benediction on us all, and conceded that she was ready to leave, if her mother promised . . .

They met Domenico in the doorway, causing a traffic jam of tragicomic proportions which ended with his left foot in the tub of soaking laundry. He went off to change his shoes. When he came back it was evident from the grease smudges and grimy hands that he had done nothing else. And he still wore the overalls that any other mechanic, following an unwritten rule of the brotherhood, would have shed at the garage. After working hours to be seen in the streets wearing the uniform of your trade is not done, a professional nicety that had escaped Domenico. Droop-seated and stiff with the usual muck of garages, his were hardly dashing. They hung on his long, disjointed frame and crackled noisily with each step he took. Unconcerned, he flopped down beside me. If the great shock of fine dark hair were ever combed out of his face, he might be quite handsome. His features are small and even. I will never know what color his eyes are, or for that matter, what interests him. Those questions he understands, he answers in monosyllables, and so by offensive persistence I learned that he was not yet a mechanic, but an apprentice, following the trade course. He had been promised a job at the garage where he goes half-days for practical training. "A mechanic can always find work" was the only statement he volunteered and of dubious wisdom. When I asked if he looked forward to going home to the much-discussed family garage, his answer was in character. "*Indifferente.*"

Bruno, the other mechanic son, must, I decided, be more forceful, more enthusiastic, but when, later that evening at Anna's, I met him again, I was not sure. The little boy in the undershirt and nothing else who spent the warm days of my first summers in Torregreca swinging on the front door and crying, had grown into a lanky man, not unlike his brother, Domenico, but much cleaner and more alert. He came shaved, combed, and dressed in immaculate, natty clothes, bringing his wife and little boy to see us. Lucetta had complained at length about the girl who had, as far as I could tell, nothing against her except that she was exceedingly pretty and was from a large town that is Torregreca's traditional enemy. She and Bruno met and fell in love in Germany. Neither family would consider their marriage. In contrast to Rosa's dilemma (and I wondered what her brother's position was in those arguments), Bruno's was never dignified by discussion. It was dismissed. Rebellion is not in Bruno's nature: it may be in his wife's. But he did find the nerve to run away with her. They had each gone home for the summer visit, and then one night simply disappeared. For a month no one knew where they were. Endless times the two families, determined to loathe each other, met and argued and catalogued heinous sins and charged negligence, until worry and exhaustion forced them to admit that nothing mattered if the children were safe. Bruno's character soundings were accurate. Several days after rage had fizzled to anxiety, he steamed into town with a new car and his bride. They must accept a fait accompli, he warned them, and they do in a truce as volatile as any in the Middle East. All bravery expended, he has lapsed back into the life planned for him by Lucetta. As far as the garage is concerned, he could go back or stay in Germany. It was all the same to him. Either way he had work. And his wife? I asked. Oh, she doesn't want to live in Torregreca. He didn't blame her. Every day she'd have to answer to his mother and nodding toward Lucetta, he added, She's hard to fight. "Ma's way is the only right way. Always has been."

Lucetta's admission that her children are "not good in school" seemed engagingly honest. Given Domenico's phlegm, not to say dullness, and Bruno's docile indifference, it may be another self-deception, a mother's legitimate defense. She has made her investment. It may or may not be sound. Only time will tell.

Domenico was impatient for his dinner. He shouted that he was hungry until bowls of *past'e ceci* and a plate of bread began arriving at the table by a modified bucket brigade from Lucetta to Chichella to Paolo to us. Finally Lucetta could leave the kitchen. Depression is infectious. Her natural exuberance would rescue me from the slag of discarded subjects. Or so I hoped, and she did not fail me.

How did I like *her* Germany? Offenbach? Had I seen the new shopping plaza? *Bella*, no? And her luminous eyes widened. Anna works there, or really, near there. She's a salesclerk in a department store. (Again!) Pride won easily over the slightest twinge of envy.

Her German's that good. She tried to get me in there too, but my German . . . no, not even my German. I can't read and write. That's the trouble. When I was little, girls didn't go to school. Eh, Chichella? They sent us to the fields or left the babies with us. So I'm what they call "analphabetic." (Her pronunciation was almost correct.) We wangled a trial for me just the same, and I've been there ever since. Not in the store. In the central place where the merchandise arrives and then gets shipped out to the stores.

Lucetta did not know the name of her job in Italian, only in German, but she could describe it in every detail: she is an inventory clerk, by her own confession an illiterate inventory clerk with a trick mental mechanism for numbers. They have always made sense to her. She recognizes whole series at a glance, seems to have an instinct for what is missing, and can transcribe the numbers quickly without error onto the forms she must file. Being illiterate is an advantage because nothing distracts her—not the name of the item or the color or anything else on the box. The words mean nothing, and that gives her a special skill. She has had regular raises. It is a good job.

"Anna's is better," Paolo grunted, generous as always with praise.

"My discount's the same," she snapped. "I get all our clothes cheap, don't I?" Chichella rushed in to describe the white batiste curtains with the embroidered border, still her favorite purchase from Lahr, then veered off to the exorbitant prices in Germany. Once more I blessed her quick wits. Dinner limped on to its logical end. Paolo's gloom, especially because it was not directed at any specific person or event, was more than our determined, slightly strained animation could penetrate. By the time we attacked the problem of how to divide three apples five ways, only Lucetta was trying and for her pains was informed that he would not go with us to Anna and Franco's. He wanted to cause trouble. He wanted attention. He succeeded in both and upset Lucetta so effectively that I began to fear another "fit." Chichella listened with her eyes lowered, apparently looking at the tablecloth that she pleated with a blunt thumb and forefinger, but actually watching Lucetta very closely. She too was worried. She must have sensed some further degeneration. Before it could happen, she interrupted.

[*222*]

"Tell you what, Paolo. I'll stay here with you. Always had sort of a weakness for you, but—of course—twenty years ... Maybe you've changed." After ten minutes of this elephantine flirtatiousness, Paolo had a silly, flushed grin on his face and had decided that, since Chichella must go to Franco's or be rude, he would come too.

Down dark stairways, into the alley, along the garage island for fifty feet, and up another dark stairway we trooped in silence. Before we reached the top, a door opened and the steps were mercifully flooded with light. Franco called out to us cheerfully. We were to hurry. He had already been cheated because we had not had dinner with them. Hurry! He handed me into an unexpected lushness of heavy pile carpet (wall-to-wall), indirect lighting, velvet upholstery, and pictures, reproductions of seascapes, on the walls. The others, arriving behind me, pushed me along a hall, past two small bedrooms and on into a large living room, another acre of deep beige carpet, where an extravagantly long, soft couch, again beige, but darker, tending toward cinnamon, and its inevitable partner in tandem, an equally long, black oak coffee table, dominated the room without in any way crowding it. Two wing chairs, several bergère chairs, a footstool, and a gaggle of end tables, each with its own mushroom growth of figurines, its own tall brass lamp and shade, had been scattered around in convenient combinations that still left great expanses of rug between neighbors. Everything that was not upholstered was black oak, spooled, knobbed, and carved into a modern synthesis of styles that may be Jacobean Biedermeier. At the end of the room was a short wall of windows disguised in billows of white batiste and side draperies and looping swags of heavy beige-and-blue-striped material. To complete the tally of what every living room must have, a small fireplace, opposite the couch, was faced in strips of polished marble and hedged about with brass rails and brass fire tools. It was also suspiciously clean, a decorative element, I decided, not a source of heat.

Stunned by the opulence of it all or the contrast with Lucetta's house, or both, I was discovered by Anna, still at the door, gaping. For the moment my mind was numbed by the contradictions, and my sincere compliments were confused mumbles. In her pride and enthusiasm Anna probably did not notice. She led me away to their bedroom, a large room with the same feeling of rugs, upholstery, and invisible lights glowing on the ceiling, all garnished with black oak, and then on to her masterpiece, the kitchen, where Antonietta was rather peevishly finishing her homework. Every conceivable modern appliance was there, hidden behind baffles in their own wall niches. The cupboards and counters of brown Formica with black-brown trim could have been the furniture for a library. In an alcove, which was almost a separate room, a large table of wrought iron and glass, surrounded by white iron chairs, was used for meals, for Antonietta's homework, and, I could imagine, dozens of other family activities. It was the real sitting room. The bathroom was large and equally well equipped. The children's bedrooms were small, Antonietta's with white painted furniture, Carlo's with sturdy pine and a bedspread and curtains of dark, determinedly masculine plaid.

By the time we arrived back in the living room Lucetta was conducting Chichella through to the kitchen. Paolo had slumped into a chair in a corner, and Carlo had appeared from somewhere. Gawky as most boys at seventeen, he was embarrassed by his parents' insistence that he must remember me. Truth was, he did not. Why should he? He could not have been four the last time he saw me, but still he blushed. He is blond, like his mother, and unfortunately has her nose without quite enough chin to counteract it, and is shy. He stayed all evening, listening intently, never saying a word unless a question was so directly aimed at him that he could not avoid it. He is training to be a bookkeeper and does not want to go back to Torregreca—ever. Franco smiled patiently at that and whispered in my ear that Carlo would leave if his mother left. If she was gone, he wouldn't last a week.

Franco is a hard man to describe, probably because he is handsome in the conventional, wartless, homogenized sense. Tall, strongly built without being fat, he has curly brown hair and features so carefully balanced that they are neither heavy nor frail. Working outside—he is a mason—has weathered his face to a perpetual tan that accentuates very blue eyes. They shine with intelligence, but above all his manner has an easy courtesy and humor about it. That was the quality I remembered from years ago and did not quite believe, and is now again, after our recent meetings, what stays in my mind. By some metamorphosis he wraps you in his grace and wit, convincing you of your own. He approached that evening with a gaiety that even Paolo could not distort. He reminded us of so much that we had forgotten about those past years. He wanted to know about everyone in Torregreca. It seemed he had forgotten no one. When he heard that we were staying at a hotel, he threatened to send Carlo to move us out—that minute, that very night. We must stay with them. He teased Chichella. He teased us all. No one was safe from his teasing or his memory. And at times he was very, very serious.

He has been with the same contractor for years and has no fear about his work. He is safe and intends to be safe. He is forty now and by his own estimate will have to stay in Germany another fifteen years. The children's future is the unknown. He knows no way to plan it. He himself was given none. To have guaranteed his own is already an accomplishment, but like any parent, he would give them more. Not in the South. He sees no future there, nor really in Italy. His children are in every true sense German, or will be, and yet he dreads the idea that, as he was in Southern Italy, so they, in Germany, will be tolerated as second-class citizens and not even citizens at that. He is bitter about many things, most especially Italy . . . but never mind. He did not want to talk about that. They were problems, like the rocks familiar to every mason, that refuse to crack no matter how stubbornly they are attacked with a hammer and chisel: the only answer is to smash away at them until they do.

If he could not reorder the world just then, that evening, he could at least enjoy what he had. Did I like his house? He was proud of it, of the way they had put it together, of its comfort. Anna. It was Anna who saw so much at the store and came home with ideas. For instance the windows. Did I realize that there were only *two* windows in the apartment? One in their bedroom and one in the kitchen. He took me on another inspection trip, this time a technical one. To give a sense of light during the day he had installed moldings that hid the actual bulbs and also muted them. The general glow was explained. He showed me the two windows, neither large. To air the apartment, the front door was left blocked open for long periods in the morning and evening. And the living room, I asked. What about those windows? Without making any fuss that the others would notice, he led me over to the curtains, showed me the layers, white batiste, beige and blue stripes, the swags—and underneath—a blank wall. All an idea of Anna's when she worked in the curtain department. She had him come to the store and see for himself. It was true: those curtain displays against a wall just as blank looked real. And so they "installed" their windows. And the fireplace. That had been his variation on Anna's scheme. He had chiseled his hole to a size he felt suited the room. He plastered it and then ordered the lengths of polished marble and put them up as decorative surrounds. The house was a series of tricks. What else could he do? Live in a dark, windowless cave? I thought of Lucetta's human kennel.

Franco and Anna have invented a place to live. It amounts to that. They have more room in which to do it, but ... The rent for all that extra room—in a city—must be ... Speculations, and for that evening I expected them to be nothing more, reeled through my head. Turning away from the "windows" with Franco, I noticed that Paolo had vanished. He had said nothing to the others. They had not seen him slip out and agreed that our good-humored chattering and reminiscences had probably driven him away. Bruno volunteered to find him and keep him company. Franco tried to discourage him.

"He's just sour, a *guastafesta*—a killjoy. Every time he comes here, it's like this. He ..." Lucetta interrupted quite good-naturedly, caught between automatic loyalty to her husband and affection for, perhaps agreement with, her brother.

"Be patient with him. He can't help it." She threw back her head and frowned at Franco. "Besides you know he doesn't approve, and then—when he's here—well, he's human. I suppose envy gets him. Not that he says much to me about it. So many other things ..."

"What does he disapprove of?" I asked with no real curiosity.

Paolo is so ready to criticize that only enthusiastic approval would have startled me.

"The house..." Lucetta began.

"We have different ideas, that's all." Franco took over from her. "*He* says save every pfennig. Never have anything nice. Don't buy anything you could possibly do without—not an ice cream cone, not a bottle of beer. Squeeze every pfennig. Take it home with you and live a happy old age. Now, *I* say—" Anna shifted in her chair, and he stopped to glance at her. She smiled encouragement, but was not inclined to quarrel with her sister-in-law. Such disputes were best left to blood relatives. "We—Anna and I—say '*Va bene.*' We have to work here, live away from home, but we still belong to the human race. We earn the money. We have a right to a decent house and the nicest furniture we can afford. Some decent clothes. *Now.* Not when we're sixty and don't care. Eh, Lucè? Eh? Eh?" He lifted his shoulders in exasperated reasonableness. Could she disagree? Lucetta sat rigid, staring at him, but would not take the bait. Finally Franco gave in, shrugging. "All right, you believe in your life hereafter, and *I'll* hope you're right, but I'll take some of mine right *now.*"

"You won't have anything to give your children. That's what Paolo thinks. You're cheating them." In spite of herself Lucetta was riled. Two bright spots of color showed on her cheekbones. "I used to think that way too—make it now, spend it now. Not anymore. A few sacrifices now and you'll be safe. Your children will be safe...."

"For God's sake, *twenty* years of sacrifices, just to go back to Torregreca and live in the *Case Popolari*—with a pension! What did *you* get out of that kind of life?" Franco sneered at her. "And I'm cheating my children. They're having the best I can give them *now.* A comfortable house and clothes they don't have to be ashamed of and good food and schooling. *Per l'amor di Dio.*" He broke off and stared at her. Her eyes were lowered and she refused to look up. "Life doesn't begin at *sixty*—and *not* in Torregreca!" Anna jumped up to offer us another liqueur from the ranks of bottles that were lined up on the coffee table, and I started asking very practical questions about rents. Between us we shut off the argument, and both

Franco and Lucetta were so eager to explain the true situation, as they saw it, that they soon forgot to carp at each other.

Paolo and Lucetta's rent is $80 a month. How much the four children living with them contribute to expenses and the garage investment I do not know. They do not, in the traditional way, hand over their pay envelopes. Making allowances for the variables (Paolo working versus Paolo drawing unemployment, Domenico's token salary, which he keeps, the waiter-son's tips, et cetera) between their own earnings and what the children probably cede to them, Paolo and Lucetta will have each month at least $1,500. Franco and Anna's monthly income is almost identical. (As a highly skilled worker with a trade and a long history of employment by the same firm, Franco earns more than Paolo and his sons. Anna's salary is higher than Lucetta's.) With two children who do not work, they, of course, have expenses the other family has eliminated. They also pay double the rent for their extra space and still save what seems a fortune to them.

"Almost a million five hundred thousand lire—*a month*! A million and a half!" Franco repeated in wonder at their riches, and then paused, half muttering rapid, gleeful calculations before he announced triumphantly, "That's between two and three times what I could make a month at home—assuming, *assuming* I had work. *Santo Dio*, a million and a half is more than a lot of people have in a year down there." He was right. In Lucania the average income per year is lower than that, but, of course, the South enjoys the highest unemployment in the country (some estimate a dizzy 48 percent of the active population) which has a house-of-mirrors effect on per capita figures: some look leaner, others fatter, no one is himself. Still, as an explanation, if one is needed, for why 70 percent of Italian emigrants are Southern, nothing else is so immediate.

"And you think I can't live decently *and* save on a million and a half *a month*," Franco went on, the old belligerent tone returning. "Even with the prices here, even with our rent? Don't forget, we don't go racing back home every year—with a fleet of cars—to show off. Don't have to. We can stay right here and be comfortable. I can't save? You're *mad!* Oh Lucetta, Lucetta, life doesn't begin at sixty in the *Case Popolari*—not even in Torregreca. It ends there!"

This same discussion would be repeated from Freiburg to Gelsenkirchen, from Düsseldorf to Stuttgart and in Milan and Turin as well. It is the common dilemma of emigrants. Two solutions are available: scrimp on life and save every coin, no matter how small, or spend moderately, enjoy a better place to live, some comfort, and save. Neither way is irrefutably right. Whichever is chosen, the principle of saving is sacrosanct.

Men who have left their families at home and live either in company barracks or in some communal quarters with other lone immigrants, spend less for a variety of logical reasons. Temptations and amusements are few and that distant family that they never quite forget needs every pfennig. The permutations are infinite. The Minister Counselor for Social Affairs and Immigration of the Italian embassy in Bonn, Dr. Francesco Pulcini, told me of a journalist friend who called him, outraged by the living conditions of four construction workers he had found in a trailer at the edge of a large building site. They had no water, no sewer attachment. The trailer, crowded to bursting with the four men, was no better than a pup tent against the German winter. To pacify him Dr. Pulcini promised to go out and see the men and do whatever he could for them. He found exactly what he had expected. The men were well paid and as a bonus had been offered free housing. That it turned out to be a trailer was not cause for jubilation. No Italian likes "temporary" housing: masonry is his guarantee of protection, but—it was free. They kept it in order, as much as suited them. They used the toilets and water at the site. They begged Dr. Pulcini, implored him not to cause trouble with the contractor. He could be forced to find other quarters for them, but they would have to *pay*. They were content as they were.

People complain that such men live like pigs. They seem to think, though heaven forbid that they should ever say so directly, that the men *prefer* to live like pigs, that they know nothing else, and are, when you come right down to it, human pigs. We forget man's greed, his monkey ability to imitate what he sees. And we forget that no matter where he lives or how, television has shown him the prosperous, to him gilded, standards of the outside world. Those men do not live in rat-infested warehouses, in the attics over horse stalls, in company barracks or cold water flats by choice. They live there because it is expedient: they can save, and they save so that they will never again live like pigs at home.

Everyone saves against the future. These days the fashion among social scientists is to deplore the immigrant's use of his savings. The new axioms have it that he will invest first in a house, one that he builds himself stone by stone on his vacations and never quite finishes. Second, he will buy durable goods—iceboxes, television sets, record or tape players, and even cars. Third and most devastating, he will not return brimming with a desire to spend his money in setting up a small manufacturing business, a cooperative, perhaps, that would benefit him and all the people of his village. He feels no obligation to import the techniques he has seen at work in other countries, no responsibility to improve the lot of his friends, while, of course, continuing to profit himself. To me the criticism is based on very faulty logic, the logic of detached men who have used villages as material for study without recognizing or sensing or having their noses rubbed in the vicious estrangements of a two-class, a Them-and-us society. The emigrant remembers the malice of his neighbors and his betters and the treacherous betrayals of both. He has learned how to sidestep them, but not how to run a business. Now, suddenly, we expect him to embrace strange, sophisticated notions of investment, of common good. We expect him to become an entrepreneur for the betterment of society. He is to be an altruist. But he knows and has always known that altruism is a trap for fools and that such an investment would be tantamount to issuing invitations to a swindle. Society did not look after him, help him. It is immune to change, but if betterment is the cry, let it better itself. *He* has ensured *his* future—I'm all right, Jack, is the philosophy, and it ends there. Any insinuation that the concept is socially immoral would be greeted with the sneer that such sanctimonious preaching of the well-heeled deserves, and labeled naïve.*

---

* One of the patterns of peasant communism, interesting to sociologists, frustrating to party organizers, is related. As soon as a peasant who has owned nothing and was rabidly in favor of common possession manages to buy a small house, a few head of cattle, a scooter per-

For the Turks, Yugoslavs, Greeks, and Spaniards, the axiom about houses may be an exact fit. For the Torresi and many other Southern emigrants it is not. Italy never quite conforms, not even in its poverty and backwardness, but why should it? It is an improvised country, created 110 years ago by amalgamating regions of such incompatible history, geography, and temperament that they shared only one common conviction: each felt all the others were out to plunder its riches. The last war left it a country of rubble and restless, hungry people and more ungovernable than ever, though a strong Communist party wanted to try. The democratic politicians set out with a great deal of foreign advice and foreign money (mostly American) to slay the red dragon. No one had a plan. No one ever does about Italy. It defies the most determined reformers, positively gobbles earnest Anglo-Saxons. They temporized. A whole fruit punch of public works seemed just the aperitivo to cheer everyone. What was to have been a pick-me-up turned into a thirty-year binge with all the stages of drunkenness—the euphoria of bogus prosperity, the reeling of more-is-better, and now the remorse and near bankruptcy of the hangover. Along with roads, dams, land reclamation, rainwater control, industrial infrastructures, and more roads—only poverty will save Italy from coast-to-coast asphalt—came public housing, and in dozens of different categories that converted the hunt for a free house into a game of bingo: houses for the poor, for "refugees" (Italians) displaced from one village to the next, for families of men lost in Libya, Russia, or just down at the end of the lane, for victims of natural disasters, which are as seasonal in Italy as the greengrocer's wares, for insured workmen, for government employees from janitors to senators, et cetera. A simple application of the law of averages means that many emigrants have these new houses and would not be inclined to build others.

Often the Torresi qualified on several counts and so gradually

---

haps, or a small piece of land, he suffers an acute reversal of enthusiasm. Sharing does not appeal to him. What is his, is his. With each step toward prosperity he is more possessive. Somehow sharing is not a human instinct. It can be learned. Mutual advantage stimulates it, but man is more prone to attacks of high blood pressure than to attacks of spontaneous sharing.

four- and five-story buildings popped up like concrete asparagus stalks on the hillside opposite town. New and old stand squared off, facing each other, ready for war.

Men who emigrate from the old town usually own their one- or two-room houses, however embryonic, and they do spend some of their first savings to improve them with new roofs, an outside coat of plaster, doomed in the mixing to peel off with the first fall rains, and inside, highly polished marble chip floors. Later, if they feel extravagant, they can invest in an attachment to the sewers and so finally acquire the coveted inside toilet. They have television sets. Iceboxes are only moderately appealing, though new stoves, real ones with ovens, sops to their wives, appear sooner or later.

The men from the new town have fewer longings to satisfy. They can tile their bathrooms and kitchens. To change the floors or put in central heating would be a bit outré. When they come back for good, they will buy overstuffed plastic leather couches and arm-chairs and dining-room suites similar in style to Franco's Jacobean Biedermeier. Having started out behind, as certified poor, orphaned, or refugeed, they now seem to be way ahead.

They *seem* to be. They have, for due cause, lived in govern-ment-built apartments, paying low rents, parts of which are credited to their eventual purchase. I know of no one assigned a house who has ever been evicted. A threat by official notice is enough to send the most blatant nonpayer of rent rushing to the post office with a money order. At the end of a specified "rent/buy" period, most often twenty-five years, the housing authority establishes the residue owed, using a formula so complex that its own accountants have been known to lose their way. Every possible factor is taken into consideration: the past, present, and future construction costs per square meter; devaluation of the lira; compound interest on the rents as paid; replacement value and local land prices. From this maze comes a figure, seldom exaggerated, which can be paid in install-ments over a reasonable time. Even a pad of printed money-order forms is supplied for the purpose. When the last has been canceled by the post office, the apartment changes hands to become the sole property of the tenant.

That one constant has been the anchor of many emigrants' careers. They have homes, physical places to go back to: they are not adrift. They continue to pay their rents, their light and water bills, and use the apartment when they can—at Christmas, in August. Some emigrants have settled permanently in Northern Italy. Their children have married there. They will not be coming back, but they too still pay their rates. If they can, they sublet. As soon as they have title to their apartments, they plan to sell. With every dip of the lira their expectations soar. Call it an unconventional savings system or outright speculation, they are the exceptions. For most emigrants, their houses are the sine qua nons of the future they have worked so hard to build.

Now even that security has exploded under them. In the spring of 1977 *l'Istituto Autonomo per le Case Popolari*, which has become the administrative octopus of the housing field, sent out notices warning that any house left untenanted for more than three months by its legal assignee would be confiscated, and presumably reassigned. No one knows whether this threat is aimed at the illegal sublessors—if so, why not say just that?—or at all families who are absent. Requests for clarification have not been answered, but the effects are already evident. In the "Villaggio" alone, out of thirty-two families, fifteen emigrated. Seven have already sacrificed the person with the least profitable job and sent him home to house-sit (in this case the units *are* double houses rather than apartments). A wife who washed dishes in a Düsseldorf restaurant, a husband with his pension who had planned to stay in Rivoli three more years until his wife had hers, an old grandmother, a man on unemployment, who, of course, now will not be able to find work, a daughter about to be married, and others have come back to wait, to frustrate the *Istituto*, and claim what they were promised would be theirs.

They have paid for those houses with their savings. Whatever else they do, whichever way they take—the scrimp-every-coin or the enjoy-a-bit-of-it-now—they save. That money is their future. For them it can never be "adventure capital." But capital it is. In nine years, between 1968 and 1976, Italian emigrants sent home more than $2.6 billion from Germany alone,[8] an average of just under $300 million a year. Those are the official figures of money imported through banks, exchanges, and post-office money orders. No one knows, no one will ever know how much money passed through the borders with emigrants returning to Italy for Christmas or a summer holiday. I know that when Chichella and I came back from Germany, she brought a million lire for her friends. In one case, Michele's, the money was to cover the current expenses of his two daughters still in Torregreca. The rest was to be deposited in various banks, postal savings accounts, and trunks. For years at Chichella's I have slept in a bed wedged between two trunks that are known jokingly in the family as the Bank of Italy and the Bank of Naples. They contain the conventional supply of extra sheets and blankets, some of her daughters' trousseau linens, *and* the bankbooks, cash savings, and rent receipts of her huge family. She is everyone's accountant. People unknown to me, and often even to her, knock on the door, mutter that they have just come from Germany and "Vincenzo sent this," or "Michele said you'd know what to do with this." And another envelope of lire has arrived to be stored in a trunk. If official remittances are $2.6 billion, the courier system may have brought in an equal amount.

To me, this, rather than the misanthropy of the returned emigrant, is the tragedy. Paolo and Lucetta, Franco and Anna, Gaetano and Bianca, Michele and Edda have sent their money home for twelve, fifteen, seventeen years, their savings. Hundreds of thousands of others have done the same. If it comes through official channels, the Italian government is delighted. In the thirteen years before the recession of 1973 the remittances of emigrants were never less than 5 percent of the Italian deficit of payments (one glorious year they were 8 percent). In 1978, after the chaos of energy costs and exchange rates, they amounted to 23 percent of the Italian deficit of payments, and it is all money that will be spent sooner or later in towns withering into oblivion for lack of money to prime their feeble commercial structures. If the money arrives with the potatoes and other presents from Germany or by private courier, it has been changed from marks to lire in Germany, relieving the German banks of the erratic lire they find so suspect. They are happy.

The tragedy is that Paolo and Lucetta and all the others who have been so carefully, furtively clever and exported their savings from a country they neither understand nor trust have cheated themselves. During the last ten years when their earnings were highest and the German mark was Europe's strongest currency, Italy (or her politicians for her) indulged in the sort of fiscal saturnalia that brought the annual increase in the cost of living to a steady 18 percent and lowered the value of the lira by more than one third. Had Lucetta and the others left their marks in a German bank, or stored them in the trunk that pretends to be part of the bedroom furniture, they would be rich today. Instead their lire are quietly inflating, evaporating where the emigrants know they are safe—in Torregreca.

There is no way to discuss it with them. I tried and watched their faces go blank with suspicion. They know me. They must know that their financial arrangements do not affect me. I would neither gain nor lose by them, but they might still salvage the money they will earn in the next few years, and yet—I was tampering with the rest of their lives and they were instantly, instinctively wary. Through the centuries they have always been the wards of *Chi Commanda* (Whoever Rules) and the victims. They despise their own government and the politicians who manipulate it. Still, faced with a choice, they chose the known evil and were duped again. They will work a little harder, a little longer, and save some more. Saving is their only future.

Cities! What can one say about them that is valid when each person concocts his own from fragments and improvises to make them serve his own purpose? A few of those fragments perceived may be common to most—as the train station is for emigrants—but no two arrangements of the rest will ever be the same. The Turin of the opera house, the graceful arcades where well-dressed, complacent couples saunter, stopping to gaze in the windows of elegant shops, or have coffee with friends, the Royal Palace and the parks that I knew, is now lost under the layers of a dozen other Turins, the cities the emigrants know: long gray reaches of gloomy avenues; dark, crumbling apartments studded with incongruous peepholes of Victorian stained glass; the towering marble corridors of the old General Hospital, which, for all its age, is surprisingly clean and efficient; the babbling chaos of the Saturday market at Porta Palazzo, a deplored Southern addition to the city, where everything from salad greens to new antiques and stolen cars can be purchased, if you find what you want before your pocket is picked; the endless, endless miles of bus and tram routes that decant people into the satellite towns; the

Piazza of Rivoli, on a sunny Sunday morning, divided in half, a no-man's-land in the middle, by two distinct, hostile groups of men, Southerners on one side, Northerners on the other, their backs turned—the suspicion, the distrust, the bleakness of exile, even if by some whim of fortune it is prosperous exile, and it seldom is.

Each of my Torresi has his own Turin, as each has his own Düsseldorf, Offenbach, or Gelsenkirchen. They do not cling together in cities. Quite the contrary, they prefer *not* to know where the others live, and if they do know by chance, are intentionally vague about them: Didn't they give up and go home? or Someone said they moved to Milan after Christmas. If they are trapped by their own absentmindedness and actually meet face to face on the street, they exchange bits of inflated information and promises to get together that neither thinks of as more than one of the rites of escape. Fathers and mothers see their grown children who have married, but they do not see their own brothers and sisters. (Lucetta and Franco are not exceptions. Only courtesy to me brought the two families together. The animosities are too raw. The evening was not repeated.) Cousins seldom mix. No one wants to know who has work and who does not. Bad news calls for sympathy and the expenditure of time and money they cannot afford and now begrudge. Good news from others depresses, is too blunt a reminder of failures which, whatever the cost in lies and misunderstandings, must be kept secret. They have reached a tacit agreement, a sort of social quitclaim: no obligations will be honored, no information exchanged, no judgments accepted. This new life is too precarious to survive the treachery of old debts and old resentments. They never trusted their friends. Relatives are no better. *Invidia* is the poison, they say, the key to every human ill. Rich and poor alike are the targets, the victims of *invidia*. Imagined or real? It makes no difference. Their anxieties—their sense of impending failure and its devastating companion, scorn, their wariness and ill will—have left them cornered. They would repudiate the past. They would share nothing, but unwittingly they do: the absolute, corrosive isolation that is their present.

The Torresi have always been misanthropic. Cities, Italian or foreign, only aggravate their natural dispositions, and Turin was neither worse nor better than any other. *Invidia* was rampant, or so each Torrese warned me about the next. The shams and smoke-screens, hastily devised, were absurd and only occasionally funny.

The most blatant and the easiest to understand was a woman named Agnese, who left Torregreca for Turin eighteen years ago with her husband and their daughter. She is a favorite local example of wealth and success. Her husband is considered amiable and physically frail. *She*, though, is a woman of iron. At first the Torresi's recital of her holdings, her shrewd deals, her methods sound admiring. Beware! Their compliments conceal barbs. Agnese is rich, or so she has convinced them, and like the rich, selfish and forgetful. You see how she ignores her father! A widower, sick and senile, she leaves him to care for himself and die, perhaps starve, in his foul hovel.

I had no reason to search out Agnese. I had known her slightly. She never lived in the "Villaggio." She had not even applied and would not have qualified: her husband had emigrated to South America and sent money back each month. I would not have seen her if, just before Chichella and I left Torregreca, I had not met her father, shuffling along one of the narrow streets that leads to the Piazza. His clothes were ragged and rank. On his feet he wore felt slippers caked with manure and his balance was uncertain. I helped him down three shallow steps. My hand under his arm must have jogged some errant brain cell. He stopped, turned to stare at me, and then smiled toothlessly.

"It's you, is it?" It seemed unlikely that he remembered and recognized me. He gummed a few phrases to himself, squinted at me again, and said very clearly, "Still traveling all the time?" I agreed that I was. Where? Oh Germany, Turin, Milan I told him, easing us both along the street. "Turin? Turin, you said? Got to see my Agnese. She's there ... and the others too. Agnese'll show you around. Knows everything. Agnese ..." For ten long minutes he clung to my arm, stumbling along, talking about Agnese. Our arrival in the Piazza and my promise, repeated half a dozen times, that I would visit Agnese in Turin if I could, finally won my release.

Agnese (and her mild husband, who is an appendage always

forgotten, but implied whenever his wife is mentioned) owns a café, which in spite of grueling hours and commercial perils is the zenith of Torrese ambition and proof per se of success. It was easy to find, just off a large square in what claims to be an independent town, though nothing, except possibly the residents' will to believe, separates it from the rest of Turin's hinterland. The outside was modest. Two letters in the electric sign blinked and the window was clouded by the milky film, part steam, part cigarette smoke, exhaust, and grime, that is the curse of industrial cities. Inside everything was long overdue for replacement. The tables and the counter were scratched, the chairs bandy-legged, some with splintered seats. Even the coffee machine had seen better days: streams of brown goo dribbled down its public face. From the next room the crash of billiard balls and the players' shouts drowned out my footsteps, but I could feel grit rasping under my shoes. The rattle of bottles suggested that out of sight there was someone behind the counter, stooping over to fill the ice-boxes.

Suddenly Agnese heaved up and surveyed the room with her usual look of disgruntled challenge. At the sight of me it changed instantly to her other expression, narrow-eyed calculation. What, now, did *I* want? Where had I come from after all these years? She disguised her reaction, of course, with smiles, wonder, and a parade of compliments so mawkish that I almost suspected her of irony. My explanation was too simple. I could feel her delving deeper and deeper in her mind for my real reason. I chattered on about her father, Torregreca, my trip. She smiled, she simpered. The probing never stopped. Her father. His vineyard? That was it. I wanted to buy it? No. Her husband's relatives needed money? I shrugged aside her preliminary wails of poverty. She didn't owe any money down there. I agreed. As far as I knew she had no debts down there *or* up here. I . . . We must talk. Where it is quieter, she insisted. Come! *He* can take the counter for a while. Come!

He was asleep on a plastic sofa that took up most of what she called "the kitchen," a blind corridor behind the café with a toilet at one end, a two-ring burner at the other under the spiral ladder-stairs leading up to their bedroom. I saw it later, a large, gloomy room. Suites of furniture—for a bedroom, a *salotto*, a dining room—

with buffets, wardrobes, cupboards, and tables were not so much arranged as impacted there. Some cabinetmaker had sated his taste for the rococo. He had covered every visible surface with veneer and more veneer, which the dampness was systematically lifting, prying up into curlicues. For very practical reasons they spent most of their time in "the kitchen."

Agnese gave me a thorough introduction to *invidia*. She started before we could settle down on the plastic couch. The Torresi are *gente invidiosa*! Malicious. You have to fight them all the time. Jealous of the bar—naturally. Jealous of her easy life. Easy life! Five in the morning to midnight, those were the hours. Always behind the bar. But for them it's the Easy Life! Of course she knew what they were really jealous of—her daughter's marriage. Eh, what can you expect? Filomena's pretty. She went to *liceo*. I can tell you in all modesty—she's brilliant. Could have gone to university, if she hadn't married. And he's an accountant. You see? Of course they're envious. He's *real* Torinese too! They live in a condominium. New. Very fancy people live there. So—you see? Too bad his mother's with them. But *pazienza*! He has a big career in front of him. Already he has a car and a color television—and *their baby*! You should see her! She's the most beautiful child—everyone says so. It's natural, I suppose, that people are envious, but—oh signora—the gossip! The bitching!

And then there's the apartment we've bought, almost bought, that is. The tenant is rich too. She doesn't know it, but we're going to raise the rent as soon as we sign the final papers. You see, someday we'll move into that—or—maybe Filomena will first, if she has more children. Their flat in the condominium isn't too large. His mamma could stay there—well—that's all in God's hands—but the apartment. You should see it. . . .

The next of her objects of envy was her son, much younger than Filomena. He was the smartest, best athlete in his class, always the best dressed. She couldn't help it if people were jealous of him: he was perfect. Eh, what else could she say? She hardly had to say more to me because I could not escape this paragon. He was, in fact, a sly, spoiled child with blond curls and a smart tongue.

Agnese rambled on, too absorbed in the architecture of the impression she was building to notice that she had overdosed me with superlatives. There was no reason to tell me all of this. I had not asked, did not want to know. Impossible to interrupt her. Words battered at me. *Ne? Ne? Ne?* the horrible verbal twitch of Turin, unconsciously thrown in after *every* phrase made me wince with irritation. Before I saw the last of Agnese, I developed a facial tic. *Ne? Ne? Ne?* Each time she said it, the right corner of my mouth jerked. Her onslaught had a progressive effect on me: from exasperation to embarrassment to claustrophobia to amusement and eventually real curiosity, which explains how I allowed myself to be involved with her three sisters.

Once she finished the review of her meager riches, she moved on to them. They were younger, had not had to struggle as hard as she. When they came North, times were already better. BUT—they're *rich* now! Rich, rich, rich! You can't imagine! *Ne?* We're so close. Their husbands—well, in all modesty, I picked them out, and they're like brothers to me. It's always "Agnese, do you need anything?" "Agnese, can I help you?" We're very close, naturally. One's a contractor, one's a *professore!* I was appropriately impressed. And their houses! Ah, signora—you *must* see them! Remembering how we lived in Torregreca, you *must* see them! One is a real villa! Just imagine. And my middle sister's café! Nothing grander in the center of Turin. *Fine, veramente fine!* Listen, come back tomorrow evening. It's our day to be closed. We can go around and call on my sisters. They'd be honored!

I was not too sure they would be, but my resistance had given way. I had to know the rest of the story. As I was leaving the café, assuring Agnese once more that I would come the following evening, a young couple arrived. What luck, she crowed. Filomena and her husband! She was plump and placid, he, tall, slender, blondish, too colorless to be handsome, too tentative in manner to be effectual. He was sent out to the car for the baby. She too was plump and placid, like her mother, a very babyish baby. I extricated myself and went off about my affairs.

Just before noon the next day I was waiting in the café of the

[*241*]

local hotel, where I had, for the sake of convenience, taken a room, when I noticed Filomena's husband come in, look around, and go back out to stand on the sidewalk by the main door. I asked him to join me. Both the people we were to meet had been caught in traffic, not unusual in Turin, and so we spent twenty minutes chatting about the only things we had in common—his wife, her family, his family, their plans. He was very mild and worried in his own gentle way that did not include protective bragging. They had been married for two years. He had no job, had never been able to find a permanent one since he left school with his diploma—as a bookkeeper. He had come to the café that day to meet a man who might be able to help him. He, Filomena, his mother, and the baby did have an apartment in the condominium that Agnese was so proud of, the basement janitor-doorkeeper's flat, in exchange for which he did the chores and a monthly breakdown of each tenant's share of heat, hall light, elevator maintenance, and the like.

Agnese had tried to convince him that he and Filomena should take over the café. They could live in the dank room above it. Agnese, her husband, and the boy would move into the newly acquired apartment, would a do daily shift behind the counter, and draw a regular monthly income from it. He had nothing against keeping a café. Please, I must understand that. But there were problems. Agnese had less than half the money for the apartment. The café that barely supported one family would not support two. There was no place for his mother. He would have to have a real job just the same, taking early morning and late evening duty behind the counter himself, leaving the other long hours to Filomena. No! First things first! He needed a job. If he and Filomena must have two jobs, one in exchange for an apartment (rents are expensive) and one to live on, then being the janitor at the condominium was far better than taking over the bar. The way he saw it, Agnese's proposition was only to *her* advantage: she would work less and the boy's future was guaranteed. Because, of course, the café goes to the boy. You know how Southerners are, signora. The boy comes first. Filomena—she's just a daughter. And then don't forget, *è gente invidiosa!* Agnese wants to be a signora, a lady of leisure. She wants to show the others and still protect the boy. After ten, fifteen years we'll be chucked out with nothing, just that much older, that much less likely to get settled. I *must* find a real job. I've got to. That would solve everything. Oh, there he is. . . . Later, as he left the café, he waved at me and shook his head: the friend had been unable to help.

That evening out in front of her café Agnese waited for me, tweaking at the collar of her silk dress, yanking down the hem where it seemed to pull. We could walk. Slowly, however, for, unaccustomed to her high heels, she could only teeter and rock along with desperate dignity. The sisters all lived within four or five blocks. First the café, with showcases full of every imaginable pastry, and a balcony, designated by a discreet mahogany and gold sign SALA DA TÈ, and mahogany counters and mahogany tables and chairs upholstered in pink velvet. We were greeted coolly, I thought, and then offered coffee. Once the sister recognized me, the tour began in earnest. I was invited (an invitation, which, had I declined, would have been converted to a command) to stroke the velvet and the mahogany and finally even the carpeting. We inspected the refrigerators, the ice cream machine, the pastry ovens, the coffee grinders. My compliments were countered by imposing price tags. The eight-year-old daughter was presented, her genius extolled, her charms displayed. Fortunately, or unfortunately, depending on your point of view, there was no piano in the café, but the child could recite for me. And did. By then the sister married to the professor had been summoned. Her husband was at a meeting. We must come to her house for a brandy. Just two steps down the street. The brother-in-law stayed behind to tend the café. As we left, I noticed for the first time that there were no customers.

The sister's apartment was in a new building with echoing halls. Upstairs, mirrors and Murano glass light fixtures and upholstered doors, onyx tables and gilt gewgaw cabinets struggled to establish their superiority over a jumble of Tyrolean peasanty—peasanty carved wardrobes, plate racks, cupboards, and buffets. Our hostess introduced each piece with its pedigree from her mental price list. Before we could finish the brandy and in spite of Agnese's best efforts, it came out that the sisters had not seen each other since

Easter. Almost six months had passed and in less than thirty minutes they were sniping at each other. *Ne? Ne?* splattered through the conversation like bird shot, lending a gentle, persistent sarcasm to the blandest remarks. I suggested we move on to the villa. The professor's wife stood up quickly, hissing in my ear, "Let's, before my husband comes home. He can't *stand* Agnese!" On our way it was agreed that I was the perfect excuse for their visit. They were dying to see the villa finished, from which I could draw only one conclusion.

Agnese's third and youngest sister was sick in bed, food poisoning, her husband said. That stopped no one. Poor thing! She might need their help. They pushed in and rushed, clucking, along the hall to her bedroom. The husband, a diffident little man, whose features, nestled in several days' growth of stubble, were indistinct, was left with me. He was bewildered and awkward, but also very kind. Conversation was not easy for him. He stammered badly until I admired the house and added that I had heard so much about it. After that all I had to do was listen to his technical explanations. He was a contractor and his pride in the house was entirely professional, which made the inevitable tour leisurely. In each room he pointed out the niceties of construction and described them in detail. The furniture he ignored, which proves that familiarity softens any shock. It was a startling collection and I cannot do it justice. There was something for every taste—a dining room straight from a Tudor manor, so many bathrooms I lost count, rows of bedrooms, an Empire drawing room (modern), and finally a red damask sitting room where the general, stiff-backed discomfort reminded me of a bishop's reception room. The kitchen seemed the only place a normal human being might sit (and from a newspaper open on the table I could guess that he had been reading there). I pulled out a chair. My host began to stammer again: this would not do. He settled me firmly back in the rigid red damask parlor and murmured on about solid walnut doors. The sisters had abandoned their patient for their inspection of the premises. Doors slammed. Giggles, then whispers loud and sibilant, swished down the halls. Disapproval brought whoops of criticism. Every nasty syllable was audible to us, sitting far away, at the other end of the house on our damask settees. Hoping to drown out their voices, I asked if he was interested in painting. Every room, it seemed, though surely not the bathrooms, had two if not three large oils, all Italian improvisations on "The Monarch of the Glen." I had found his hobby. He was a "collector" and as though the mere saying of the word released magic gasses, he began to swell, to blow up right before my eyes with pride. Very complex field. He would try to explain some of the finer points. Where his analysis of the cost/size ratio might have taken us I will never know.

"*Basta*, Stefano! Do I have to do everything? Can't you at least get them a *liquore*?" a shrill voice called from the hall, followed by the appearance of an extraordinary figure in the doorway, a very thin young woman, her face waxy, wearing a green satin negligee trimmed with long, scraggly, rather limp plumes that had never been the glory of any bird. The youngest and richest of Agnese's sisters was obviously ill. She pushed two lank strands of dark hair back from her face, and I stood up.

Our exit had an "abandon ship" quality about it, but bearing in mind the dispositions of the three viragoes in my charge, speed and authority, not grace, seemed desirable. Once out in the street they soon forgot that they were miffed with me and devoted themselves to dissecting the vulgarity of the villa, a complicated process because they felt that they must also impress me with the cost of each item they deplored. As we were about to separate, Agnese and I to go to the left, the other two, to the right, the lady of the bar gave her final judgment.

"She *is* such a slut too! Won't lift a finger. He even does *the cooking.* God *knows* how she ever caught him." Once they had gone on, Agnese picked up the subject.

"*I* know how she caught him—and so do *they*. She teased him into raping her right in the front hall of the old building where my sisters used to live. Our brothers-in-law did the rest. He *had* to marry her." She sighed. "That one always gets what she wants, but don't think the other two are any better. Why, do you know . . . ?" Her heels clicked and clacked to the rhythm of their infamies.

Agnese and Company are, for me, personifications of *invidia* and its twin evils: the envy you feel toward others and the envy you imagine, in defense of your own self-respect, that others feel toward you. They are extreme examples that prove the wisdom of their choice and the choice of most of the Torresi: isolation, no matter how depressing, is better than the full blast of pernicious *invidia*.

Not four blocks away, Giulia, a woman who grew up with Agnese and her charming sisters, lives and has lived for seventeen years. When I visited them, each was elaborately surprised to hear that the other was still in Turin: surely *she* left years ago. When confronted with the exact address, Agnese dismissed the family as *gentalia*, not really meaning rabble, I think, but people beneath her notice. Giulia was somewhat kinder: *she* was one for minding her own business, unlike others she knew, and she certainly did not have time for the game of airs and graces. Giulia never has had.

During her years at the "Villaggio" she had at least one child, sometimes two, at the nursery. Two more she bundled off each morning to school and still there was always a baby that she toted around with her as casually as she might have a bag of shopping. Whatever she did—working in the fields, washing at the fountain, chasing children, or just gossiping—she did it at full speed, arms twirling, eyes flashing. Her sheer physical energy was impressive. Less obvious, but ultimately more powerful was the mind that churned along at the same pace and would not be denied. She must know. She must understand. Having collected the facts and fictions, she could turn her own very particular logic and savage sense of humor loose to dissect and rearrange them. Her conclusions were unorthodox. The neighbors should have been shocked and were not. The simplicity of truth attracted them: her opinions *sounded* right. No issue was ever quite decided until Giulia had her say, and though her advice might not be followed, it was never forgotten: too often she had been right. She did not aspire to the office but always was the unchallenged oracle of the "Villaggio." and of all the women by far the best company.

According to Giulia, daylight hours were for work. The break she allowed herself late each afternoon was a compromise between duty and the requirements of her psyche. She felt guilty about going out to her front gate, so she took the baby, balanced precariously on one arm, and stood, knitting, her needles flying back and forth across the rows of yet another sweater. As long as she worked, she was not really slacking. She could justify waiting for her neighbors to pass. As they came along the road she called out to them, teasing them, casting her verbal flies at them as shrewdly as any fisherman in pursuit of a timid trout, and they always stopped. They counted on her for a joke, bits of news, even secrets. One by one the crowd grew and with it the roar of voices that brought children up from their rubble piles to stare. At the very center of it all, Giulia waved and nodded and pointed at people who were trying desperately to squeeze in a word. They shouted and laughed and sometimes ended up arguing, half jokingly, and Giulia shouted and laughed and argued louder than all the rest, her eyes sparkling, her cheeks, normally so rosy, now fired red by her own feverish animation. Everyone enjoyed her afternoon break. It jarred them from the apathy that the pattern of yesterday, repeated today and to be repeated tomorrow, imposed on their minds. Without her they would have plodded home, spanked the children, eaten supper, and gone to bed. She reminded them that they were alive: the end of the day was brighter, almost gay.

When Giulia's husband arrived, everything changed. She would abandon the group with an abrupt good-bye and follow him into their house. In a few minutes they might reappear to sit on their front steps talking quietly to each other, but more often than not, once the door closed, they were neither seen nor heard until the next morning. Her husband, a peasant converted by the times to an unskilled construction laborer, was a neat, mild man who worked hard, paid his debts, and stayed at home. He did not sit around in wine shops or play cards with the other men. Politics did not interest him. He adored his children, who never strayed far from home when he was there, hoping that he would want to do something with them and usually he did. He was the first of the men to see the advantage of planting a vegetable garden in the plot of land at the side of the house. Other improvements followed which his neighbors with less imagination copied. They could not dislike him. He gave them no cause. He earned general, uneasy respect, as most enigmas do, because no one could think of anything against him.

Giulia's ascendancy over the nursery mothers was one of those unexpected gifts. What she could not accomplish by her transparent logic, she did by force, bullying and threatening and reminding them all that whatever we agreed to do, she would have to do twice as much (because she had two children in the nursery). Convinced that she would be just as outspoken in the general "Villaggio" meetings, I primed her quite shamelessly. From what I heard the women saying, I knew she had done her spadework. They were upset about certain problems—an oven, garbage collection—and determined now with Giulia's prodding that *we* could plan to correct them. I faced the first meeting without a qualm and was taught a lesson in passive resistance, which is exactly what I deserved.

We all agreed something must be done. My proposal of a simple communal oven that we could build ourselves was answered by the men with the traditional negative: the town council must provide such services, therefore it was pointless for us to bother. We must wait and it would be given—someday. That, at least, warned me away from the question of garbage collection, which clearly was the responsibility of the town administration. I persisted with the oven: it was not a public service for which they could expect public funds. On the other hand I had arranged for a small piece of land to be deeded to me, the British Committee had agreed to give me $500 for basic expenses. If the men would give two days' work apiece, we could have our oven ... and I waited for Giulia to come to my rescue. She sat mute, staring at the floor. The objections were legion—all from the men. I would "own" the oven. I would *not*: they would. I must run it for them: I would *not*. They must run it themselves, deciding on turns, choosing the baker, ordering (and paying for) the wood.

About one Southern characteristic I was not naïve: they will set up obstructions as long as you bowl at them. I would not play that game. It was useless to discuss such details if the men would not give the two days. They shrugged. No objection. Time, free time, was the one commodity they had in abundance. Then came the voice of doom and from a weedy little man who was so chronically unemployed that he had lost the urge to work: no, he would not agree because there would be no accident insurance and *with the blasting* inevitably someone would be hurt. There would be *no* blasting, I insisted. Giulia sat mute. They knew the piece of land. It was in the center of the "Villaggio." No blasting was needed. The town surveyor had drawn up a very simple plan for me. I showed it to them. Today with Xerox machines I would probably have copies made for each of the men, but there were none such then. The men studied it. Giulia and her cohorts sat mute. Eventually the meeting was disbanded. One point of agreement had been reached: the oven could not be constructed because the men working without accident insurance would be in danger of injury *from the blasting*. This in spite of the fact that most agreed there would be *no* blasting. Giulia had never said a word: neither had any other woman.

For several days Giulia avoided me. She did not come to the nursery, nor did she hold court at her gate. I waited. Finally one afternoon she came to pick up her children. The front hall was full of women. Giulia sailed in, an Amazon ready for battle, her cheeks flaming, her arms waving, and her voice at full volume. I had no right to be cross with her! What could *she* say in a public meeting? At home, yes. But not in public. And I *had* to know that! She had done her best, but I couldn't expect her to say anything with the men there. I couldn't. The others agreed obediently. Again she had organized her support. I startled her by laughing.

After that I always went from house to house, discussing any project with one man, or sometimes two or three together, never more. The public meetings became *pro forma* sessions to ratify private agreements, which is hardly in the purest tradition of "community development" and neither democratic nor educational. However— given a choice between the projects getting started or the projects being permanently bogged down in the dogmatic practice, futile in itself, of democratic process, I took the heretic's way. One project realized, one success, leads to others, and "democratic process" will sooner or later, assume its proper role. Our meetings were held with all due formality. The men had already committed themselves and even if one of those catch-all objections, like injury from blasting, came along and they were tempted to agree, they would look around sheepishly, shake their heads, and decide against it. I had learned, but I never told the women why I laughed the day Giulia roared into the nursery to face me: this ferocious woman I considered so formidable was afraid of me.

Seeing her in Turin was a shock. I have always thought of her as large and commanding. She is not over five feet two, which says a lot for the power of personality. Now she is completely gray, very pale, and much thinner. For the last seventeen years she has worked in a factory that makes headlights. The fumes from hot rubber being shaped in molds have brought on chronic bronchial asthma. The climate of Turin does not help. In three years she will have her pension and finally return for good to Torregreca. All of her children except the youngest girl are married. The young women work in factories, the men as skilled workers in factories. One is a book-keeper. Her children and their husbands and wives all sound Northern, Torinese, until they are angered: then the Southern accents, the dialects they grew up with at home, come flooding out. These dregs of language are all that is left. They have no nostalgia for the South and will never return. Giulia's mild, quiet husband has been as consistent as I would have expected. He has never been without work, has never been more than an unskilled laborer, but he was shrewd enough to insist, always, on the legal insurances, and so now, after thirty years of work, he has retired on his pension.

Giulia works forty hours a week making headlights. Saturdays she does as much of the week's shopping as she can and cleans—and when Giulia cleans, it is a total turnout—her large, sunny apartment filled with Louis XIV reproductions. Ormolu cascades from every possible corner, and satin upholstery flashes. The floors are polished marble, the rugs deep. Inside, luxury as Giulia must have imagined it. Outside, the view over an extensive factory is less than luxurious. Humpy vacant lots abut two sides of the building and on Sundays are crowded with cars. Undoubtedly the neighbors' children come to their parents for lunch, as Giulia's do, bringing their husbands and wives and the whole herd of grandchildren. In the afternoon, when they have finally gone home, Giulia knits and dozes in front of the television. Except for fleeting glimpses of the train station, she does not know the center of Turin.

Giulia is well dressed, well spoken, and she admits, as she would never have in the past, that she is tired, so tired. Asthma keeps her short of breath. The days seem long. Each night, foggy. The energy for rampages of wit and rage has been drained, but the mind and the will to understand can still drive her to unorthodox conclusions and even action. It was Giulia who first told me that the tenants of the "Villaggio" had received notices warning of the eviction of any family that left a house unoccupied for more than three months. Back in Torregreca she found that her neighbors were frightened and worried too. They talked and they talked and they talked until many convinced themselves that nothing could happen. If it did? Time enough to think up something then. Giulia was not convinced. She did not argue, which was unlike her. Instead she wrote a letter, requesting clarification, and sent it by registered mail to the address on the notice. There was no answer. The silence seemed ominous. She wrote a second letter and persuaded her husband to stay behind in Torregreca, visibly, publicly camping alone in the house. There has been no acknowledgment of the second letter, which, in a country where registered mail is sacrosanct and government agencies required to answer it, is more than ominous.

Her eyes flashed in the old way as she told me, and two unhealthy blue-red patches stood out on her cheeks like splotches of enamel. She could still be angered. She was willing to fight, but she could not find the enemy. She was also afraid. Could I pry an answer from the agency?

My adventures in the housing maze became a nonmilitary spy story. First, the agency that built the houses had suffered cosmetic surgery, which left it with a new alphabetical conundrum for a name. Then it was taken under the wing of the Ministry of the Interior, a damp, dark, treacherous place indeed, where mold led quickly to decomposition and to burial in an unmarked grave. I will admit that the agency had an unconventional and therefore in-convenient policy about housing: units were not legal tender for political debts. Ergo its demise. Of twenty-five *thousand* govern-ment-sanctioned agencies, this is one of the half-dozen that has *ever* been suppressed. Interestingly enough, though nonexistent, the hous-ing agency has telephone numbers and postal boxes. The voices that answer are courteous and vague. You are connected with an inside line of a detached section of the Ministry of the Interior. They can-not give you any information and refuse to reveal their address. Me-chanical devices carry on, sending out notices and receiving answers that are beyond their capacities to decipher.

Never for a moment did I give up the idea that there was a human brain behind it all. Eventually the best lead seemed to be a vast atomic cloud of an agency, now called, after numerous reincar-nations of its own, IACP—*Istituti Autonomi per le Case Popolari.* Dur-ing the recent fiction of government decentralization it had, by a process of bureaucratic fission, proliferated into autonomous regional offices, some twenty, and from there into provincial installations. The head of the local office that has jurisdiction over Torregreca was a teacher who could not be present in the mornings, napped in the afternoons, and vanished toward sunset, presumably to his office, long since closed for the day, to sign whatever papers had drifted up on his desk.

On my tortuous journey I met some very nice people, but of course only after I had managed to poison or otherwise circumvent the ushers, those surly despots who rule (and lounge) in the cor-ridors of government office buildings, rejecting all legitimate visitors as either invisible, in the wrong place, or outside the scheduled "re-ceiving hours." (Unemployment may have its minor compensations. I heard recently that in the last civil service examinations given for ushers by the Ministry of Foreign Affairs, 75 percent of the appli-cants had university degrees. Assuming that the *"dottori"* meet the requirements, we civilians may, someday, be treated as other than bearers of pestilence or machine guns.) Everyone who actually had an office and a desk tried to be helpful. They referred me to others like themselves. They made suggestions, the most practical and often repeated being, "Don't you have any friends who can find out from the inside?" I had not overlooked the underground route, and so it is that after fifteen months I have the answer to Giulia's query, an answer so Italian, so unlikely that it must be right.

The teacher-director of the local *Istituto* was (and probably still is) a Socialist. In the last years the Socialist party has been scrabbling for votes. Thousands of people who were not assigned units in public housing still want them. They vote. Emigrants often do not, and furthermore emigrants were not actually living in the houses. Before the plan for confiscation could creep to its logical conclusion, the political balance in the region shifted, the teacher's term ended, and in his place a Communist was appointed. Communists are not against scavenging for votes either and are much more astute than the Socialists. The discontented are their natural prey, the emigrant, the epitome of the good prospect. For years the Communists have proselytized in Italy, meeting trains in Milan and Turin, helping emigrants to settle, to find work and rooms; in Germany, where activity of foreign political parties and foreign unions is illegal, the Italian Communist unions have set up offices of their assistance committees, which are open to any Italian, Communist or otherwise, union member or not, in need of help.[9] No charge is made for services. The party would ingratiate itself with the emigrants. There are so many of them. They all have a vote. Nothing will be done to anger them. Certainly a Communist, appointed director of an *Istituto Autonomo per le Case Popolari*, is not tempted to evict them from houses legally assigned to them, and so for all the wrong reasons, the mystery ends in the right way on the usual discordant Italian political note. Giulia and her neighbors are safe for another few years. I told her. She can spread the news as she chooses. She was the one who had the courage to fight.

Giulia knows where most of her Torresi neighbors live in Turin, but she never sees them: "Once we're back home, we'll see too much of each other. Why bother here?" Each must make his own way, seemed to be her idea, and they are doing just that, the variations being exactly the same as those I saw in Germany. For every Giulia, there was a pinchpenny or a semifailure, families living six in a sub-let room or in one of those alluvial semi-underground storerooms that every storm floods with water and sewerage. They resort to any subterfuge that will keep the secret of how they live. Several of the sons have "gotten in trouble," one daughter has left home and "set herself up" in a rented room. There was no point in asking, As what? One woman lives in a state of terror that she will be caught with her *amante*, a taxi driver originally from Palermo. They are the exceptions. The adults drudge from day to day, month to month, interned in the family, the local café, and the local factory. They do not seek each other: the Torinesi certainly do not seek them. The young, still believing in the elusive "life" a city is supposed to offer, ramble the streets, searching, and end up accepting anyone who will accept them. Someday many of them will go back to Torregreca and grow old spinning yarns about the rich world they lived in up North, and no one will contradict them, for each has at least one secret to hide.

And there are those who will never go back. One Saturday after-noon Chichella and I went to see a woman who had gone to Turin only six months before with her considerable family—ten children and her sick husband. She had been home in August, telling every-one about the café she had bought, by which we knew she meant that she had scraped together enough money for the down payment. She is a good press agent for herself. The mayor was convinced that the bar would be the meeting place of what he was pleased to call "The Young Torresi Club," a group of recent emigrants, footloose and lonely. Long before we arrived, the boys had fallen out over politics, and the project, like most such Torresi associations, had dis-integrated into rancor and finally disbanded. Melina was not dis-couraged. Business was good. She would supervise this bar on a side street—in Turin, but just barely—while she hunted for another, larger, better-equipped one closer to the center. Four of her sons took turns serving behind the counter. It was a haphazard operation. They talked to their friends and ignored the stray customer. No table was ever cleaned off, dirty glasses lined the counter. The jukebox bellowed. And still the café made money. Melina knew that she had reached the end of the rainbow.

She herself was a revelation. The city! The city! So much to see! So much to do! So much money—and so easy to come by it! Three of her sons have found jobs with small firms—a painting contractor, an electrician, a plumbing supply dealer. The painter was hired as a *stuccatore*, a skilled category, so naturally he is paid more than the others, but they are learning a trade. In time . . . ? You see how they stole from us in Torregreca? For exactly the same work the *stuccatore* received half as much there. *If* he could make the people pay. Not in Turin. Full *stuccatore's* pay. She talked about it at such length that I finally asked how much he earned and was told what I feared, had not wanted to hear: he is paid exactly the going wage of an *unskilled* worker. The other two boys are paid 33 percent less than the going wage for their days as simple laborers. I said nothing. She was aglow with prosperity. Why discourage her? Never before had life been this happy.

The two youngest children, girls, are still in school. The eldest son is married and lives with his in-laws. For the past ten years Melina's husband has had a regular job in Torregreca. (For many years a militant Communist and so informally blacklisted by the local powers, he marched into party headquarters one evening and interrupted a discussion to tell his comrades that they were fools. Idiots! They had watched for twenty-five years while every bastard and thief in town professed to be Demo-Christian and was given a job. And what did they get? *Nothing!* Well, not him! This was his notice. He was through and to prove it he tore up his membership card, threw the pieces on the floor, and left. The next morning he appeared in the Piazza wearing the uniform of a municipal road-maintenance man.) Even a regular job can do little more than keep ten children from starvation. Now he was ill, seriously ill. His salary continued, augmented by the free-running gold of Turin. Between the bar, the boys, and Melina's husband, the family has $1,500 a month (after the regular note on their loan for the bar has been paid), gold indeed compared to $400 a month in Torregreca and tiny amounts the boys might dredge out of odd jobs.

Expenses in Turin would be much greater. Rents, for instance. At home they had a two-bedroom apartment with a dining room and sitting room where the overflow could sleep on fold-up beds, all for $20 a month, naturally in public housing. Melina waved the problem aside. Across from the café she has rented a two-room apartment where she, her husband when he is out of the hospital, and five children eat and sleep. The four boys who tend, if that is the proper term for their casual attentions, the counter eat at Melina's and sleep in the storeroom behind the café, amid an indescribable smelly mess of broken chairs, old tarps, crates of empty bottles, hanks of uneaten pizza, bins of dirty paper napkins, and piles of abandoned raincoats and umbrellas. Melina cooks for them, acts as general business manager, and has a great deal of time to discover Turin.

At home Melina's wardrobe was far from elaborate. Summers were easy: a few cotton dresses in various stages of raggedness and floppy open-backed slippers would see her through. Winters she was layered in shapeless skirts and as many sweaters, often patched with different colors of yarn, as she needed to keep warm. For weddings, funerals, and Sunday mass she had one decent, if simple, outfit. Chichella and I were not expected that Saturday at the café. She did not know we were in Turin and yet we found her in a dark gray wool dress, not *haute couture*, but a very good copy, and high-heeled black kid pumps. When we went out, a dark gray tweed reefer, silk scarf, black kid gloves, and a black kid purse completed the ensemble. Melina has taken to the city with such exuberance her long, thin face has changed. It has relaxed and a few extra pounds have done the rest to smooth out, fill in, the creases around the large melancholy brown eyes and the deep lines around her mouth that seemed brands of a despair so intense that she had to force it to stay inside, under control, by frowning. She always had a slow, gentle smile, all the sweeter for being rare. Now it is constant and a bit secretive, as though she were in love, and she is—with a city, with prosperity. She could talk of nothing else. Even in drab anonymous neighborhoods, jostled about by crowds on the sidewalk, she would stop dead and announce, "I feel like I'd been born all over again—and this time with everything, just *everything*!"

[256]

We had only come to call and after we had had coffee and sat talking for an hour or so, I started collecting my things. We must ... Where were we going? I had a list of people I wanted to see, all of whom lived relatively near Porta Palazzo, where on Saturdays the enormous and supposedly dangerous market is held. The chance was too good to miss. She would go with us and be our guide. She knew all the tram and bus lines, all of them, could take us anywhere by the shortest route. At the time I thought she was boasting. Eight hours and untold miles later, exhausted and bleary, I was willing to admit that she knows the Turin transit system better than most motormen.

On the first of our many trams, she and Chichella amused themselves imitating a slack-jawed conductor whose intellectual powers were strained by the simple business of making change. Passengers seeking directions set him babbling absurdities and eventually, insults. We sat one behind the other in single seats, Chichella at the front, Melina in the middle, and I at the back. After a few blocks Melina turned around to me and whispered,

"Don't they talk funny up here?" The accent in Italian, not dialect, sounded very pleasant, but I smiled. She and Chichella carried on in their Torrese dialect, ignoring me. When we had gone what seemed a long way, she must have noticed that I was restless, because she turned again to reassure me, this time in a normal tone: she had nothing to hide. "Don't worry. I'll tell you in plenty of time to get off. I know right where Porta Palazzo is." She picked up her conversation with Chichella again, their voices neither loud nor self-consciously soft. They knew that I was the only person on the tram who could understand them. A nicely dressed woman about my age, who had been standing beside my seat, leaned over and said quietly, very courteously,

"I beg your pardon. I believe you're not from Turin, and I couldn't help overhearing what that woman said to you. About Porta Palazzo ...?" I nodded, agreed that I was not from Turin, and let my sentence hang there, inviting her to go on. "I'm sure you'll understand. I just thought I should tell you, the city is very dangerous these days—so unlike it used to be. Those Southerners have changed everything." Her head bobbed in Melina and Chichella's direction. "And Porta Palazzo is very dangerous. Very dangerous, indeed. Don't trust those two women. You can't tell *what* they're planning. Southerners are so treacherous, you know. I just thought—well, I thought I should warn you." I knew that my face had stiffened in useless resentment, but some even more apparent change in my manner had made her doubt the wisdom of her remarks. She backed away from me and was soon lost among the people crowded around the middle door. She meant no harm, quite the contrary. Undoubtedly everyone else on that tram shared her opinion and had not been kind enough to warn me of what is, by now, a canon of life in Turin: Beware of *all* Southerners.

Düsseldorf was not too different. There, after a long day spent with a young Torrese family, one I had known extremely well, I asked Pietro, the husband, if he could show me the city. Unemployed and plagued by a grab bag of problems, which, wherever he is, he acquires with startling ease, he had been talking about the only work he had been offered (by Italians he had met in Germany), as a waiter in a bar. So far he had refused to take the job. He would have to be away from home at night. The pay was too little, 1,200 DM ($600). He had been making twice that much. Tips would help, I offered. He doubted it. Germans didn't go in for tips. They would not double his salary, that was sure. He went on with suspect enthusiasm to talk about nightlife in Düsseldorf, about the bars, restaurants, and pizzerias on one particular street, closed to traffic, in the center of the city. He had friends who had leased franchises there. Some were doing well, others not. They were all being milked by a new Italian protection Mafia. The police were suspicious.

I was torn: it could be true; it could also be a harmless fiction. Pietro is thirty-eight. For the last eighteen years, and never by choice, he has shuttled between Torregreca and points of emigration, staying at home as long as there was work (he is a construction carpenter) and then, resigned, leaving again for a Northern city. Sometimes his wife and children have gone with him, sometimes not. So three years passed in Turin, two more in Milan, four years in Düsseldorf on two separate stints, and now finally Düsseldorf again.

He had been there a year. I had never listed the places quite that methodically to myself before. Cities. Why, I wondered, always cities? Did they stimulate his imagination? Were these bars and Mafia and police the result? I doubted it. He is one of those people to whom so much happens in the normal-abnormal course of life that he does not need to attract attention by exaggeration. I wanted to see his Düsseldorf, real or invented. He had already whispered that, if we could escape from his family, he had a problem he wanted to discuss with me. I could guess: his mother-in-law, who has been one of the unmitigated trials of the last fifteen years. Pietro jumped at my suggestion of a tour, assuming it was a stratagem. Ten minutes for him to shave and change and we would be off. He was happy: he could worry out loud about his mother-in-law. I was happy: I would see his Düsseldorf without seeming to spy. And his wife, for whom the humors of others are contagious, turned into a tornado of gaiety, rushing around the small apartment, searching for things he did not want, shouting additions to our itinerary, instructions as to what trousers he should wear, admonitions to me about the dangers of dark streets. She was so excited that she forgot to sulk about being left behind, a temporary oversight we were to pay for later.

Pietro and Liliana live on the southwest edge of the city, not far from the river docks and the bridge to Neuss, in a neighborhood of small factories and battered buildings that look semi-condemned. Their windows are blacked with soot, some even boarded over, and the doors, stripped raw and ribbed by weather, might not have been opened for years. They seemed deserted, but here and there a grayed glow of light proved that within there was human life.

Once in Istanbul I tried to imagine the insides of the rickety buildings that paraded by the windows of my tourist bus. Part adobe, part timber, they could have been medium-rise rabbit hutches with lean-tos that bulged out from their walls like tuberous growths to dangle precariously in space. The stone and brick of Düsseldorf's fringe looks more solid than the slapped-together tenements of Istanbul. I know now that the protuberances *are* there, at the back—shower stalls on balconies that sway as you cross them, toilets in little three-foot-high carbuncles opened off stair landings, sagging jetties, loosely anchored onto rooms, serve as kitchens—and the stairways feel as I think those in Istanbul would. The steps are splintered and sink creaking to your weight. Soft scuttlings warn you of a presence, there in the dark: human or animal, you will never know. A toilet flushes right by your shoulder. The air is thick and rancid with cabbage. You trip over a mound of trash, dry trash, not garbage. Doors open. Doors close. Footsteps approach and remain bodiless. Whimpers and groans: a baby cries. A tap leaks. Suddenly the floor jitters in answer to the tonnage of a passing truck. The sounds and smells, the decay of poverty, are all there, just as I imagined them in Istanbul. They do not show from the street: that is the difference.

At a little after seven those streets were dark and lonely. The city council must be saving electricity. The lights, distant one from the other, deepen the shadows, making them sinister. Pietro and I hurried down the broad avenue. Our voices echoed, amplified by the dark, or perhaps unconsciously we did talk that loudly to warn of our approach: better not to surprise anyone in such a neighborhood. Four long blocks and we reached the main tram line, and soon after, the brilliant safety of a tram car. It glided along, smoothly, quietly. There were still seats. I sat just in front of Pietro, who leaned forward, murmuring the squalid details of his mother-in-law's saga.

For the last twelve years she has lived in Düsseldorf and worked as a ward orderly in a hospital, which has, unknown to its administrators and medical staff, supplied half the households of Torregreca with towels and sheets. At the very top of the building where Pietro and Liliana have three rooms on the second floor, his mother-in-law lives with an unmarried daughter in two small rooms, sharing a toilet on the landing below with the tenants of two floors. Originally for Pietro the ease of finding the apartment outweighed the disadvantages of proximity. Across from his mother-in-law in another small room lives a married daughter, rebaptized Kiki in Germany for trade reasons, I gather. She was the immediate problem.

A year before she had married a German laborer. Six months later she gave birth to a son, officially his child, and then threw him out and returned to her more amusing professional activities, but now with a fixed income from the city of Düsseldorf as the separated and destitute wife of a German citizen. To satisfy the welfare authorities she does go each afternoon, looking like a modern Medusa in leather "hot pants" studded with silver, suede thigh boots, and stage makeup, to clean a warehouse. The baby is an inconvenience. Her younger sister is a full-time clerk in a shop. Liliana also works in the afternoon (not, however, with her sister) cleaning offices, and although she objects violently—scenes have swept over the building like tidal waves—Kiki tosses the baby on Liliana's sofa and tells the children to keep an eye on him. Often Kiki is late coming home, so her gentlemen callers settle on the couch too and must be entertained by the children. Mario, at thirteen, understands the "arrangement" and tries to push his sisters, Rita, who is a quiet, wise eleven, and little Pina, a flirtatious four, into the kitchen "to play." Rita obliges. She likes to read. Pina, who will sit in any man's lap and burble at him, usually eels her way back into the sitting room. Eventually Kiki breezes in, only a few steps in front of Liliana, berates the children for not feeding the baby, slaps them around, curses her own caller, and if she is lucky, flounces out before Liliana catches her. If not, then another tidal wave thunders down on the neighbors.

While Pietro was telling me all this, half of which I had guessed just following the sequence of the afternoon, I glanced around the car. Men read newspapers. Three boys joked loudly with two pimply girls, and two middle-aged women who had at first talked pleasantly to each other, now sat staring sideways over their shoulders at me, relishing some shared antipathy. I turned back to Pietro and listened absentmindedly. I looked up quickly. They *were* staring at me, the corners of their mouths tight with disapproval. There must be something conspicuous or scandalous about me. My clothes were European, dark, not flamboyant, conventional, warm city clothes like theirs, slightly less shabby. Pietro? Nothing about him was remarkable. He is a strong, solid man, taller than I, but not tall, with short bristly dark hair, brown eyes, and a soft, deep voice that lilts when he is amused. He had just shaved and put on clean

[*261*]

clothes—a polo shirt, a light gray sweater, darker gray wool trousers, and a windbreaker. He was very neat: even his shoes were polished. Perhaps they knew him and thought Liliana betrayed. I asked him. He shook his head without interrupting his tale. He couldn't stand it anymore. Mario said that if Kiki hit him again, he would hit her back. Rita had developed a queasy stomach and cried at the first words of a disagreement, no matter how minor. His mother-in-law denied that Kiki's callers were other than "friends," saw no reason why the baby should not be left with the children, and accused Pietro and Liliana of being mean-spirited toward a sister who had had such "bad luck." Liliana's disposition, never temperate, had suffered. At times Pietro thought he would lose his mind. He had to find a way out.

"Why not move?" I asked.

"Expensive. First, at least, I have to get a job. Where we are, the rent can slip for a month or two. Another landlord—who knows? And it would have to be in the neighborhood. Mario already takes three trams to school. I don't want to get farther away—and Kiki could still . . ."

Damn those two women! They glowered at us, beaming such concentrated venom in our direction that I lost the thread of Pietro's logic.

"Ah, we're almost at the station." Pietro had ducked down to look out the window. "Might as well let the others get off first. It's a long stop."

Already people were bunched up around the doors. The two women stood up. I expected them to join the queues. Relieved, I turned and looked out the window too: a large amorphous brown building, a typical 1880s station, loomed over us. Suddenly a spate of German crackled in my ear like static. I wheeled around and there, standing above us, were the two middle-aged women, their faces twisted and growing pink with rage. For an instant I did not believe they were talking to us. Words spewed over us, and there was no doubt, because the women so obviously did not doubt: whatever their cause, they were convinced and self-righteous. Pietro stood up slowly, dazed, and tried to interrupt. I heard myself insist with calmness I did not feel, "I'm sorry. I do not speak German. Really, I do not speak German." One of them stopped and leaned over closer to squint at me. "I do not speak German," I repeated idiotically in German. "I do not speak German."

"*Lügnerin!*" she spat at me. Later my dictionary told me that meant liar. The other woman muttered something that sounded like "whore" and probably was, since the German word is *Hure*. Pietro had found his voice and was shouting at them: I was not German, I did not speak German, and of course I lost the rest. After one last volley at him, they marched stiffly down the car and got off. We followed at a safe distance. I never really saw Pietro's face until we were in the street. It was deep, angry red, and he was scowling.

He refused to tell me what they had said about him. The expurgated version of my guilt was that a woman my age should have better sense, more dignity, than to cavort with an Italian gigolo. They had mistaken me for German. I was a collaborator, if there can be such in peacetime. Pietro was radically miscast. His monologue, poured softly into my ear over the entire route, might have seemed assiduous attention, the suave Italian bent on seduction, but under the circumstances, the verb *cavort* strikes me as a clue to the ladies' fantasies. Their prejudices were less subliminal.

Each of us had determined to make a joke of the incident for the sake of the other. The effort should have suffocated the evening in brittle good humor. Somehow we avoided that extreme. The ladies receded and were lost, as they should have been, at the tram stop.

Pietro was disappointed in the station. It was almost empty, he claimed. Streams of people came and went along the tiled corridors leading to the tracks, but they did not satisfy him. The lobby should be crowded with emigrants. Several dozen Turks stood in silent little groups, watching the main doors. Pietro ignored them. Near the station buffet he spied a friend from Torregreca, a tall, thin young man with bushy eyebrows and a stormy, resentful expression. As soon as he saw Pietro, he rushed toward us, waving and smiling. Pleasure had erased the frown that ten seconds before had seemed a warranty of his disposition. He was glad to see us, both of us. He remembered me from his childhood: I did not remember him, though I knew his parents. We must have a beer with him. To my surprise Pietro said we had an appointment. Then he would come with us. He didn't have anything better to do. Well, no, that wouldn't do either: this was a business appointment—of mine. His friend looked dejected. The eyebrows pulled tight again over his eyes, concealing them and with them any prickles of frustration or anxiety.

Pietro had already turned away when I asked the young man what his name was, what he did. He deserved that much interest from us. Gianni, he said, shaking my hand for the second time, and he was unemployed "right at present." He was beating around for a job, had been for a month. Then tonight, right here in the station, the police had picked him up for illegal porterage. His second time. They said a third time and they'd send him back to Italy. Could they really do that? I had no idea. Like everyone who has struggled through a German station with bags, I had cursed the nonexistence, the absolute nonexistence of porters. What could be the harm, if he was willing to carry bags and found someone willing to pay him for the service?

"We'd better go along, signora." Pietro came back a few steps, took my arm, and then turned to Gianni who stood looking lost and worried. "*Guaglió*, there's always the tire factory." His voice rumbled off into a nasty wheeze: the tire factory must be synonymous with the cemetery.

Once we were safely on another tram, I asked Pietro why he hadn't wanted Gianni to come with us.

"Signò, it's like this." Deep thought brought back the dialect. "Today, the way things are here, you don't give nothing away free. Nothing! He's a bright kid, quick-moving. Make a good waiter, wouldn't he? And if he heard us talking to these friends of mine— tonight where we're going—he'd know there was a job. Right? Just the kind he'd like to have too. No. Don't give nothing away free. Take care of yourself. Mind your own business. Let him find his perch. I've had to often enough. Won't hurt him to do the same."

He took me to a square with a park and fountains in the center. We studied the windows of beautiful shops. The clothes were stunning. So were the prices. We converted them and groaned. We passed several of the "fancy" hotels, as he called them, very slowly. He craned around to watch the people who sauntered in and out, oblivious of his curiosity. I offered to buy us a drink in whichever of the hotels he chose. He stared at me, shocked. We couldn't. You wouldn't dare. Do you know how much it would cost? I did, of course. To reassure him I pulled out 50 DM, three times what we would spend, and handed them to him. He would not have to be embarrassed: he could pay. No, no. They wouldn't let us in and besides . . . His voice petered out. He wanted to and at the same time was afraid. He did not quite dare. I could have insisted and, since, I have regretted in some ways that I did not. It would have been interesting to see his reaction, the reaction of the hotel staff and the customers, but not interesting enough to make him feel scruffy and out of place. We went on to the pedestrian island and the street of bars and restaurants, where he could be a Cicerone, not a Yahoo.

Again he was disappointed by the number of people. Most nights the crowd was so thick you could hardly get through. It was a little after eight, early for such places, I suggested. And it had begun to drizzle. We went the length of the street, stepping just inside the doorways he chose, presumably the bars his friends managed. They were either deserted or jammed, Stygian dark and pulsating with dreary rock music. The puzzle of such places is why one bar is popular and its immediate neighbor with the same prices, size, blackness, and racket is not. Emptiness attracts no one. I was surprised that we did not go inside any of them. Pietro only allowed me to peek in, then steered me away along the street again.

When we came to the end, he turned into an alley and into another and we were at the back doors of the same bars. Curious. I had never seen the *back* door of a bar. The noise and bottles and dirty glasses and waiters rushing wildly in all directions, grabbing up whatever they needed or could reach, probably were all normal enough: the caterwaul of four or five languages was less so. Turks, Greeks, Italians, and a few Germans howled at each other in their own languages and seemed to make themselves understood. A lot of the confusion had to do with food—plates, dirty and clean, silver, steaming pots, men trying to serve from them—but I never really found out whether what I called bars were primarily bars, primarily restaurants, or more likely bars with limited menus of food that would keep the customers drinking. Pietro would allow me to look through the service door. Nothing more. Finally I accepted that my respectability was more valuable to him than the comprehensive inspection of a bar was to me.

The managers were men in their thirties, experienced in the pitfalls of emigration and cities, Italian and German. They had learned the odd assortment of skills misadventure teaches, especially in cities—courtesy, the clichés of language vital if they were to be more than slum rowdies, and the trick of absolute stillness, both physical and vocal, that can be mistaken for attention and is something more, a wary listening to vibrations only men as tough and determined can hear. The threat was always there, unspoken, cold, and blunt: Don't push me.

They were glad to see Pietro: about me they were uneasy. We did a lot of explaining. They were friendly and cautious. Mention of the protection Mafia brought lifted shoulders, heads cocked to one side, and silence. Whatever they might tell Pietro, I was a different matter. Emigration was my subject, and I decided to stick to it. They became restive, their answers, evasive. Men who seek kitchen work are unskilled drifters, gypsies by disposition. No problem of work contracts or pension payments. They want money now, tonight. Tomorrow they may show, they may not. Never have the same help for long. That's why they needed one regular Italian waiter who spoke German. The other waiters could be German for all they cared, but one, at least, must be *di fiducia*, be trusted to keep an eye on the front and an eye on the "hired muscle" in the kitchen; that was why they wanted Pietro. My impression, no more than an educated guess, is that the old Italian system has moved to Germany: the men do not simply wander, they are shifted from bar to bar deliberately, hired and paid on a daily basis, never working in the same bar so long that the police notice, never insured and never declared employed.

By 10:30, after several more long streetcar rides, we were home. Liliana had waited to have supper with us and complain. The children watched television. The set, like all the furniture, was a trophy from a weekend raid on the castoffs put out on the sidewalks to await the garbage collectors. An old American film with the original soundtrack and German subtitles was being shown. Mario and Rita (Pina was blissfully intent on the action) read the titles very carefully and then explained the plot to me. They were right too.

Later I was reminded of them so often that in spite of myself they became symbolic of Italian children in German schools.

Pina, a bouncy four-year-old with ringlets and sapphire eyes, went to the neighborhood nursery school and came home each day not quite sure which language she was speaking. German. Italian. They were the same to her, one as easy as the other. More often than not she brought little friends with her, and they sprawled out on the kitchen floor to play. If Liliana, Pietro, and I talked, they turned around to stare at us. We sounded funny, but they were too busy, chattering themselves, to be interested for long. By the time Pina starts school, she will have acquired the same burden of slang, dialect, and accent that the other children in first grade must unlearn. She should have neither more nor less trouble than they. No one need worry about her—unless suddenly in third or fourth grade she is uprooted, taken back to Torregreca, and put in school there. Critical as Italians are about what has (and has not) been done for their children in foreign schools, they have not provided or even planned any help for many of the same children, who do return in midscholastic career and must adapt to a new language—Italian—for their studies.

Rita and the others her age who have started school in one country and must continue in another with a new language, suffer. Nature and chance have been unkind to Rita. She is a sallow pudding of a child with a broad flat face, hazel eyes usually cast down, and stringy mouse-colored hair. She has never been vivacious. Even at home she always played slightly apart from the others, with them

[267]

and yet separate. I have seen her watch them, her eyes wide and expressionless, as though they interested and repelled her, and she were trying to decide which reaction was the stronger. She did not have an easy time in school. The Torresi teachers, usually so generous or so lazy that they fail no one, were irritated by what they took to be her refusal to understand. They threatened her, they screamed at her, and finally one forced her to repeat a year. If explanations make sense to her and she grasps the principle, she is very quick to arrive at conclusions, even projections of the theory. If the explanation does not explain, at least to her, then repetition of it is useless. The problems will remain unsolved and questions, unanswered. Her teacher would have to discover what she does not understand and approach her explanation from another angle, one of the basic elements of teaching, I would have thought, but beyond the ability or inclination of Torresi teachers. Theirs is a pedagogy without frills. *This* is the explanation, *that* is the answer, and failure to grasp is obstinacy. In Torregreca school was an unpleasant battle for her, in Germany it became a mute torture.

Again, about the education of immigrant children, the member governments of the European Common Market stipulated agreements, and again they established an equality that, so far, only Italians can enjoy. (Many of the same provisions have been written into immigration contract agreements between Germany and non–Common Market countries. Whether or not there are special arrangements, immigrant parents who have children in Germany must send them to school.) Italian children in Germany have the same right to an education as German children and the same obligation of attendance. Special classes, *classi d'inserimento*, would prepare them for their gradual absorption into normal German elementary and secondary classes. A year of concentrated German with the other regular subjects taught at first in the native language, then gradually more and more in German, should be sufficient, according to the plan, for complete integration. Of necessity the specifications were broad to guarantee the autonomy of each *Land* and its right to devise its own independent school system. Each would supply the German teachers who would teach the language courses and the supervision consonant with the local system.* The Italian Ministry of Public Instruction would be responsible for the assignment of Italian teachers, preferably with *some* knowledge of German, since by the end of the year they would be expected to teach the regular curriculum almost completely in German. (Fifty percent of the cost for the teacher was to be reimbursed by the Common Market through a network of interlocking committees.) To each *Land* the Italian Ministry would also appoint its own school supervisors, who would be in charge of the Italian teachers, any Italian parents' committees he might be able to organize, and "after-school" groups where the children would be helped to do their homework. Liaison was the Italian supervisor's role. All responsibility and authority rested with the *Land's* supervisors. Their decisions would be final, which sounds like cause for resentment, almost an invitation, and has been for German and Italian supervisors alike. Their comments, usually tactful, on "the situation" do not conceal their frustration. Occasionally the bitterness spits out in print:

> ... While Greece, Italy, and Yugoslavia were entitled to evaluate the work of their teachers in Germany, their officials could do so only in the company of German officials and school heads. "Attempts by foreign inspectors to intervene or in any way shape the teaching of foreigners must be rejected." [10]

The quoted statement was made by Dr. Franz Domhoff of the Ministry of Education for North Rhine-Westphalia.

On paper the plan was simple and fair. Like most modern social legislation, it lost in translation to fact. So much depended on the integrity and conscientiousness of the *Länder* and the Italian Ministry of Public Instruction (not, in the case of the Ministry, the two qualities that flash most insistently across the mind). As it turned out neither party was fired with enthusiasm. The *Länder* had and have some legitimate problems: a shortage of classrooms and of

---

* Each *Land* also has the right to set its own numerical minimum required before a *classe d'inserimento* must be provided. For instance, in Bavaria a class must be established if twenty-five children or more need it. In Hessen, twelve children are enough. The divergence speaks for itself.

teachers trained in the techniques of teaching language to foreigners. The Italian Ministry, although besieged by an army of unemployed teachers, has been slow to appoint them to the supplementary classes. Those who have been and who do report, having failed to discover some mortal illness or other cause for leave of absence, do not know German. They seldom have even the vaguest urge to learn it. They will never be able to teach in the language. The Italian supervisors have ranged from energetic, intelligent men, who are thwarted at every turn, to those arrogant incompetents who think service abroad will look impressive on their records. The embassy and consular officers who represent the Italian government (and with it the Ministry of Public Instruction) in Germany are, at least officially, responsible for the presence and efficiency of the Italian staff in supplementary classes. At times they must despair. Their pleas, their threats, their reports, their thunderings have been useless. The Ministry of Public Instruction will function as it chooses, and since it chooses to consider the teachers detached to Germany unimportant, the program is doomed to limp, embarrassing officials, enraging parents and convincing the Germans, once more, of Italian irresponsibility.

The results have not been consoling. Where they exist at all, the supplementary classes tend to be scholastic checkrooms or worse, one-room multiclass Italian schools. In that one room forty children can be preparing, in theory, for eight different German grades with eight different curricula, though none of the teaching is in German, *or* forty children from eight different classes can be studying eight different Italian curricula in one room. In either case the children are neatly isolated from the German classes and have no prospects of ever joining them. They have been permanently shunted off into a one-room–one-teacher multiclass school. Northern Italian educators and sociologists claim this makes them "doubly disadvantaged": it is a deplorable repetition, in even more confusing circumstances, of the school conditions in Southern Italy. This question of one-room-one-teacher multiclass schools seems to have become a fixation with them.[11]

Southern children *are* disastrously underprepared for school in

Northern Italy or abroad and their parents are themselves often illiterate, which these authorities would explain is the result of the isolation of Southern villages, the lack of highways, transportation, and so the predominance of one-room multiclass schools where the children learn little or nothing. There are, of course, one-room schools in minute settlements (not really villages), especially in the mountains of Calabria and the interior of Sicily, but nothing like the numbers suggested. In the early 1960s there was a rush to build country schools. They had hardly opened before the joys of consolidation and busing became fashionable and they were closed, the pattern that has been repeated so many times in so many countries. Torregreca, with officially only 8,500 people (and actually 4,500), lost on a mountain ridge in the far corner of a province, has four nursery schools (places for 500 children), along with elementary schools, lower and middle schools, *Liceo Scientifico*, a small trade school, an agricultural school, and a nursery and elementary teachers' training school (private). Only university is lacking. Squadrons of buses and minibuses from dozens of surrounding villages, small and truly isolated, converge on the town twice a day and have since the early 1960s, as they do in towns all over the South. There *are* some one-room–one-teacher multiclass schools in the Southern mountains (and in the Northern too) but they are not the cause of the abysmal record of Southern schoolchildren in the North and abroad: that is all credit to the way the existing schools function—more specifically to the ignorance and the laziness and the *mala fide* of the teachers.

The Ministry of Public Instruction and the *Länder* did not conspire to ignore the situation, to block the supplementary classes, but they have in their independent ways done the least that could be expected. For once the least, so convenient to them, has been the best for the very children they were to help. Most Italian children (90 percent) do not have the "advantage" of a supplementary class and so are simply thrown into German school classes.

Where, small town or city, becomes the vital question. Small children, who reach Germany still under school age and live a more or less "village" life, play with other children, learn the dialect, and seem to hold their own in first grade. They, like little Pina in Düsseldorf, have the same lacunae and the same bad habits to unlearn as the German children. Those who arrive in time for third or fourth grade suffer. Often they repeat a year, some even two, but again the size of the community helps them. They play with other children, they run errands to shops, the neighbors talk to them, and slowly the gap of language closes.

Cities are more difficult. Unless small children, like Pina, can go to nursery school—and again there is a scarcity of nursery places and a strong, entirely understandable feeling that German children should have priority—starting first grade is like pushing them out to sea in an inner tube. Given time and help and a patient teacher, they will learn the language. They are lucky if they have all three. Children who come into a German school at third- and fourth-grade levels are the real victims. Often, in the absence of a supplementary class, they are given a summary oral quiz in German and then banished *in perpetuum* to a class for children of subnormal intelligence. It is quick, practical: the child is out of the way—in school *and* out of the way. What is in 99 percent of the children a language deficiency turns into a mental deficiency. If the child understood German, the result might be the same. A six-year-old from a Southern mountain village would give bizarre explanations of subways, airplanes, and telephones, or none at all. They are beyond his experience, and he pays the price.

After the elementary grades, secondary schools await them. Those who started in normal German classes and managed to finish them, go on without trouble. Others who started midway or had trouble or arrived after their elementary classes, ready for secondary school, have only one hope: what I would call "differential" schools and the immigrants call "international" schools, which should not be confused with the private "International Schools," attended by the children of diplomats and foreign businessmen. In the "international" schools a language compromise has been made: German, German history, civics, and the like are taught in German *and* at the same time Italian, Italian history, geography, and mathematics are taught in Italian (and now where the number of students warrants, in Spanish, Greek, and Yugoslav equivalents). Eventually the children leave school with a diploma that is valid both in Germany and Italy and are eligible for (and by German law to fulfill their school obligations required to take) the two-year professional (trade) training courses.* But "international" schools are not available everywhere. The alternatives are dismal. Children can sit, silent, mystified, and resentful, repeating the same secondary classes until they outgrow their desks and are given a certificate of "attendance." They can be sent home to school, compounding their confusion. Or they can become truants, ambiguous ones at that: truants before the law—with their parents' approval and encouragement.

Mario, Pietro's thirteen-year-old boy, did what I would have imagined impossible. He reached Düsseldorf just before Christmas. In January he went into the middle of his second year in secondary school, an "international" school, and at the end of the year was duly promoted to the next class. He is a steady, solemn boy who works hard. Although Liliana and Pietro speak German quite well, they do not write it. They were of little help to him, except that they had one very sound idea: the television set. During one of their weekend searches through castoffs, they found it, along with a kitchen cabinet, lined up neatly at the curb, ready for the dump. It was relatively new, appeared to be in good condition and, they decided, worth the investment to repair it. Worth it, that is, in the help it could be to the children. At first Mario had no friends, so he had plenty of time to watch the sports events, cartoons, and science-fiction films that were his natural choice. He says that without them he would never have heard enough German to understand it with ease. Once he did, the rest came automatically. He tells Rita that she must listen, must listen all the time, very carefully, and she will understand. She tries. She listens so intently that her concentration takes on a physical dimension, like a thick fog that slowly fills the sitting room, obscuring everything in it except the granular shadows

---

* Very, very few immigrant children are scholastically able to go on into the higher or technical schools. German authorities complain that relatively few take the professional training courses. Often with the repetition of classes they have satisfied the number of years in school required by law.

on the screen. Sometimes you see her eyes, heavy-lidded, staring at it with dislike. She does not give up. She persists and she understands what she hears, but for her understanding has not been the open sesame to reading, writing, and proper answers in school. She broods about it.

One day she came home from school and without hanging up her coat or even putting down her books, stalked through the sitting room, where she, Pina, and Mario sleep, into her mother and father's bedroom and closed the door. Pietro looked at me, surprised. Usually the first thing she wants to know is "What's for lunch?" We decided she would be out in a few minutes and, I am afraid, forgot her. Almost an hour later we realized that she was still there. Pietro went into the bedroom. In a few minutes he came out carrying her, no mean feat with a stocky eleven-year-old. Her head was pushed down against his shoulder. He talked very gently in her ear.

"If you don't believe *me*, ask the signora. She always tells the truth. Doesn't she?" He shook her playfully. She nodded without lifting her face. He sat down on the sofa (another sidewalk find) with Rita in his lap and went on talking quietly to her, waiting for her to lift her head. When, finally, she did, he said, "Now ask her."

She inspected our faces very carefully, as though to make sure we were really the people she thought. After long seconds she looked down at her hands and muttered, "They move away from me at school. They won't sit by me or play with me because ... because they say I stink. Do ... do I?" Now that the statement was made, she looked up at me, her eyes wide and timid and hurt. One thing that still surprises me is that she never cried. She brooded, she worried, but she did not cry. (I could have cried for her.)

She is the only non-German child in her class and one of only four in the neighborhood elementary school. Her schoolmates, like all children, had sensed a failure, the perfect butt without defenses or defenders, and had started their campaign. Rita was failing the fourth grade. Pietro and Liliana were bitter. The teacher should do more to help her. She should keep the children from teasing her, excluding her, but most of all she should help. The Ritas, Giovannis, and Carlos, according to their mothers, need just a "little bit" of help, a "little bit" of encouragement. A little bit? They need an entire language!

I tried to reason with Liliana and Pietro. Did they remember the summer their American cousin came to Torregreca? What funny clothes he wore? How incomprehensible everything he said was? How they teased him? That was different. No, not really, and what would have happened if that cousin had stayed on in Torregreca and gone to school?

Reason may be on my side, but parents, worried and hurt because their children have been hurt, are beyond the reach of reason. Pietro and Liliana and the dozens of other parents I talked to are right: they cannot be objective about their children and if they could be, their children would be much less secure. I persisted, knowing all the while it was futile. They would blame the teacher. But the teacher must take her class, perhaps thirty children, over a set block of subject matter in a given period of time. She can explain the basics. She can supply additional material, examples, illustrations not in textbooks. She can repeat and dissect concepts not understood. She can review and point out and question, but she *cannot* bring twenty-nine children to a standstill while she teaches one child the very language of the discussion, which the others already speak. No, they argued, their Rita, Giovanni, or Carlo had a right to help.

That they needed help, we all agreed, and one of the more probable ways would seem to be "after-school" groups organized especially for them to complement the rather short European school day. Games and various recreational activities can be offered and homework can be done under the supervision of a teacher who does have time to help and in cases of pronounced difficulty can work out special study plans, almost tutoring. The use of a classroom (or more) *after* the school day is over should not present complications. There remains the teacher's salary, which with everyone involved claiming lack of funds, has become a major hurdle and explains why relatively few "after-school" groups exist. They are available to 6.6 percent of the Italian schoolchildren in Germany, which, as it happened, did not include a single Torrese child.

From what I read, the "after-school" groups, rather than concentrating on scholastic improvement, seemed to provide the release of tremendous pent-up physical energy, aggression, and frustration, which are the children's not-so-surprising reactions to their anomalous position. The groups that I saw confirmed what I had read. The teachers struggled along, discouraged by the classroom teacher's lack of cooperation and by the children who were restless, impatient, unable and unwilling to understand. Exuberance was more obvious than passion for learning. After a long afternoon with one such group in a small town, I went in search of the mothers, who had by then come home from work. (Many Italian women work, legally, which is one of the premiums the Common Market bestowed with equality. The families of other foreign immigrants are not as free to work—legally.) I talked to twelve women, mostly Calabrian and Sicilian—incidentally only one of their children had ever been to a one-room multiclass school in Italy. They were delighted with the "after-school" group. It kept the children off the street, out of trouble, the least they should expect from a country that insists, but *insists* on keeping children in school after their time. What else should they be doing then? Working, of course! From which I can only decide that the mystique of education, like some dyes on synthetic cloth, has taken unevenly. If parents feel school is unnecessary, a waste of time, the children cannot be expected to consider it more seriously. The attitude is not common in Southern Italy and in this instance I suspect the answers are misleading, perhaps defensive. The women did, I believe, feel guilty about leaving the children to their own devices all day, every day—but I could go no further. I had myself become one of those "investigators" asking personal questions of unknown people. I can, at least, resist specious conclusions.

Only a Solomon would dare to assess the accusations of the school authorities, German and Italian, and lay guilt where guilt belongs. No special wisdom or intuition is needed, however, to understand that the formal integration of immigrant children into German schools, guaranteed by agreement as their right, meets with apathy (if not open obstruction) from the authorities of the different *Länder* or that the Italian government has been derelict, shamefully so, in the execution of its responsibilities. Diplomacy required a show of noble intent. Integration is on the record, proof for all to see and talk about, but is not a crusade—just another token. It could never really have been otherwise when a German teacher can talk about the inability of the "Mediterranean races" to understand "our" (i.e., Anglo-Saxon) concepts of responsibility, reasoning, and citizenship, and when an Italian school supervisor, speaking of Italian immigrant children, can tell a German school principal, "They were born in the mud of the *mezzogiorno*, let them die in the mud of Germany."

This year Rita is repeating the fourth grade. Liliana and Pietro talk of sending her home to Torregreca, if she fails again. Another problem must be solved first: they are on such bad terms with their relatives that no one is willing to keep her. Rita's years of brooding are not over yet.

Pietro worried about Rita. He worried about his mother-in-law, his sister-in-law, and about where he could find an apartment that was far enough away from them and still near enough Mario's school, but most of all he worried about finding work. Even being unemployed was a full-time job. He spent much of each day in a tour of offices that had to do with his immediate problem.

On his arrival a year before he had gone to work in the infamous tire plant, one of six men on a team assigned to operate two enormous molds. People came and people went in that section. The work required stamina, not skill, and because the men could communicate what little they had to say in obvious gestures, any man who was healthy, whatever his nationality, was hired. They were well paid, but no one lasted long. The miasma of steam and hot rubber picked them off one by one. Pietro worked there six months and ten days, just long enough to be eligible for unemployment compensation, only partial at that, because he was not dismissed, he quit. He had not been sure he could last. Once he had asked to be transferred and was sent to a section where raw rubber was processed. It was worse. He went back to the molds, drank milk as prescribed by the plant doctor against the toxic effects of the fumes, took aspirin for his persistent pounding headache, and lost 17 kilos (37.5 lbs.) in the bargain.

After he quit, he spent a month at home. He physicked himself, gobbled liver purifiers and kidney flushers, and worried. When he felt better, he was surprised and a little disappointed. Thoughts of a disability pension had danced in his head. Instead he went out looking for work again and found a job with a subcontractor who specialized in the mounting of "structures," which seems to mean any combination of a framework and attachable panels, from oil storage tanks to Quonset huts and geodesic domes. His crews might work in Duisberg one week, Munich the next, and Hanover a month later, which explains why the men were paid so well: 2,200 DM ($1,100) a month.

From Sunday night to Friday night they were away from home. (*N.B.* Absence from home did not worry Pietro in a job he liked.) They had to pay for their room, board, and transportation. They could pig it, four to a room, cooking on a gas ring, or they could throw their money away at the Grand Hotel. The contractor did not care. He had to know that, wherever he sent them, they would be present and able to work five days a week. Much of the work was outside and so subject to weather. There were delays. Often consignment dates were not met. For each extra day the contractor paid a fine. Fines could add up, at times leaving less in hand than he owed the crew. He had a foolproof system: he vanished, stranding three or four workers, taking the others with him to an unannounced destination. Pietro spent four glorious months on the mounting crew. He worked hard, saved a lot of money, and saw every city of any size in Germany. He was quite prepared to continue. Then the contractor disappeared, and he and three other men were left behind, unpaid.

At the Düsseldorf employment office the clerks just smiled. It was all familiar, a routine bit of chicanery for this gentleman. Pietro need not worry. He would be paid as soon as the next contract was settled, which was reassuring, but not at the moment helpful. He must file unemployment applications, register for employment, start the involved process of claiming his back wages from the subcontractor, which he did, naturally, through the Italian union assistance committee, *and* go the rounds in search of work. He said it was like his first days in the army. Everywhere he went there was a crowd of men, the same men, all wanting the same thing, pushing, staring blankly into space, carefully ignoring each other so that no courtesy, no bit of free advice, no surrender of place in line could be claimed. In the army those silent struggles had been for uniforms and toilets and meals, all things that seemed important then. In Düsseldorf they were bitter contests for jobs.

Immigrant laborers are, by definition, unskilled. There are exceptions. Some have trades, but not trades that will support them at home. Travel means trauma: their own cities frighten them; a foreign country is like falling off the edge of the earth. Only the desperate leave and certain tragic corollaries follow. They have minimal educations by the standards of their own countries (Turkey, Yugoslavia, Greece, Spain, Portugal, and Italy), whose standards are, in turn, well below those of industrialized Northern countries. (Italy, always a contradiction, manages to fit both categories. Underindustrialized and overpopulated, it has a plethora of schools relentlessly educating the city young in nonskills and a scarcity of professional schools in the South.) Their wives may have less education, never more. They do not know languages, even their own. Their traditions, customs, and food are conspicuously different. Their families are large and continue to grow and with them grows the pressure on the country of immigration to supply housing, schools, and the other public services—garbage disposal, transportation, utilities—that we take so for granted.

Immigrants who are construction workers and content to be such, seem to settle in more easily than those with industrial ambitions. The benefits and drawbacks of their work are known. The foreman may be a bastard. Winters can be so severe that contruction is halted. The muscles ache. Flu and colds and mashed fingers follow each other with dreary regularity—all that is true, but Italians have an innate affinity for stone. They understand it and what they are asked to do with it, and they know that on any construction crew they will find other Italians. They may not like each other: but even quarreling and hate are signs of life and familiar. In Germany, Switzerland, and France they can make their peace with the familiar. The unknown life of a factory disorients the mind, the body, and finally the sense of life itself.

Every worker arrives with his own dowry of problems and ignorance, social factors which, however agonizing, do not concern the personnel director of a factory. His duty is to find and hire efficient labor. The plant manager sees them from a slightly different, equally impersonal point of view. He has no time to coddle them. He wants an operation that runs smoothly. He needs to be sure that the men hired are capable of the jobs assigned to them and, in a very loose sense, of getting along with their fellow workers. Nothing more.

Rather than visit huge industrial complexes where sheer size and number of workers reduce contact to a minimum, I talked to the personnel managers and plant managers at half a dozen small and medium-sized factories. They were honest, hardworking men who tried to be fair. They were also human and had their preferences and their prejudices, based on experience or interior chemistry. Their opinions varied in emphasis, not substance. Unfortunately. If a Turk, a Greek, a Spaniard, and an Italian of uniform inexperience applied for work requiring no skill, the Italian would be the last choice. He might hold his own against the Yugoslav, although those who had actually employed Yugoslavs were loud in their praise and placed them well ahead of Italians. Why?

Their reasons were very clear. 1) Italians are too independent; they move on if not satisfied. 2) Italians do not learn German: *all* of the others, they claimed, do better. 3) Italians are not interested in courses, often given by the management, to earn their qualification in a skill. 4) Italians lose more workdays to ill health than the others. Willful absenteeism was implied, never stated. 5) Italians are never active in plant unions, which in Germany, beyond their traditional domain of wages and shop problems, are powerful in certain specific sectors of the management.

What, at first glance, is a blanket indictment of Italian immigrants in all respects, *except*, curiously enough, the quality of their work, begins to crumble under inspection. The Italians are less desirable because they do not do what the management thinks they have some moral, as against financial, obligation to do. They ought to

———— (fill in the blank) because our modern industrial ethic prescribes it. For their betterment, of course.

Taken one by one the criticisms are revealing.

Italians are too independent: they move on if not satisfied. There is a difference between hiring a man and buying one. The Italian, armed with Common Market equality, is not chained to one job. He can look elsewhere, if he does not like the work, the pay, or his foreman. The Turk, Greek, Spaniard, or Yugoslav cannot—legally. They acquire their jobs under special contracts and are imported, like any other merchandise. No doubt it is convenient for industry to have men who cannot leave, as it is convenient for industry to have the right of block dismissal at the end of the contract, if the men are not needed—and their automatic repatriation without damage to unemployment figures or compensation funds. The criticism, translated, is that Italians are undesirable because they cannot be manipulated.

Italians do not learn German: *all* of the others, they claimed, do better. I did not make a survey of Italian workers in Germany, nor would I be a judge of their fluency in German. Many Torresi have worked in plants for years and manage enough German. Pietro, for instance, in the shopping we did together, in his conversations with the employment authorities and the waiters in his friends' bars clipped along at a furious rate. I am sure his accent is atrocious and his grammar a travesty, but no one had trouble understanding him, which is the point of language. He has his limitations. If he was asked to discuss the Industrial Revolution, its social and philosophical aspects, the responsibility of management to the worker and vice versa, it would be beyond him in German—and Italian.

Italians are not interested in courses, often given by management, to earn their qualification in a skill. As soon as Turks, Greeks, Yugoslavs, and Spaniards know German well enough they throw themselves into courses.* They can go home with a trade and be

---

* Actually German government figures tell another story: 6 percent of all immigrants take courses for semiskilled qualification, which is no more than factory orientation for their specific job, and only 2 percent take courses for definite trade specialization.

privileged workers, sought after and highly paid by the blossom-
ing (?) industries of their own countries. German industry offered,
spontaneously, its contribution to the social and economic improvement of countries less prosperous. The Italians are not interested.
Their hosts are offended and disillusioned. They should not be.
Their preconception, not entirely disinterested, was that this system
would comply with their non–Common Market agreements, keep
the immigrants settled and quiet for as long as they stayed, and send
them back to their homelands as skilled men who would prosper
and so not be tempted to roam. The logic is almost logical: unskilled
laborers abound in Turkey, Yugoslavia, Greece, and Spain; trained,
skilled men are scarce. But in Italy skilled men are not scarce. Jobs
are—particularly in the South.

Italian industry, so creative in most ways, is also creative in
mismanagement. The techniques are simple: overhiring, inefficient
planning, eternal refinancing, each new transfusion funneled, not
into the ailing business, but somehow into directors' (too often political appointees) pockets or their pet projects. Those management
features, coupled with general government policies and the Christian
Democrats' weakness for union blackmail—if you do not give us the
increases we demand, the Communists will take over—has brought
Italian industry to semisolvency (or semibankruptcy) which, always
endemic, now threatens to become epidemic. Another practice com-
pounds the problem: if a company is ailing, the directors try with
some fancy political footwork to sell it off to the government holding company, which *guarantees* mismanagement and losses, now
minor matters, neither real nor worrying, because the taxpayer pays.
For many industries, tottering under the weight of their own perennial blunders, the interest costs on borrowed capital and wage hikes
(now with an automatic escalation clause tied to the cost-of-living
index), 1973 and the oil crisis meant collapse. Some companies hus-
tled into bankruptcy; others work on limited schedules. The result:
fewer jobs. More skilled workers are and will be unemployed. Some,
especially those with automotive skills, were trained in Germany.

Italian workers, even the least indoctrinated in union lore, are
pragmatic. After a day of heavy work, an immigrant in Germany

does not see the sense of learning a skill that he probably will not be encouraged to use there and knows he cannot use in Italy.

Italians lose more workdays to ill health than others. Willful absenteeism implied, never stated. I asked if we could compare the record of German workers with those of foreign workers. None of the personnel or plant managers objected. It might take a few minutes to dig out the figures. When they arrived—without exception—they disproved the statement. Foreign workers in general showed a fractionally higher number of days in a year that they are away from work because of illness. Throughout, the Italians were in the middle of the foreign band, neither the worst nor the best. The personnel managers and plant managers were surprised themselves. Their *impression* had been that Italians lost more days: their impression was honest, if wrong.

Many of these men spoke English extremely well, but to be on the safe side and courteous I always had an interpreter with me. One of them was a young university student, whose English was proficient and whose manner was particularly pleasant. Her opinions were, as far as she had formulated them, liberal. Immigration was by no means a favorite subject. It was a situation/problem that she had grown up with and assumed, as I think I would have, that her country was doing everything possible to make it profitable and painless for everyone concerned. She went with me to a medium-sized plant outside Frankfurt, where, as it happened, the personnel manager spoke English and the plant manager did not. I had warned her not to be surprised by my blandness. She should translate my questions and the answers to them, ask questions of her own if there was any doubt about the fullness of the answers, but that under no circumstances was she to tell me her impressions of their real opinions, their prejudices or half-truths. While we were there. Once we left, I would be very interested. She, of course, had not heard the story as often as I.

She was very alert and careful in her translations and added some questions of her own that made the men relax. Much of her conversation was, of necessity, with the plant manager who was a gentle, pensive man with a slow smile and a quiet sense of humor.

The personnel manager, whose attentions never wavered from me, was a much more aggressive, younger man bent on making a point. He accepted without too much consideration, not enough anyway, my professed attitude of we are two Anglo-Saxons discussing the difficult matter of "those others." My interpreter was thrown slightly off balance by this new persona. She hesitated, looking puzzled, then remembered my instructions and plunged on with her questioning of the plant manager.

After an hour and a half we left, and I was treated to the full force of her irritation, surprise, and shame. The condescension, the arrogance of our plant manager (who had not seemed arrogant to me) and our personnel manager! Foreign workers were not men they employed. They thought of them as serfs, interchangeable, obligated to work and obey and disappear from sight on command. They would not dare treat a German worker, even a totally unskilled one, as a specimen of a lower order. I understood her reaction: mine had not been too different that day and many others. What worried me was an inevitable side effect. Of all infectious attitudes, superiority is the most virulent. Management with its contempt for foreign laborers issues an official license to the Germans who work with them: immigrants can be despised with impunity. Their days must be long, lonely, and bitter.

As a consolation I reminded my interpreter of the plant manager's suggestion that perhaps immigrants had a slightly higher absentee rate because they had to take care of all administrative formalities for themselves and their families, whereas German wives could do most of it for their husbands. She countered with the personnel manager's parting remark to me: "We needed the Italians in the sixties. I guess we'll just have to put up with them in the seventies."

Italians are never active in plant unions, which, in Germany, beyond the traditional domain of wages and shop problems, are powerful in certain specific sectors of the management. Over and over again this was cited as typical of the Italians' failure to integrate. At several factories the personnel manager and the plant manager talked enthusiastically of a Turk or Spaniard, a Greek or Yugoslav who was on the union council and widely respected. There was never more than one, which did give an aura of "the house immigrant." He had always been elected in the normal way. By whose votes? By the Turks, the Spanish, the Greeks, or the Yugoslavs, whichever was the majority within the minority and organized. Because they tend to come under group contracts, one or the other will always constitute a majority. The Italians seldom do and are not association-minded. Instinctively they distrust other nationalities, their would-be co-members, and problems of language and historic antipathies further inhibit recognition of their common interests. As the Communists' efforts at union organization prove, immigrants can be convinced and will finally act together. If immigrant employees of a German factory remained the same over a period of years, long enough to trust each other and the representatives they elected (and voting in a bloc, they would elect a higher number), if they *did* finally act together, I wonder how German workers, their union representatives, and the management would react. Theory is one thing: practice is another. As I have said, the immigrant is, by definition, unskilled: preferably he should also be docile.

For once the Torresi were unanimous: to join a union in Germany with the idea of participating is a waste of time. German workers, through their representatives, control the unions. They should: they are theirs. They will continue to control them with or without the votes of foreign workers. So be it. Italians have nothing to lose. They share *every* benefit the Germans win—without cost to themselves. In that one respect, contrary to the Bible, they reap without sowing.

On the first of October 1977 Pietro was collecting unemployment compensation and looking for work. By February of 1978 nothing had changed. Government payments and odd jobs kept him and his family alive. He still resisted his wife's nagging and refused to work as a waiter. In my travels I had met a contractor in a large town not too far from Düsseldorf who employed just under a hundred Italian contruction workers, skilled and unskilled, among them half a dozen

Torresi. He required them to sign a two-year contract. In exchange he guaranteed work, full salaries with all insurances and contributions paid—and a house. I suggested Pietro should talk to him. He did. He came back admitting that the Italians were there, the houses too, that everyone spoke highly of the contractor, but . . . well . . . he guessed he wouldn't go there. The only real excuse he offered: there was no "international" school in the town. Mario would suffer. Poor Mario who hates the city and longs to be in the country! Liliana accepted the reason as valid. She did not know, as I did, that there *is* such a school in the town.

Pietro went back to see his old foreman at the tire factory. The section was all Turks now. They could not get anyone else. *Va bene,* signora, that I had to leave Italy to find work and it will always be hard work that no German wants—but—I don't have to sink to the level of the Turks! They take what no one will touch. The rubber molds! Let them! But not me! Italians, who were themselves the Turks of the early immigration years, consider themselves the gentlemen of immigrants now. A pointless snobbery, but they worked hard for this right of pretense and they protect it. For once they are not the lowest, the most despised, the *Terroni*—they think.

Finally in June of 1978 Pietro went to work in a factory that manufactures detergents, which would not, a priori, seem an improvement. How long he will stay there is hard to tell: at least six months and ten days.

Cities and their industries, both so foreign! Why do immigrants cling to them? Not for money. Whatever more they may earn, they have to spend. Reaction, I believe, plays its part. Immigration means failure; for some the failure of the system, for others, like Pietro, more morbidly self-conscious, their own. In small towns, the Torregrecas, it also means humiliation to the Pietros. When they leave home, they admit defeat. To go to a small German town, another Torregreca, however prosperous, confirms their defeat. To leave for something better relieves stigma: factories, industrial cities, modern life. Cities offer them a kind of defense. They also offer true isolation—loneliness, distrust, bitterness, alienation—all the bleakness of exile. It can, at least, be suffered in privacy. So, if it comes, can another defeat. Cities give them the public illusion of success; the pale, private illusion, as a few are honest enought to admit, is the *possibility* of success. But without some defense, either reason or appearance, without illusions, even the palest, the human being cannot survive.

Epilogue

My pursuit of emigrants made me—*nolens volens*—an emigrant too. A year of perpetual motion, in places not strange of themselves, only strange to me, left little time to think. People and places jumble together and confound. What memory has lost, my notebooks and tapes retain in their dates, their summaries of conversations, their hurried impressions. If I need them, they are there, just across the desk. For months I have not looked at them. They cannot tell me, now, what I need to know.

How does the *potatore* of olive trees know which branches should be cut, which trunks should be sliced and pared and hacked almost in two, if the tree is to be saved and grow strong? Experience? It helps. It confirms what he senses, for he *senses* a drain on the tree, a distorted growth or the rot so pernicious and invisible. His saw and ax prove him right. There is no such proof for ideas, for opinions, and yet if they are to be sound, they need the same treatment. Judicious plowing and proper doses of fertilizer, or with ideas, experience and research, are not enough. They still need to be pruned, the trunks tested, suckers removed, branches must be trimmed, a shape imposed. The human being as pruner is fallible. He has some choices about which there is no doubt. Others, he only *senses* are right. He must trust his intuition, a most capricious tool. Decision is not a scientific process. For months I have wished that I had a saw or an ax. It is too late now: the choices have all been made, the shape imposed. I know what I think and must stand on it.

Chichella has played her own particular part in it all, from our first trip to Germany to the last evening of the Festa this summer. We do not always agree. We bicker amiably over impressions. On questions of theory, international trade, laws, or analysis of trends, she defers to me, commenting with a pride that suggests she has resisted a vice, "Of course I don't read all that junk you do." In matters of the past, I defer to her. The present is an open battlefield. She has a knack, almost a theatrical trick, of re-creating any scene. If I say, "How did we ever start talking about...?" she reels back through the dialogue, picks up her cue, and starts forward again with words, action, and nuances. She is a research assistant *per eccellenza*, rather like having your own "instant replay" mechanism. She pooh-poohs it as just another compensation for illiteracy. She may yet convince me that I am "disadvantaged."

She gave me four eyes, two points of view, and some surprises, the first of them the least expected. Chichella has always been a silent traveler. She is uneasy between places, neither here nor there, so nowhere, and she has a definite tendency to be carsick. Her remedy is to settle her body bolt upright, well braced, and allow her mind to slip away into a therapeutic lethargy which only arrival can shatter. Maybe once an hour she will make some sudden comment—"You know he died?" or "I wonder why the geraniums wilted"—in a distant, autistic voice. Sometimes she answers questions, sometimes not. As a companion she is a patient corpse, whose spirit seems to be of two minds about transmigration. She is no trouble and no company: the alternative would be far worse.

I had worried about our long trip, about the effect it might have on her, and about the Alps. Our first twelve-hour day to Saronno she spent deep in her trance. The second morning I headed for the Saint Gotthard Pass with trepidation. Geography is vague to her, and I had not mentioned the mountains, but they were there shimmering in the clear, clear light. She started, looked frightened for a second, and then began twisting around to see out the windows. She may even have thought she had dozed off into the other world. She was terribly excited. The houses with their steep thatched roofs, the cascades of water, the splendor of great rock spires that caught the sunlight, small boys stumbling through pastures behind their cows—everything seemed to delight her. She laughed and smiled and pointed. She tried to imagine what life would be like in those houses perched on the slopes, and soon she forgot to worry altogether. By the time we reached Lucerne, she had also forgotten that curves make her dizzy and sick. There was so much to see, so much that was different. The light, the houses, even the people were different.

The Alps converted Chichella. She would have been converted much sooner, she said, "if there was anything to see in Italy," a judgment so final it could shake even Sir Kenneth Clark's urbanity. Under the circumstances, I did not quibble. She is a relaxed passenger now, a jaunty tourist, tireless in her curiosity, and best of all, she knows that she can talk without courting the disintegration of body and soul. We chattered through four thousand miles, avoiding thruway lag and establishing what must be a record for continuous debate.

From Freiburg to Heidelberg to Offenbach and Frankfurt and on to Düsseldorf, through our detours to villages and our picnics at the side of the road we talked of what we had seen, the people, their present and what might be their future. The only taboo was Edda. Sisters-in-law celebrate their incompatability. I refused to discuss either with the other. Chichella's verdicts on the adults were harsh. She spun cocoons for them from the historical and genealogical threads of their lives. Each was a stark individual, precisely rooted in his unique past. The present was only part of the story and the future would lead irrevocably from the other two. She was not easily impressed. She does not believe in new virtues or the death of old vices.

Leniency and fanciful hopes, she saved for the children. About the half-grown she tried to be realistic, as she is about her own children. They are here, now, ready for some kind of life and little has changed. About small children her objectivity collapsed. She did not see them as combinations of their fathers and mothers, those people she had already stretched and mounted as neatly as butterflies. The young raise flurries of tenderness and optimism. They are small, defenseless, and strangely themselves. They must be different. For us puppies are not the snarling watchdogs of the future, nor tiger cubs the predators. These children would not be the unemployed, the whores, the masons, or the laborers of the future. They would have better food, better schools, better clothes, and so a better chance and better lives. I wish I thought so.

We swept back through Switzerland, the debate lively as ever. Northern Italy was yet to come. Chichella surprised me again at the border, where one lone guard looked out, bewildered, over a kilometer of cars that swarmed and growled and jockeyed for places at his gate, the only gate bv. Well-dressed older men shook their fists at each other. One beautiful young woman yowled obscenities at anyone who resisted her bumper. A mild-looking man in a gray suit got out of his car and kicked savagely at his tires in frustration: the radiator had boiled. It was irritating to have hikers with backpacks stride by us. Cigarette wrappers and plastic bags and the litter from picnics shuffled and flipped about in the plumes of exhaust, and Chichella, the experienced traveler who could now compare Italy to other countries, went into paroxysms of *autocritica*. Why was Italy so messy? Unruly? So disorganized? As we finally neared the gate, she found a new target: the guard. His shirt was dirty. Why didn't they make him straighten his tie? Throw away his cigarette? In Germany ... He was surly about the date on my passport: he could not find it. He waved us through with a flip of his hand. In France the guards bowed and saluted. ... Every other Italian car was motioned to the parking lot, where dozens of drivers, waiting for inspectors, squabbled with each other about who arrived first. Chichella assumed that our obvious respectability had saved us the trial. No, my American passport, I explained. I am a certified tourist: Italy tries not to offend its largest source of income.

The homecoming she had looked forward to was a shock. The

frenzied traffic made her flinch. The ladies' room at the gas station was dirty. The Neopolitan station attendant tried to shortchange me of 10,000 lire. My acid remarks were compliments compared to Chichella's. Italians have no pride, no dignity. There was trash everywhere and the noise—it gave her a headache. Suddenly chaos struck her as chaos, not the freehand confusion she had always accepted as order. For the first time in her life she saw Italy as others see it, and was ashamed.

Our days in Turin and Milan, our visits depressed her further. The Torresi were aggressive in their well-being. They were rich. They were the smart ones. They were safe and at home. They—They—They. They seemed blind and trapped by their own resentment, unable to see any contradiction in their imitations of the very attitudes they resented. In long years there they had endured enough condescension from Northerners to learn the manner. The *invidia* that they had brought from home as a mere cutting has grown into a choking vine, and a Melina is warning that innocence is dangerous. Chichella and I were both glad to leave.

She was quiet again on the trip South. Not for lack of scenery—she admitted that she had never really looked before. She was thinking, deciding about something. When we were off the thruway and less than a hundred miles from Torregreca, I asked her the one question I had avoided all those days. I had wanted to wait until we were back in a landscape that was familiar and close to home. What did she think now about emigration? Her answer was her last surprise.

"Twenty years ago—when my husband died—if I'd known Germany is like it is, *I* would have gone there. *Si, signora! With* the children. Wasn't anybody to keep them. And we'd have made out all right. I'd be rich now, not just safe, and I'm lucky to be safe." She hesitated: safety outweighs almost all temptations. "I'll tell you another thing. If it weren't for losing my pension, I'd go right now, *today!* Not to a city and *not* to the North—that's like changing one pair of wornout shoes for another—but I'd go to Germany. *Right now.* Twenty years ago—if I'd just gone then. But I didn't know, signò. What do you ever *know* in Torregreca? We would have been all right. Better off than we are today and happier—*ma* ..." The rest of the way to Torregreca she was quiet, but she nodded often, abruptly, as though she approved of the points in her own silent argument.

I agreed with her then and still do about herself and without qualification: She is a survivor.

In the next ten months I was in Torregreca often enough to inspire a new generation of rumors: through some secret pact with The Authorities (unspecified), I had taken over the nursery again; I opposed the marriage of Chichella's daughter (actually I was her witness in the wedding); I was going to manage/own the *salame* factory! All flights of fancy that honored me with varied, fugitive powers. When I came back for the Festa the second year in a row, the Torresi reversed themselves. I am, after all, only a woman. My reappearance was a simple matter of *cherchez l'homme!* They watched me very carefully. They had nothing better to do.

Torregreca has for too long had a regular gait—one step forward, two steps back—to change. Last year's Festa was so gay, so profitable, so un-Torrese, that this year's must fail. Since the Torresi have a fatal skill, the opposite of a green thumb, they went one better: there was *no* Festa at all.

No lacy ornaments festooned the streets, no bands played, no chairs were put out in the Piazza, and no "Lioness" from anywhere came to stomp and snarl. Last year's still threatened to sue the *comune*. The actor had. No one was willing to be chairman of the Festa committee, which boasted a healthy deficit and a portfolio of accounts due. For a while there was even some question about the Madonna: would she or would she not be transported to the cathedral? The curia was said to feel that, under the circumstances, this might be the moment to respect the calendar and reinstate the original date, later in the fall, for her annual outing. No one was quite sure what the decision had been until one evening, in the semidarkness, she *did* wobble down the road on the usual blue truck, which was decked for the occasion with white tablecloths, large lace doilies, and some wilting gladioli. By the time she and her twin-axled litter reached the Piazza, the loungers had gone home for supper. She was unattended at the cathedral and several days later without fanfare she was hauled off home again. The Festa had disintegrated, and the final proof, if more were needed, was both negative and irrefutable: each evening at sunset the seneschal of the aqueduct valves shut off all water to the town.

Two things remained resolutely the same: the weather, which by day was clear and warm, by night cool to cold; and the returned emigrants who, dressed in their city clothes, cruised gently back and forth in their quiet cars. They were depressed. The days limped along, never seemed to pass. Their quarters, either cot dormitories with relatives or makeshifts with the skeletons of comfort they themselves had left behind, were not inviting places to spend a day. They must be outside. There was nothing to do. Their children were peevish. Grumbling was a very temporary pleasure. They did a lot of it just the same. This was the ultimate betrayal! The town had never offered anything in fair measure. Not schools! Not work! Not food! Not public services! And now not even a Festa!

The Communist party had thought to take up the slack (and win a captive audience) by organizing one of their summer hoedowns called a *Festa dell'Unità*. They offered three activities: political speeches, contests of *ballo liscio*, the old dances—the waltz, tango, and fox-trot—newly fashionable again, and donkey races. The program as printed on the poster looked all right. The reality was disappointing. The gaiety opened in front of the elementary school with several political speeches, about an hour's worth. Then a record, played on an old bent turntable that was attached to an even older, broken amplifier, boomed and crackled its music over the crowd and was accompanied by the master of ceremonies' voice, booming and crackling too as he bellowed, "*Ballo liscio!* Everybody dance the *ballo liscio! Ballo liscio!* Everybody dance the *ballo liscio!*" The children, hundreds of them, were eager to oblige. The only other *ballerini* were old couples. The sets seemed geared for their endurance. They were very short and gave way to more political speeches. The donkey races, which might have added a change of pace, proved hard to organize: the student-youths of today do not crave such bucolic amusements, and there are few donkeys left, none of age and condition to race. The *Festa dell'Unità* went on for a week. One evening, part of one at least, was enough for most. The emigrants sneered. They had not come home to listen to that crap. What did the Communist party think they were—cave dwellers?

The days were dreary. We milled around, trying to invent things to do, which sooner or later, *faute de mieux*, brought us to the Piazza, the stage on which hundreds of little scenes were played out for the bystanders. Late one of the first mornings I was in Torregreca, I too went to the Piazza to buy, or try to buy, a newspaper. (That day the train skipped us.) I had to pick my way through groups of men and around cars. I skirted a semicircle of silent men, listening to one man who stood in the open space they had left, talking and gesticulating emphatically. What did he have to say that was so fascinating? I wondered. From my brief sideways glimpse he looked very sleek: carefully combed dark hair, well cut, a clean pink jaw, and a tan suit of fine, fine herringbone material, so well fitted it might have been upholstered on him. I had passed him when he spun around and called after me,

"*Ehhhh, ciao, signò! Ciao! Come va?*" I waved vaguely and hurried on with my head down. That sort of familiarity would keep rumors flying! Who in the world was he? From the café, while I had my coffee, I watched him. The group split up into twos and threes, and he started walking slowly back and forth across the Piazza, his arm around the shoulders of his companion. On the third turn I recognized Paolo. The depression and listlessness of Offenbach had been replaced by brisk, expansive gestures, a quick smile, bright eyes. He put a friendly hand on men's shoulders as they passed, stopped to have a whispered conference with the deputy mayor ("business with important people" would be the interpretation), and disappeared with his friend into another café.

Ten minutes later a long low car with a German license plate, a VW Passat, cobalt blue and immaculate, swept in a wide arc around the Piazza and stopped by the monument. I admired the courage of the driver, who had never slowed down, but assumed the crowds would part—and they did. In a few minutes Paolo came out of his café, shook hands with his friend, waved at others, and walked quickly over to the cobalt blue Passat, which two or three men had already stopped to admire. Paolo talked to them, smiling, and then got in the back seat and was driven away, still smiling and waving two-finger salutes to friends with languid majesty.

Lucetta had not come with him—no one knew why—nor had the boys, but Rosa and her sister served loyally as chauffeur and footman. They polished the car every morning, they washed it twice, and morning and afternoon they drove him in town. He kept a schedule well calculated to coincide with the peak audience: he arrived at ten-thirty and was called for at noon; at exactly six he reappeared, stayed an hour, and again was picked up. Rosa always drove with her sister sitting beside her, both looking straight ahead, unaware, as far as you could tell from their expressions, of anyone, just as the caryatids had been last summer. This summer they were not dignified in shame: they were confident in superiority.

People were agog with the news that Paolo had bought "apartments" in Rome. And the car! Just something he felt he deserved after all these years of sacrifice, he said. It was new, of course, and costly, but ... (not quite as costly as he led them to believe, but at least $7,500). Personally he advised real estate. Protection against inflation. Good sound investment. Each to his own choice. *Liberissimo*, naturally! But he'd say real estate. Men began to speak of him with puzzled respect. (Did they notice that for three weeks he wore the same suit, shirt, tie, and shoes? I doubt it.)

Anna and Franco were home from Offenbach too. Though Paolo was not on their list of visits, Chichella and I were. I had seen them strolling along the road, talking to each other, not paying the slightest attention to the people who passed them. Most of their friends in Torregreca were gone, they said, or too many years had passed, or maybe they had changed. They weren't sure. People treated them like strangers. They were. In their nice casual clothes they might have been any middle-class couple come to the mountains for a brief holiday. They did not stay long. Carlo and Antonietta were bored. In truth, so were Franco and Anna. They left ten days before they had planned. Franco said he might be back in 1988—or better 1998. Either would do. Nothing would have changed in Torregreca.

I had missed Edda and Michele. Their trip had not been a success really either. Michele had wanted to stay "at home," a telling remark. He only came to satisfy Edda. He spent most of his time at Chichella's sitting on the balcony, talking to her if she was there, reading, dozing, if she was not. Edda was busy elsewhere, picking fights with her relatives. Nicola has his car: his job was too new for him to have a vacation. Michele left me a tin of my favorite German cigarettes and a message: if I would come to see them soon, he would organize another dance!

Bianca too had come and gone. She must have been following a private scorched-earth policy. She had offended everyone. "Who does she think she is," they kept asking each other, "to give herself such airs?" She has promised never to come back again. They say good riddance.

For several days Melina paraded up and down on the road, almost as though it were the *Corso* of Turin, spreading the good news that she had bought another café, larger, closer to the center of the city. Her clothes were admired, and she knew it: during her stay she changed them twice a day and never once repeated.

Each day I made my calls, as many as I could before a sad, heavy weariness overtook me. At times I was an awkward visitor. Tales of splendor and prosperity had to be very carefully fashioned, if I was there listening to what friends and relatives were told. I knew the truth. One afternoon I went to see a woman who lives now in a busy town near Milan where thousands of men are employed by one dominant company that processes food. I had spent just one morning with her there, sitting in her large, cold living room on bulbous fake-leather furniture, but it had been long enough for her to give me a running account of the last years. For twelve years she had cleaned the local post office from four in the morning to eight and from eight to noon had cleaned and cooked for a teacher. The director of the post office assured her that she was *effettiva*, that is legally, permanently hired, insured, and eligible for a pension in time. Two years ago when she needed a hysterectomy, she discovered that she was not *effettiva* at all, had no insurance and no payments toward her pension. The operation was taken care of by her husband's insurance—he is legally employed by the processing company—but she is still trying to reclaim the withholdings so thoughtfully deducted by a clerk in the post office. "I wonder what he does for pocket money *now*!" she spat at me bitterly. I could hardly blame her.

This summer her husband amused their neighbors by appearing late each afternoon on their balcony in his pajamas to stand, leaning on the iron rail for an hour or more, watching people pass on the road below. I had seen him and been amused too. He gave Torregreca a strange touch of certain seaside resorts where in the first fifty years of the century such a display was a mark of gentility.

When I arrived his wife, dressed in her dark silk print dress and high-heeled pumps, was sitting in the kitchen with an old aunt and two cousins. Already on the stairs I had heard the harsh staccato sounds of her voice. She speaks only Milanese now and was probably talking about her diet. She has bored everyone with it, urged them to try it: grilled meat or steamed fish twice a day, boiled, unseasoned vegetables, milk, I seem to remember, and no wine. It will never catch on in Torregreca. She fussed over me, yelling more than seemed necessary. For whose benefit? She made a pot of coffee. It was just beginning to hiss when her husband shambled through the kitchen in his pajamas and went out onto the balcony.

"Coffee's almost ready," she called after him and turned back to us with a shrugging smile. "All these years up there—*sapete*—habit. He can't do without his nap and a bit of air on the balcony. We have a beautiful balcony...."

"Every day...?" asked one cousin.

"But his job...?" murmured the other.

"No, no—supervisors—you know. They have different schedules, time off..." Her voice trailed away. She had remembered I was there. "Well, that is—ah..." She stopped herself and glanced again at me. What would I say? Her husband is a loader on the shipping platform. Her apartment is large and new. In a climate as cold and foggy as Milan's, balconies are ornamental. She does not actually have one, and if she did it would overlook a large freight yard. To reassure her I talked at length about her apartment, the furniture, the floors, the bathrooms, all the things she would be proudest of. Then I drank my coffee and left as soon as courtesy allowed.

She was no worse than the others. They exchanged lies like Christmas cards. Each afternoon I went home and puzzled over those lies and the hints—not quite lies, that implied without claiming, a status, a well-being or the hardware to establish them—that I knew were fictions. Who were they for, those lies? For their friends? To impress them? Or for themselves? And each evening while Chichella and what we still call "the children" watched television, and long after they went to bed, I sat at the kitchen table, forcing myself finally to do my job of pruning and decide what I think about emigration.

At two o'clock on my last night there, I finished as precise a statement as I am capable of, one that is more detached, perhaps, than I feel, but one that I believe to be true.

Migration is as old as recorded history. Nomads, indeed, preferred it as a way of life. For all the others it has been the last resort, the price they paid for being the weakest members of their societies. It was their last chance to survive and always the last, dread resort: satisfied people do not leave home; prosperous people do not welcome them and the poor are their natural enemies. Today in the Western world, limited in space and driven by economic fears, it can only be an act of desperation, endured by immigrants and hosts alike without gratitude or sympathy, a placebo, not a cure. No matter what the moral bleatings of politicians—exploitation, conditions, rights— emigration suits the governments concerned too perfectly for reform. Mediterranean countries, overpopulated, without industries, and never the most stable, must siphon off their hordes of unemployed (the younger the more dangerous)—or explode. For them emigration is a crucial safety valve. The industrial countries of northern Europe have prospered so efficiently that they have exhausted their supply of unskilled labor. For them immigration is the expansion of industry and the continuance of vital services—or, failing it, the collapse of both. The *system* works. Governments, cabals of politicians, have evaded one problem for the time being. They have temporized, but out of sight *is* out of mind.

It is patently moral, and just as patently silly, to say, Halt the system! Exclude *all* emigration! It is exploitation! Invent a new system! To dismantle what exists is easy. To erect a new structure, assuming it would be better, takes time. The millions, 5.5 million in Europe alone (2 million of them Italians), who would be thrown back automatically into the marginal existences they have escaped, would create chaos, perhaps worse, in their own countries. And what of the industrialized countries? Germany, for instance? Three million immigrant laborers suddenly missing in the structure: they must have been doing something.

Time is the crux. The industrial countries are prospering *now*. The Mediterranean countries are relieved of the crush of their own populations *now*. Surely it is now that they must plan for reasonable development which could in some imaginable future absorb their excess manpower. International blackmail, better known as diplomatic pressures, will be needed. Mediterranean countries have a penchant for planning—not doing. And they will answer pressure with pressure: industrialized countries should build factories where the labor supply exists. Businessmen are known for many things, but seldom stupidity. It would take a naïve one, indeed, to move into today's Italy. The climate in Greece, Yugoslavia, Turkey, Portugal, or Spain may be better. I doubt it, just as I doubt that the Mediterranean countries will do more than plan unless forced, unless they are threatened and the threat is real, one that would hurt them if it were carried out, like, among other things, the reversal of emigration itself.

The Common Market is not an international welfare agency. Its basic policy, enlightened greed as I called it, is very schematic. Prosperity depends on increased employment and increased production, which is futile if there are no more consumers. The solution is obvious: start the Italian progression all over again with Turkey, Greece, Portugal, and Spain. Accept them in the Common Market, give their laborers the equality that only Italians enjoy at the moment. They will earn, become consumers. The people they leave at home will have more and will become consumers too. The *system* will work. It will work so well, in fact, that there will be an excuse for national quotas or time limits—no immigrant could stay in any country more than five years, for example—which the industrialized countries secretly want and have wanted. They are still guaranteed a surplus of unskilled labor for a limited number of jobs. Immigrants will compete directly with each other, each equal, unskilled, and docile, no longer protected by contracts. Wages could even fall, an employer's dream, and in the bargain he would choose any nationality he happened to prefer. The labor market is finally under control.

Quotas or time limits offer another advantage. They eliminate a problem the industrialized countries, most notably Germany in the Common Market, deny they have. Germany is *not* a country of immigration. It insists it is not. Immigrants are not to settle permanently. Citizenship, except through marriage, is kept carefully out of reach. Yet some Italian immigrants have been in Germany for twelve or fifteen years. Their children have grown up there. Those children have little or no contact with Italy. No friends there, no real ties there, and no possibility of work there. *They* will *not* go home. They are semiskilled, at best, working today and planning to stay in a country that is methodically mechanizing its industry to the very limits of known technology and intends to eliminate those that cannot be mechanized. More skilled workers will be needed. The Italian-German immigrant youth will be phased out. As things stand now he will stay, discontent, disruptive, and almost certainly redundant in the new industrial scheme, a "displaced person," not through war, but immigration. With quotas, and their implied rotation of immigrants, or with a time limit, *he* could be sent home and too, there would never be others like him to plague countries that will not accept permanent immigration.

Emigration *is* an unnatural act between consenting adults, but it suits the governments concerned too perfectly for reform, much less destruction. If it cannot be condemned as immoral, it is still a system, like any other, only as valuable as its results. Systems are abstract, so must the results be: emigration relieves demographic pressures in underindustrialized countries and supplies unskilled labor to industrialized countries where it is scarce. The formula is simple and proves that the *system* does, indeed, work.

And those unskilled, docile ergs that I insist are people. What has it done to them?

With all its brutalities and its discriminations and its wrenches, emigration has given my Torresi, at least, the only chance they ever had or ever will have for a decent life. They take with them that *x*-quality, inbred and inescapable, for success or failure, but they can act now where success is possible and failure, not inevitable. They have worked and they have suffered and they have cheated and they have misunderstood. They have been foolish in many ways: short-sighted and greedy. They have been abandoned almost without help. They have had to learn on their own. They have ignored much that would have been of value to them. They have bought, gorged on much that was useless. They lie to each other about what they are and what they have. I think I would do *all* of those things, if I was new to life. They want to learn. They will learn. They want to live. Anyone who sees Southern Italy for the first time is overwhelmed, often frightened, by the savage vitality of its people, suppressed but waiting to get loose. They wait for what did not happen to their fathers, is not happening now, and will not happen, hoping to live. They want so desperately to live, and they *know* they have not, so far.

Below in the courtyard I can hear them, packing their cars. They move slowly, as though the bags were heavy and they, reluctant. Each time the whispers stop, doors close, and an engine starts, I am relieved.

I hope—for them—that they are strong enough not to wait longer, that they never again listen to the noble hypocrisies of Italian politicians, that they are strong enough to leave Southern Italy and go anywhere that there is work, but that they go—and go now.

 *Notes*

1. This statement has been repeated in every edition for the last ten years. The most recent available is *Compendio Statistico Italiano,* 1977 edition, published by the *Istituto Centrale di Statistica,* p. 48, n. 2.
2. *Aspetti e Problemi dell'Emigrazione Italiana all'estero nel 1976* (Rome: Ministero degli Affari Esteri, Direzione Generale Emigrazione e Affari Sociali, January 1978), p. 83. An interesting sidelight (p. 23, same source) is that the number of Italians employed in Germany has dropped from 1973's high of 450,000 (or 72.3 percent of the Italian community) to, in 1976, 280,000 (or 49 percent of the Italian community). As a direct result of the recession many men were out of work and went home. The families of men more fortunate came to Germany to live (and save money).
3. Ibid., p. 83, n. 7.
4. Ibid., p. 84.
5. *Sozialpolitik in Baden-Wuerttemberg Leistungen und Perspektiven* (Stuttgart: Ministerium fuer Arbeit Gesundheit und Sozialordnung Baden-Wuerttemberg, 1976), p. 58. For the record, the other large foreign nuclei are: Yugoslavs 23 percent, Turks 21.4 percent and Greeks 11.3 percent. Of these foreign workers, 75 percent have been in Germany more than three years, and 43.6 percent more than six years. In industrial areas the foreign population averages 14.5 percent of the total—in Stuttgart, 16.3 percent.
6. *Aspetti e Problemi,* pp. 292–3.
7. Elaboration of figures of the *Istituto Centrale di Statistica* quoted in *Pirell Rivista d'informazione e di tecnica,* no. 11/12 (November-December 1970), p. 64, published in Milan.
8. *Aspetti e Problemi,* pp. 286–7.
9. A federation of Demo-Christian, Social Democratic, and Communist unions represents about 60 percent of the Italian work force, but the individual unions within the federation maintain the independent umbilical attachment to their parent political parties and can in many instances—assistance being one of them—function quite outside the federation. The Communist party uses other, more overt approaches to indoctrination of emigrants—see *Presenti e In-*

visibili, Storie e dibattiti degli emigranti di Campobello, edited by Chiara and Giovanni Commare, published by Feltrinelli, 1978—but the union assistance committees have been effective seines of unaffiliated and discontented emigrants.

10. From a resumé of comments made by Dr. Franz Domhoff of the Ministry of Education for North Rhine-Westphalia, quoted in *Problems of training foreign workers and their cultural integration with special reference to young people. Summary report on an International Seminar held in Bergneustadt, 5-8 December, 1972,* p. 2, published by the German Commission for UNESCO, Friedrich Ebert Foundation.

11. Two examples of the many: Dr. Vittorio Gazerro, an Italian school supervisor in Hessen during the mid-1970s, states (*"Doposcuola come recupero educativo degli Svantaggiati,"* published in *La Vita Scolastica* [November 16, 1976], p. 4) that a quick survey of the Italian children in *"classi d'inserimento"* in his district showed that 65 percent had attended multiclass, one-room schools at home; Giovanni Pellicciari and Adriano Baglivo of the *Centro Orientamento Immigrati,* in their book *Sud Amaro—Esodo come Sopravvivenza* (Milan: Sapere, 1970), use these conditions, which they describe as general and apparently accept as such, to explain the pathetically inadequate level of Southern children who were studied in Northern schools.

About the Author

An American who has lived in Italy for the past twenty-five years, Ann Cornelisen was born in Cleveland, Ohio, spent much of her childhood in Chicago, and attended Vassar College. In 1954 she went to Florence intending to study archeology; instead, she spent ten years with the Save the Children Fund, setting up nurseries in impoverished villages of southern Italy. Her first book, *Torregreca*, was published in 1969. Since then, she has written *Vendetta of Silence*, a novel, *Women of the Shadows*, and *Strangers and Pilgrims*. She has held a Guggenheim Fellowship, and in 1974 she received a special award from the National Institute of Arts and Letters.